Web Usability

A **USER-CENTERED** DESIGN APPROACH

Web Usability

A **USER-CENTERED** DESIGN APPROACH

Jonathan Lazar

TOWSON UNIVERSITY

PEARSON

Addison
Wesley

Boston San Francisco New York
London Toronto Sydney Tokyo Singapore Madrid

Publisher	Greg Tobin
Senior Acquisitions Editor	Michael Hirsch
Editorial Assistant	Lindsey Triebel
Managing Editor	Patty Mahtani
Cover Design	Joyce Cosentino Wells
Cover Image	© 2005 Scott Fattig / Corbis
Supplements Supervisor	Jason Miranda
Media Producer	Bethany Tidd
Senior Marketing Manager	Michelle Brown
Marketing Assistant	Dana Lopreato
Senior Manufacturing Buyer	Caroline Fell
Text Design, Production Coordination, Composition, and Illustrations	Gillian Hall, The Aardvark Group

Access the latest information about Addison-Wesley titles from our World Wide Web site: http://www.aw.com/cs

Many of the designations used by manufacturers and sellers to distinguish their products are claimed as trademarks. Where those designations appear in this book, and Addison-Wesley was aware of a trademark claim, the designations have been printed in initial caps or all caps.

Library of Congress Cataloging-in-Publication Data

Lazar, Jonathan.
  Web usability : a user-centered design approach / Jonathan Lazar.-- 1st ed.
    p. cm.
  Includes bibliographical references and index.
  ISBN-13: 978-0-321-32135-0
  1. Web sites--Design. 2. User interfaces (Computer systems) I. Title.

  TK5105.888.L3975 2005
  006.7'019--dc22

                              2005018218

ISBN 0-321-32135-9

1 2 3 4 5 6 7 8 9 10—CRS—09 08 07 06 05

Preface

Web sites are most effective when they meet both the content and usability needs of their users. The best way to ensure that a Web site meets the users' needs is to involve the users throughout the design (or redesign) process. The question is "*How* do you involve the users?" This book answers that question by presenting a process-oriented approach to designing user-centered Web sites.

In Web site design, it's not sufficient to present design guidelines to interface designers and tell them to design sites based on those guidelines. Nor is it appropriate for interface designers to substitute their own design likes and dislikes in place of the needs and desires of the users. Designing a Web site is a process. Just as you don't start erecting a building by pouring concrete (first you must plan the building design based on topography and the needs of the companies and people who will inhabit the building), when building a Web site, you must create a plan that is informed by understanding the needs of those who will use the site.

How is a Web site designed? Web site design is a challenge because it bridges two fields, graphic design and usability engineering, which have different points of view about what makes a good user interface. An interface should not be designed solely on visual appeal or the number of people who will visit the site. At the same time, a text-only Web site will have no appeal. The appropriate balance is a Web site that is functional, easy to use, appropriate, visually appealing, and suitable for users who have disabilities. This type of design is possible if you truly understand who the site's users are, and what they want and need. The most important theme of this book is—*know thy users*!

The design suggestions in this book are not based on my personal opinion. They are based on the research about how users interact with Web sites. In many places, actual design guidelines from research are included in the text.

Real-World Approach

Keep in mind that there is never a perfect design that will work for every site and user population. The key is to understand the design that is appropriate for each specific site and its users. Understanding the context of the users, tasks, and environment is the key to choosing an appropriate design. That's why this book takes a real-world approach to Web site design. There are many hands-on examples throughout the book. These examples are, in many cases, short case studies showing how a specific user involvement or interface concept was applied in a real-world project. In some cases, these hands-on examples include specifics about how to implement a concept in a real-world project, such as a sample form or task list. Either way, these hands-on examples help link the theory with the practice. Another way that this book provides a real-world approach is through four major Case Studies that appear at the end of the book.

Each chapter ends with a series of discussion questions to stimulate in-class conversation. A Design Exercise in each chapter challenges students to apply these concepts in a real-world example. A Suggested Reading list provides a list of books, journal articles, and conference papers for additional information on the topics presented in each chapter.

Who Should Read This Book

This book is geared toward undergraduate and graduate courses in which students study the process of Web site development, Web interface design, or a combination of both. The text provides information about Web usability and the user-centered design process for creating Web sites.

In a Web Design course: A course in site design might focus on interface design, the development process, or both. This book covers the development process (Chapters 1–4 and 9–11) and Web interface design (Chapters 5–8). In these courses, it is also expected that some basic amount of Web programming will be taught, either using HTML and JavaScript or a Web development application such as FrontPage or Dreamweaver. It is expected that many of these courses will be project-based, and so the Addison Wesley instructor resource center (http://www.aw.com/irc) provides a number of resources related to Web projects in a classroom setting. The general public also can access the Web-Star survey and project deliverables at http://www.aw.com/cssupport.

In a Systems Analysis and Design course: Chapters 1–4, which focus on cost-justification, site mission, target user population, and requirements gathering will be very useful. Chapters 9–11, which focus on usability testing, implementation, marketing, and evaluation, are also appropriate for use in this course.

In a Human–Computer Interaction course: Readers will be most interested in Chapter 1, which presents user-centered design concepts for the Web; Chapters 5–8, which focus on conceptual and physical design of the Web interface design; Chapter 9, which focuses on usability testing; and Chapter 11, which focuses on evaluation.

In a Web Programming course: The material in Chapters 5–8 (conceptual and physical design of the Web interface) and the information about automated usability testing tools in Chapter 9 will be most useful.

In addition, this book can be useful for those in the Web development industry who want to include users in the development process but are unfamiliar with the standard processes, tools, and techniques of systems analysis and design or user-centered design.

Case Studies

User-centered design is a development process. It's nice to understand the steps in the process, but it's necessary to see how these concepts are applied in real-world settings. Unfortunately, many companies do not publicize their design processes or methods for fear of providing valuable information to their competitors. It can be hard to find public information about how user-centered design is actually used in organizations. For that reason, this book includes Case Studies about real organizational Web sites. They are excellent learning tools, which show how theory is applied in the real world. They help students understand the challenges, trade-offs, and adjustments that do not usually occur in theory, but are an everyday part of the working world.

This book includes four Case Studies of actual Web sites that were designed or redesigned with user-centered design methods. They represent four very different organizations: a large for-profit corporation (Kodak), a non-profit professional organization (ASHA), a governmental organization (Cancernet), and a sports league (NFL). Each case highlights the needs of different types of organizations and different types of users as it relates to user-centered Web design.

Three of the sites were redesigns and one site was an entirely new design (NFL). Two of the Case Studies were written by information technology professionals within a client organization (Kodak and Cancernet) and two were written by outside consultants (ASHA and NFL).

Supplemental Materials

The following materials are available to all readers of this book at http://www.aw.com/cssupport:

- Project templates for use in classes
- Web-Star survey
- Research papers on web usability topics

In addition, qualified instructors can access the following secure supplements at Addison Wesley's Instructor's Resource Center (http://www.aw.com/irc):

- Powerpoint lecture slides
- Responses to discussion questions
- Responses to design exercises
- Sample syllabi

Acknowledgments

First, and most important, I want to thank my close family, those who have mentored me and influenced me the most. My parents, Drs. Libby Kumin and Martin Lazar, and my grandparents, Berniece and Herbert Kumin and Mollie and Aaron Lazar, have always provided love and support. They made sure that I grew up appreciating everything that life has to offer, and my responsibilities to the world, as well. I also thank Phyllis and Milton Shuch and Joel and Sandy Lazar, just for being the amazing people that they are.

My work in this field would not be possible without the support of Towson University. Chao Lu and James Clements have always been very supportive of my human–computer interaction work at Towson University, and were integral in turning the Universal Usability Laboratory from my dream into a reality. I also collaborate regularly at Towson University with Alfreda Dudley-Sponaugle, Heidi Feng, Doris Lidtke, Gabriele Meiselwitz, and Kathy Wang.

In addition to my colleagues at Towson University, I am lucky to have many supportive colleagues in the human–computer interaction community with whom I collaborate on a regular basis, including: Ben Bederson, Brad Hodges, Julie Jacko, Anthony Norcio, and Andrew Sears. Jenny Preece and Ben Shneiderman are not only excellent colleagues, but also inspiring human beings!

I thank Kisha-Dawn Greenidge and Jessica Lawrence from Towson University, who served as graduate assistants during the writing process, helping to track down screenshots and permissions. Thanks go to Sam Houston for providing the Web site stats, and Dick Horst at UserWorks for providing the usability lab pictures. Portions of Chapter 11 were reprinted with permission, from a paper that I co-authored with Jenny Preece.

The Case Studies that illustrate the user-centered Web development techniques in real-world settings are a major component of the book. My thanks go to Jori Clarke, Sanjay Koyani, Craig LaFond, Janice Nall, Theresa O'Connell, and Jack Yu, who wrote the Case Studies and were the actual developers responsible for the projects. Thanks also go to the Eastman Kodak Company, the American Speech-Language-Hearing Association (ASHA), the National Football League (NFL), and the National Cancer Institute (of the U.S. Department of Health and Human Services) for giving permission to publish the studies. In addition, every screenshot that appears in the book appears with the permission of the sponsoring organization or company.

Thank you to the reviewers of the book, who provided much useful feedback. They are Dennis G. Jones, Tarleton State University, Don Turnbull, University of Texas at Austin, Catherine Hayes, Washtenaw Community College, Jo Wiley, Western Michigan University, Deborah Carstens, Florida Institute of Technology, Laura Frost, Walsh College, Louisa Ha, Bowling Green State University, Jody Blanke, Mercer University, Larry Wood, Brigham Young University, Valeri Scott, University of Maryland, Baltimore County, Jonathan Knolle, California State University-Chico, Kenrick Mock, University of Alaska-Anchorage, William P. Cantor, The Pennsylvania State University-York, and Richard Hall, University of Missouri-Rolla.

Of course, a book isn't published without an excellent publishing team. This team included Michael Hirsch, Pat Mahtani, Joyce Cosentino Wells, Gillian Hall, and Kathy Cantwell. I'd specifically like to thank Lindsey Triebel at Addison-Wesley for her diligent work at securing permissions to use many of the images in this book.

No list of thank yous would be complete without mentioning Meg Richards, who introduced me to human–computer interaction many years ago. Always remember, when you change one person's life, you enable them to change the world.

About the Author

Dr. Jonathan Lazar is an Associate Professor in the Department of Computer and Information Sciences, in the Fisher College of Science and Mathematics at Towson University. He is founder and director of the Universal Usability Laboratory at Towson University. He is also an Affiliate Professor in the Center for Applied Information Technology. He currently serves as Director of the Computer Information Systems undergraduate program. At the university, Dr. Lazar has received the "Excellence in Teaching" Award, and the "Business and Community Outreach" Award.

Dr. Lazar has published over 60 technical papers on topics within human–computer interaction related to Web usability, user-centered design processes, assistive technology, and human error and frustration. Dr. Lazar serves on the editorial boards of the Journal for Informatics Education and Research and the Information Resource Management Journal. Dr. Lazar has served on the program committees for the ACM Conference on Human Factors in Computing Systems (CHI), ACM Conference on Assistive Technology (ASSETS), Human–Computer Interaction International conference (HCII), Online Communities and Social Computing (OCSC) conference, and the Universal Access in Human–Computer Interaction (UAHCI) conference. Dr. Lazar is a founding member of the ACM CHI US Public Policy Committee.

Contents

Chapter 2   **Defining the Mission and Target User Population**   **29**

Chapter 3   **Requirements Gathering–What Information Is Needed?**   **51**

Chapter 4 **Methods for Requirements Gathering** **75**

Case Study B   **asha.org**   **309**

Case Study C   **CancerNet**   339

chapter 1

Introduction to Web Usability

After reading this chapter, you will be able to:

- Describe why user-centered Web sites lead to organizational profitability.
- Understand why users are often frustrated with Web sites.
- Differentiate between the five major types of Web sites.
- Explain how to define the user population and the user task needs.
- Understand the stages of the User-Centered Web Development Life Cycle.
- Justify the costs incurred when users are involved in a Web development project.
- Apply traditional project management techniques to Web development.

Introduction

The Internet and the World Wide Web have become an integral part of our world. In approximately one decade, the Web has grown from a theoretical concept to a daily reality. Most companies, nonprofit organizations, schools, and universities have Web sites. More information is made available on the Web every day. The number of current Web users is so large that it is impossible to count them accurately. The Web has become ubiquitous in much of our society.

When the Web was first introduced to the public in the early 1990s, the primary concern was to make sure that the technological infrastructure worked. Now that the infrastructure has stabilized, the challenge is to design Web sites that meet the needs of the people who use them. These people, known as users, are your company's customers or employees, your organization's members, your school's students or faculty, or people simply seeking information. Most of the time, Web site users have diverse backgrounds and varying reasons for visiting a site. Therefore, we want to ensure that all users with various technologies, ages, computer knowledge, and disabilities have an equally enjoyable experience.

Users want a site that is easy to use, loads quickly in their browser, and allows them to complete tasks without frustration. To create a site that satisfies its users, a designer should focus on two factors: content and usability. These standards apply to all types of Web sites, whether they provide information, entertainment, or e-commerce. For example, a user will not purchase from an e-commerce Web site that does not offer competitive prices or quick product delivery (the content). Nor will a user purchase from a Web site that is complicated and frustrating to use (the usability).

The world of Web design began to change around 2000 when "the dot-com bubble" burst and many e-commerce companies went out of business. In the years prior to 2000, companies often pushed their Web sites online in a matter of weeks. Usability was not a priority, and the difficulty people experienced when using the sites turned users away. Since the dot-com bubble burst, things have changed. Companies focus more on usability as a means to keep their customers satisfied and their companies profitable. Organizations are increasing their Web development project timelines and focusing more on user involvement by incorporating the concepts of user-centered design into their projects. As a result, more Web sites meet the functionality and usability needs of users, leading to increased site hits, additional e-commerce transactions, and a more satisfied user population.

Web developers should not substitute their own personal preferences for the principles of user-centered design. What a Web developer might consider "cool," a user might consider annoying. A Web developer's perceptions and knowledge base can be quite different from those of the targeted users. The only way to know what users want, what they know, and what technology they use, is to get them involved in the site development or redevelopment!

This book guides the reader through the process of designing or redesigning a Web site that incorporates the input of the end user. In order for a site to be successful, it must offer content that users want and it must be designed so that users can easily access it and navigate through it. History shows that a site that does not include the user in the design process will most likely fail.

Unlike traditional informational systems, the Web has a short history. The theoretical concept of a "web" of information was first introduced by Vannevar Bush in his classic 1945 paper titled "As We May Think." The technical foundation of the Internet, on which Web traffic travels, has been around since the early 1970s (although not in its current form). The technical infrastructure of the Web, including the standards for HTML and HTTP, has existed since the early 1990s, but the Web has seen widespread acceptance only within the last 10 years. As the Web grows and matures, there is a new focus on the user when designing sites. With more experience and research, and with the benefit of hindsight, we have a better sense of how to design and redesign a successful Web site.

Why Focus on the User?

User-centered Web development refers to design processes for designing or redesigning a Web site that meets the needs of the user. A related term is Web usability, which refers to creating Web sites that are easy to use. Companies, nonprofit organizations, and government agencies are adopting the user-centered approach to Web design as they develop new sites and redesign existing ones. Users are satisfied with Web sites that are easy to use and that help them complete their tasks easily. Users return to these sites, leading to positive results for the sponsoring organization.

Greater Profits

User-centered Web development often comes down to dollars and cents. Companies realize that poor Web design means lost revenue. For example, in the late 1990s, IBM's Web site was very difficult to navigate. The two most used features on the site were the search function and the help button because potential customers did not understand how to use the site. After a multimillion-dollar Web site redesign, sales increased 400 percent and help button use decreased 84 percent. The functionality of the site stayed the same—users could perform the same tasks as before—but the redesign effort made the site easier to use. And as a result of the redesign effort, users were more satisfied (Tedeschi '99). When Macy's made their Web site search engine easier to use, the conversion rate (the rate at which site visitors are "converted" into buyers) increased 150 percent (Kemp '01). Staples.com incorporated user feedback to simplify their online registration pages, leading to a 53 percent decrease in registration drop-off rate (the number of people who begin to register but fail to complete the process) (Roberts-Witt '01).

Some companies refuse to discuss, publicize, or even mention the amount of user involvement in the development of their Web sites. They view their focus on user input as a competitive advantage and are hesitant to share this information with their competitors.

Reduce User Frustration

Unfortunately, for many users, the Web is still difficult and incredibly frustrating to use. The terminology is confusing, pages take too long to download, and there are many additional annoying features. Studies of both novice and workplace users find that people, on average, waste 40–50 percent of their computer time, primarily due to poorly designed interfaces (Ceaparu '04a; Lazar '05a). From a user's point of view, this is disappointing and worrisome. From an organizational point of view, this significant amount of unproductive time wastes huge amounts of money.

Even small changes in a Web site interface can result in large improvements in user performance. For example, on one U.S. government site, users reported task success rates as low as 20 percent. However, when this same Web site was redesigned for improved usability by rearranging hypertext links and descriptions, success rates doubled and frustration levels dropped (Ceaparu '03; Ceaparu '04b). When companies redesign their Web sites for improved usability and functionality and involve users in the process, there is usually a positive outcome. For instance, e-commerce sites that are redesigned to be easier to use result in increased traffic to the site, more loyal customers, and significantly higher sales (Marcus '02). For nonprofit or strictly informational sites, involving users in Web development can lead to positive outcomes, such as favorable organization perception, better company name recognition, and increased organizational membership.

Consider the Web site for Magic Hat Brewery, as shown in Figure 1.1 (see color insert for full color version). It is unclear what the various components of the Web page do and how the overall graphic relates to the company and product. It is a nonstandard and unpredictable design, which can confuse users.

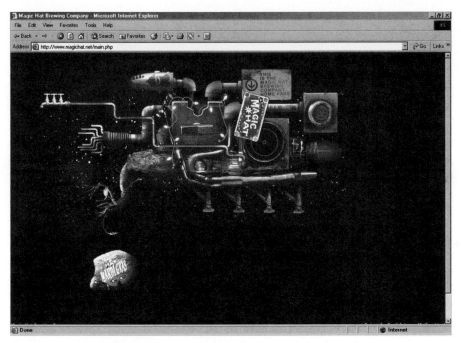

Also in the
Color Insert

Figure 1.1 A nonstandard Web page design, which can confuse users.

How Is the Web Different from Traditional Information Systems?

The Web environment is a paradigm shift from past software development. Traditionally, software applications were designed either for a group of users within an organization (such as a custom payroll system) or for the mass market (such as a word processing application). For users within an organization, it was possible to determine exactly who they were and what their computing environments were. For mass market software, programs had minimum requirements (such as 8 MB RAM, 50 MB free hard drive space, and so on) and were developed to work on one platform only (such as IBM PC). Web sites however, are very different because they can be accessed by people with various technological environments, using any platform and browser, anywhere. Therefore, a Web site has to work with hundreds or thousands of possible technological environments.

Given the inherent unpredictability of the Web environment, some take the "least common denominator approach," arguing that Web design should be simple, without graphics and plug-ins; with paragraphs of text only. This book does not advocate that course. Rather, graphics, plug-ins, and metaphors should be used when appropriate. It's important to strike a balance. Users don't want to see page after page of long paragraphs of text. At the same time, too many graphics, animations, and plug-ins can be overwhelming. The point is to determine what is appropriate. How many graphics should be on a page? How many plug-ins must be downloaded? The answers to these questions partially depend on the users. What connection speeds are likely? What plug-in applications are already available? How much experience do the users have? Simple text-based pages are not appealing. There needs to be a balance—a visually attractive Web site that offers alternative interaction for users with disabilities without being overwhelming. The key is to determine what is appropriate—to create an inviting presentation that does not confuse users in any way.

This is challenging. Web users are the most diverse of all computer application users. When the Web was introduced in the early 1990s, new groups of users who had never used computers before went online. Up to that point, computer applications were used for workplace-related tasks, such as number crunching, desktop publishing, and transactional information storage. When the Web came along, the promise of consumer information, e-commerce, health information, online communication, and other tasks appealed to all people, regardless of age, computer experience, job, or economic status. That's what makes the Web different—it appeals to everyone! But if it's hard to use, it loses its appeal, despite its promise. For instance, a recent study from the Pew Internet and American Life Project found that 42 percent of people in the U.S. don't go online, mainly because the experience can be frustrating and problematic. These are not people who have never been online; many have been online, found it to be problematic, and have decided to stay off-line. What does that say about the future of the Web?

No User Training

When people use a traditional software application (such as a spreadsheet or custom student records database), they receive training and/or read documentation. Users may feel comfortable only after they complete a training session or read handouts or books about the software application. If users move from one brand of software to another (such as from Corel WordPerfect to Microsoft Word), they must be retrained, or at least receive documentation about the new program. This rarely happens with Web sites. People usually don't receive training or documentation about using a Web site; but even if they did, it's questionable if they could overcome a confusing interface. Since Web site training or documentation is rare, a site's usability is extremely important in determining user success.

Users of major software applications that are delivered via a Web browser interface (e.g., through an intranet) receive documentation and training because these applications are similar to traditional software applications. Users access these applications daily and perform hundreds or even thousands of possible tasks. These sites must have user involvement through development because users must specify the task structure.

Intranets or desktop applications are fundamentally very different from Web sites. Web sites resemble "walk-up-and-usability" interfaces, such as ATM machines or voting machines. Users must be able to use a Web site successfully, in a short amount of time, without any prior training or documentation. Users expect that Web sites will operate similarly. For instance, if most Web sites use blue text for hyperlinks, then users will expect that blue text indicates a hyperlink. If most e-commerce Web sites use the shopping cart and checkout metaphors, then users will expect these terms and may be confused when other terminology is used. The conformity of Web site design can actually facilitate users' task performance.

Predictability Means Easy Use

When users browse the Web they are dealing with two different interfaces: the Web browser interface and the Web site interface. The Web browser interface, consisting of the scrollbars, buttons, menu bar, and other traditional user interface widgets, stays relatively consistent from site to site. However, the Web site interface changes from site to site. Colors, layout, terminology, and navigation are different on each site; the user has to adapt and adjust to each new interface. Interfaces that act in unexpected ways or use unclear metaphors can be especially problematic. For instance, one e-commerce bookstore took an unusual approach to their Web site design (Nielsen '00). Instead of the standard use of shopping carts and checkout (which most people understand from their real-world shopping experiences), the online bookstore used the metaphor that one placed books in a bag and then proceeded to the exit. For most people, placing items in a bag and then going to the exit suggests shoplifting! Using nonstandard interfaces that users are not familiar with, and that they cannot pick up easily, can cause problems.

As software application uniformity found in Word, Excel, and Access was a successful strategy for the Microsoft Office Suite, similarity among different Web sites is beneficial because it allows users to carry over their knowledge from one site to the next. Think about it—if Microsoft Word acted differently every time we accessed it, wouldn't we become quickly frustrated? In fact, due to the nature of the Web (a distributed network with numerous components that are all susceptible to failure), the Web experience is inherently unpredictable. Errors occur frequently, and many errors are not due to the actions of the users. Users may get a "404-File Not Found" error, a local network error, or a "server cannot connect" error. All of these are unpredictable and the user cannot change this. Therefore, because the browsing experience is inherently unpredictable, the interface must be as predictable as possible.

Traditional Development of Information Systems

Information systems are never designed beginning with the coding. Rather, a series of steps takes place to ensure that the system is built properly. This is similar to an architect's approach when planning a building's construction. Many steps occur before the bricks are laid and the concrete is poured. In computer design, these steps (stages) are known as a development model or a life cycle model. The most commonly used development model is the Systems Development Life Cycle (SDLC), also called the waterfall model. Although the exact life cycle steps differ depending on the project, most versions of the SDLC model include similar steps. These steps include a large component of requirements gathering to fully understand the problem, using traditional techniques such as user surveys, interviews, and document analysis. Most versions of the SDLC include testing to ensure that the system works properly, and training and documentation to ensure that users can use the system successfully. Other life cycle models, such as participatory design, focus on including users in all design phases. More information on participatory design is available later in Chapter 1.

New Challenges in Web Development Projects

Web development projects must face obstacles that were not a consideration in traditional information systems projects. Web sites must be designed so that they work with a number of different browsers, such as Internet Explorer, Netscape

Navigator, and Firefox; and with a number of different browser versions, such as versions 3.0, 4.0, and 5.0. The same HTML code (and JavaScript) can appear differently depending on the browser in which it is displayed. Therefore, thorough testing must be done to ensure that Web pages will appear appropriately (or appear at all!) in a number of different browsers. Web designers must consider that users view Web sites using monitors of different sizes (from 21-inch monitors to laptop computers and smaller), and that they might have slow Web connections (less than 56 kbps) (Shneiderman '00). All of these factors influence a Web site's usability. Some sites are frequently visited by users from outside the site's country of origin. This poses new challenges because multiple versions of a site may have to be developed or the single version must fulfill the needs of a multicountry user population.

Usability is more of a concern in developing Web sites than in traditional information systems. In many traditional information systems, such as transactional systems, the system is designed for daily use and the user population is well defined in advance of development. The user interacts with the traditional information system frequently, and with regular use can learn about and possibly get used to parts of the interface that might be confusing. However, Web sites are different. Because a user may access a Web site infrequently, the site must be easy to use each time it's accessed. Web users must be able to figure out immediately how to use an interface. If previous knowledge is required, the interface is confusing, information is not easy to find, or the user has to ask for outside assistance, he or she might visit another Web site because there is virtually no cost involved in switching. Because of these specific challenges, user involvement is extremely important in Web site development.

The Role of Users

Since there are many challenges in developing Web sites, the chance of a site being difficult to use and ultimately a failure increases. However, using a structured methodology increases the chance that a Web site is easy to use and successful. In some cases, it can be challenging to define your user population and determine how to include it in the development process. However, ignoring your users when designing your Web site is a recipe for failure. If you do not include your users in the design process, there is no way to know whether your Web site provides the content that they require, or whether they find the site easy to use. This problem is illustrated in the Hands-On Example on page 18, "Redesigning

Web Sites: The Need for Requirements Gathering." In this example, user involvement during a redesign process for the College of Science and Mathematics Web site at Towson University revealed that the site did not offer the content users were interested in. Therefore, even if the site had been 100 percent usable, users would not visit it, simply because the information they wanted was not on the site. User involvement can also be beneficial later on with user buy-in. When users are involved in system development, they are more likely to use it because it's hard for them to reject a system that they helped to build!

User involvement sounds like an ideal method for ensuring a positive Web development outcome. But what level of user involvement is sufficient or appropriate? How much time can users offer to developers? Users are not willing to spend personal time helping developers if it does not have a major impact on the users. However, if users expect to use a system daily, it is in their best interest to make sure that it meets their needs and is easy to use. For some systems, it may not be necessary to have users involved at every stage. There are many different purposes of user involvement as follows:

- to understand who the users are
- to understand what the users want to achieve with their interactions
- to understand what types of interfaces the users need
- to test early prototypes of interfaces
- to test fully functional interfaces
- to get user buy-in and later acceptance

Different types of Web sites require different types and levels of user involvement.

Types of Web Sites

At a broad level, there are five different types of Web sites: e-commerce, informational, entertainment, community, and intranet. Many sites offer features of more than one of these categories. For instance, Amazon, an e-commerce site, also offers communities where customers can discuss the products they have purchased.

E-Commerce Web Sites. The main goal of e-commerce sites is transactional: products, services, and/or money all change hands. E-commerce sites include business-to-consumer (B2C) sites, such as L.L. Bean, business-to-business (B2B) sites, such as CDWG.com, and marketplaces that connect consumers to consumers (C2C), such as Ebay. The end goal of these Web sites is to sell products or services, or to facilitate transactions. While some sites actually sell products, others help to facilitate transactions by linking buyers and sellers. Nearly all of these sites have an end goal of profitability.

Informational Web Sites. The purpose of informational sites is to provide information about a company, organization, group, hobby, or activity. Informational sites offer information, similar to that found in pamphlets, handbooks, or other types of printed items. In fact, the goal of many informational sites is simply to replace printed materials. Consider a university. Most universities have thousands of individual Web pages on their site. These pages include information on course schedules, faculty phone numbers, art and cultural events, student clubs, and sports scores. Prior to the Web, most of this information was printed on paper and distributed.

Entertainment Web Sites. An entertainment site offers content with an end goal toward recreation, amusement, or distraction. This can include audio clips, video clips, comic strips, and other types of downloads. Many of these sites are either subscriber-driven or advertiser-driven. That is, the services on these sites are made available through revenues from sponsors or subscription fees. These sites frequently use plug-ins, such as those for streaming audio or video.

Community Web Sites. Community Web sites offer a location where people with shared interests can communicate about their common topic. The community members use computer-mediated communication tools, such as list servers, newsgroups, bulletin boards, and chat rooms. Many community Web sites also have information about the shared area of interest and offer downloadable files. Some of these online communities are based on professional communities (e.g., CHIplace, for people who work in the area of human-computer interaction) or physical communities (e.g., the Seattle Community Network or Blacksburg Electronic Village).

Intranet Web Sites. Many organizations have started to implement intranets, which are organizational information systems delivered through Web browsers. Typically, intranets are password protected and unavailable to the public. These intranets offer information about organizational events, data, transaction processing, file uploads, and many other features, which are usually dependent on the mission of the organization and what types of transactional support they require. Intranets have many benefits because they improve communication and data sharing within an organization. Extranets are similar to intranets. They allow different organizations to share data and communication when they are collaborating. For instance, an extranet might be created to support the employees of five different organizations as they collaborate on projects, or to help companies communicate and process transactions with their subcontractors, suppliers, and distributors.

Regardless of the type of Web site, user involvement is necessary. However, the type of user involvement and when in the development process it should occur, differs due to two main factors: the population definition and the task definition.

Defining the User Population

It's important to determine how well defined the user population is before development (or redesign) begins. Who are the targeted users and how much is known about them? For some types of Web sites, such as intranets, or other password protected sites, the population is very well defined. Only certain users have access. These might be users within a specific organization, members of a distributed team, or something similar. For these types of sites, the dividing line between users and nonusers is very clear. Even if these sites include tens of thousands of users or multiple user groups within the population, the user group is well defined. We know in advance specifically who the users will be.

Other types of Web sites have user populations that are not well defined prior to development. These sites, including news sites, such as CNN.com and Washingtonpost.com, search engine sites, such as Google.com and Yahoo.com, and e-commerce sites, such as Ebay.com and Amazon.com, are targeted toward a majority of Web users. With these sites, there is no defined user population, but realistically, the developers are targeting all Web users.

While the two previous paragraphs discuss Web sites that are used by a small set of users or those that are used by everyone on the Web, the reality is that most Web sites lie somewhere between these two extremes. Most Web sites are targeted toward certain users. There might not be clear borders around this user population, i.e., they might not all be within a certain organization or on a password control list, but the developers and the sponsoring organization have a good idea who the users are. The users may share certain characteristics—live in a certain area, be interested in a certain hobby, be a certain age, or have a certain profession. The users have something in common that draws them to the Web site; that is what establishes them as the targeted user population. More information on defining the target user population is available in Chapter 2.

Defining the User Tasks

Another important factor associated with population definition is task definition. It is important to ask how much is known about what tasks users want to perform before the development (or redevelopment) begins. Are the tasks that users want to perform well defined? For instance, the tasks of a newspaper or a search engine are defined well in advance. Search engines have been around for approximately 10 years, and the task of searching for information is a well-defined task due to decades of research from the library science community. Newspaper Web sites also have a long history to build on. Online newspapers, such as *The New York Times* or *The Washington Post*, mirror their paper versions in many ways. Therefore, the tasks of these Web site users tend to be well defined in advance of development. Even if new features that are unavailable in the paper versions are added to the Web site, the core tasks remain the same.

Tasks can be undefined for other types of Web sites. For instance, for a company intranet, the tasks must support the job tasks at the organization. These tasks are usually not simple information seeking tasks, but rather complex tasks. For instance, an intranet might need to include features such as database access, chat rooms, shared whiteboards, work schedules, and other advanced applications. The tasks for an intranet are not simple because an intranet mirrors the extensive nature of an organization. To understand fully what users need from an intranet, we must understand what those users do. We must understand the goals of the organization and how various people and divisions interact with each other. Therefore, we must conduct a thorough job of requirements gathering and task analysis. In addition, intranets are used to support community development in diverse places such as Roxbury, Massachusetts, and Celebration, Florida. In these cases, tasks are relatively undefined before development; therefore, requirements gathering is an especially important activity.

The previous two paragraphs describe extreme examples of tasks that are well defined or not defined at all in advance of development. Most Web sites fall between these two examples. For most sites, we can determine what users will want in terms of tasks. For instance, if users call looking for information, or send e-mails asking for help, it's possible to get a good sense of what those users need. Questions and requests from users, in any communication format, most often are good places to start to understand user tasks. The paper materials that users rely on are also good sources for understanding user tasks. People who deal with users regularly are good resources for understanding user tasks. On the other hand, users themselves may not know what they want because they've never been asked or thought about it. Until users give feedback about what information they want and what types of tasks they want to accomplish, it's impossible to know what content and tasks will meet their needs.

How do the user population definition and the task definition affect the levels of user involvement needed? The Task-Time-Population Model of user involvement, as shown in Figure 1.2, provides some guidance about what level of user involvement is needed (Lazar '04).

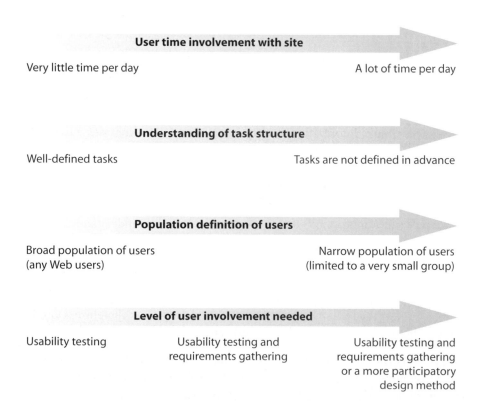

User time involvement with site

Very little time per day   A lot of time per day

Understanding of task structure

Well-defined tasks   Tasks are not defined in advance

Population definition of users

Broad population of users   Narrow population of users
(any Web users)   (limited to a very small group)

Level of user involvement needed

Usability testing   Usability testing and   Usability testing and
                           requirements gathering   requirements gathering
                                                         or a more participatory
                                                         design method

Figure 1.2 The Task-Time-Population Model of user involvement.

Another way to determine how much user involvement is needed is by answering the following questions.

How much is known about the tasks?

The less that is known in advance, the more user involvement is needed.

How often will users be using the Web site?

High levels of user involvement are needed for Web sites that will be used regularly.

What is the user population like? Are there users with disabilities? Older users? Younger users? Inexperienced users?

Knowing the user audience is important. Specialized user populations need to have more involvement.

Will user acceptance be a problem?

Increased user involvement can help with buy-in.

Participatory Design. Participatory design is a methodology where users are actually members of the design team and take part in all system development discussions. The idea of participatory design is that users have the right to determine the technology they will use as part of their work. Participatory design is most appropriate when user tasks are relatively complex and not well understood before development. For instance, the participatory design method was used when developing technology to be used by teachers in Montgomery County, Virginia (Carroll '02). The idea is that teachers are the ones who truly understand what takes place in their classrooms, and they have a right to determine what technologies are used as a part of their job.

Participatory design is an ideal methodology; however, its use is limited due to the intense time commitment that users must make. Due to the nature of most Web site use (used for small periods infrequently), the costs involved in using the participatory design method generally outweigh the benefits. However, there are specific types of Web development projects where participatory design is definitely appropriate, such as cases when users will be using a system daily (an intranet), or when there are special circumstances that make it risky to develop a system without the full involvement of the users (see Hands-On Example, "Using Participatory Design with Older Users," on next page).

Hands-On Example

Using Participatory Design with Older Users

The Participatory Design methodology was used to develop ezSIS, the ez-Senior Information System Web site. The development team consisted of approximately 15 people (5 developers and 10 users). The users were seniors (in their 60s and 70s) living in retirement communities near Detroit. Additionally, 318 user surveys were collected, providing information about user computer knowledge and experience, domain knowledge, and frustration. Based on the decisions of the development team, changes were made to meet the specific needs of the older users. For instance, clickable objects on the Web site were designed larger to facilitate targeting the object with a mouse. The site was made to minimize the use of additional browser windows because the users found them confusing. Also, the users preferred larger font sizes. The inclusion of users on the development team that drives the development process is the foundation of participatory design (Ellis '00).

The User-Centered Web Development Life Cycle

The Web development team must follow an orderly process to create a successful Web site. This doesn't mean that all Web site development projects proceed in the same manner or that all projects use the same methods. Different projects have different purposes (informational, e-commerce, community), organizations are different (corporate, nonprofit), users are different (people with disabilities, children, novices), and access to users varies (face-to-face, postal mail, e-mail, phone). Therefore, the specific methods used are different but the goal remains the same: to gain a better understanding of the content and usability needs of the users.

Ideally, users would be involved with every stage of development. However, for most Web sites, this is an unrealistic goal, since users will not have the time to commit to the complete project. The client organization may not want to spend the time and incur the costs involved with user involvement at all stages of development. There are two major stages of development where user involvement is especially helpful: requirements gathering and usability testing. These minimum levels of involvement ensure that the Web site being developed (or redesigned) will meet both the content and usability needs of its users.

The following is a Web development life cycle model that is centered on the needs of its user population. The model was developed by the author and defines the development processes actually used in industry. The User-Centered Web Development Life Cycle model, illustrated in Figure 1.3, has seven stages.

Stage 1: Define the Mission of Your Web Site and Its Target User Population

The first stage is to decide the mission and user population of your Web site. What is the goal of the site? Is the site expected to advertise a product, provide information on upcoming events, or collect names for a mailing list? How will the site be evaluated for success? A popular quote is "If you don't know where

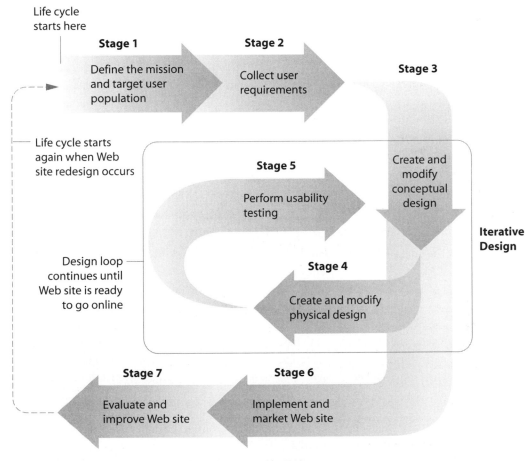

Figure 1.3 The User-Centered Web Development Life Cycle.

you are going, you are never going to get there." Applied to Web site development: If you don't know why you are developing a Web site, chances are you will not meet your goal. A parallel decision is to decide who the target users of your Web site are. Are they from a certain geographic area? A certain age group? A certain area of interest? A certain cultural group? For whom should the Web site be developed?

Defining your target user population has ramifications for the requirements gathering (see Stage 2) and the Web usability needs.

Stage 2: Collect the User Requirements for Your Web Site

The second stage is to collect requirements from the targeted user population. There are a number of important requirements to be discussed at this stage. What are the technological characteristics of the users? What browsers are they using? What connection speeds are they using? What type of Web site do they like to visit? What content and information are they interested in? What task goals do they have? What features would encourage them to revisit your Web site and what elements would keep them away? Do they have preferences regarding Web site design? A short case study from Towson University highlighting the need for requirements gathering appears in the Hands-On Example below.

Hands-On Example

Redesigning Web Sites— The Need for Requirements Gathering

The College of Science and Mathematics (CSM) is one of six colleges at Towson University. A redesign for the CSM Web site was planned for fall, 2001. Surveys were created and distributed among the faculty, staff, and students to help determine the task needs of the users. The tasks were not well defined before user involvement. A representative sample of surveys was collected (>70) from faculty, staff, and students, with most respondents indicating that they did not visit the CSM Web site regularly. When asked what content they were interested in, most respondents asked for content that was not currently on the site. For instance, survey respondents were interested in lists of college-wide committees and minutes of previous college council meetings. Neither of these resources was available on the existing CSM site. Redesigning for improved usability would not have drawn more people to the site because even if the site was 100 percent usable, the information was not what people wanted. It was critical to consult the users to determine their task needs.

Stage 3: Create and Modify the Conceptual Design of Your Web Site

At this stage, the development team must plan for the conceptual design of the Web site. For instance, how will navigation be provided to the user? What overall information architecture will be used? What page layout will be used? What color schemes are appropriate? Will there be graphics? What content must be developed? At the conceptual design stage, the development team must decide what the Web site will look like in order to create detailed specifications for the Web programmers. Techniques such as paper prototyping and card sorting might be helpful at this stage.

Stage 4: Create and Modify the Physical Design

This stage covers coding and technical development of the Web site. During this time, the developers actually create the code for the site. They may use hand-coded HTML and JavaScript, or a Web development application (such as FrontPage or Dreamweaver). Frequently, designers use a Web development application to get a head start, and then edit the code and fine-tune it to meet their needs. At this stage, functionality testing is performed to make sure that the code is correct and that any scripts and applets work properly.

Stage 5: Perform Web Site Usability Testing

At this stage, testing is performed to ensure that the interface is easy to use. Testing can be done with both interface experts and representative users. First, experts can help identify obvious major interface flaws. Next, users can attempt to perform sample tasks on the Web site to help determine the overall match between their task needs and the interface. The testers provide feedback on the Web site, point out problem areas, and possibly provide suggestions for improvements.

Stage 6: Implement and Market Your Web Site

Decisions about the site's URL and where the site will be hosted should have been made in this stage. The Web site "goes live," and users around the world are able to access it. The Web site must be marketed through traditional marketing (tote bags, fliers, etc.) or electronic marketing (search engines and Web rings) to the target population of interest.

Stage 7: Evaluate and Improve Your Web Site

Periodic evaluations of the effectiveness of the Web site should be performed. User feedback should be considered to determine if the site is meeting the needs of its users, or whether it might be time to redesign or make improvements. Content should always be kept up-to-date.

Cost Justifying User Involvement in Development

To involve users in a Web site development process takes time and costs money. Sometimes it's necessary to justify to managers or other decision makers why time and money must be spent on user involvement. A Web site can be built without user involvement (although it shouldn't be), and for those unfamiliar with user-centered design techniques, it can be unclear why time and money should be spent on user involvement activities. User-centered design techniques improve the quality, appropriateness, and effectiveness of a Web site. These benefits are sometimes hard to measure. At the same time, the costs of user involvement are relatively easy to measure (time spent interviewing subjects, distributing surveys, taking part in usability tests). This is the classic challenge of cost-justifying usability engineering activities: the costs are incurred today and relatively easy to measure; the benefits are hard to measure and occur in the future (Bias '05). However, the challenge of cost justifying a user involvement activity shouldn't automatically stop those user involvement activities from occurring.

There are economic benefits to including users in Web development projects, which in the end produce more successful Web sites. For instance, consumers frequently cite ease of use of an e-commerce site as more important than product cost (Marcus '02). Research has shown that when information is made available through a Web site, the costs associated with transmitting that information in other formats decreases (for instance, fewer calls to a help center or customer service line, or smaller distribution of printed pamphlets, brochures, or catalogs). Brief examples of sites that were redesigned and gained great financial benefit are included earlier in the chapter. The argument for user involvement can be made by predicting and estimating the future benefits of user involvement in a Web development project. The sidebar indicates some of the benefits of user involvement in Web development, for different categories of sites.

When making an argument to budget for user involvement, the relevant metric (as shown above) should be chosen, and both costs and quantity for that metric

Hands-On Example

Measurable Benefits of User Involvement in Web Development

Informational Web Sites:
- Lower distribution costs for printed information
- Increased donations (for a nonprofit organization)
- Increased membership
- Fewer telephone calls with questions (including customer service)
- Improved organizational name recognition
- Higher user satisfaction

E-Commerce Web Sites:
- Increased number of sales/transactions
- Increased site traffic
- Increased customer retention
- Increased return visitors
- Decreased number of errors in business transactions
- Fewer number of dropped shopping carts (higher number of completed transactions)
- Fewer number of calls to customer service

Entertainment Web Sites:
- Increased site traffic
- Increased number of click-throughs (for advertising-supported sites)
- Increased number of subscriptions (for subscription-supported sites)

Community Web sites:
- Increased number of community members
- Increased number of resources made available to the community
- Increased amount of time spent on the site ("stickiness")

Intranets:
- Increased transaction speed
- Improved information sharing within the organization
- Improved user (employee) productivity
- Reduced training costs for employees
- Higher user satisfaction

(Marcus '02; Mayhew '03)

should be estimated. For instance, on an intranet within an organization, it could be estimated that user involvement would make a specific screen (e.g., a login screen) easier to use. Maybe it would speed up the time for a user to access the intranet—on average three seconds for every login screen. How many times a day does the average user access the screen? How many users use the screen daily? How many times is the screen accessed yearly? While three seconds may not seem significant, if you consider that the login screen is accessed 10,000 times a year, that translates to 30,000 seconds saved by users yearly, which is equivalent to 500 saved hours. That's a measurable amount of time, and there is a related value of 500 hours of productive employee time. This is the classic way to estimate the benefits of user involvement activities.

For other types of Web sites, the appropriate metric should be chosen and the values estimated. For instance, say that on average, 5000 shopping carts are dropped (the transaction is not completed) a year, with an average value of $100 per shopping cart. Estimate that improved site usability will lead to 10 percent of those dropped shopping carts actually making it through the checkout. That means that 500 more shopping carts, with an average value of $100 per cart, would be checked out over a year for an increased revenue (in that year) of $5000. Neither of these examples even considers cost issues in a multiyear period, which can be much larger (e.g., more revenue or saved time). While it's impossible to know in advance exactly what the financial benefits of user involvement are, by estimating some possible benefits, it can help to convince decision makers of the need for user involvement in your Web development project.

Sometimes, people argue that a Web site should be launched and user involvement will happen when the site is redesigned in the future. From a cost-justification point of view, this argument makes no sense. Designing the site correctly in the first place is much cheaper than fixing usability flaws after the site has been implemented. The stage of development in which user involvement takes place correlates with the cost of the fixes. That is, the longer a developer waits for user involvement, the more likely fixes will be expensive and time-consuming because the current state of the site will not be close to matching what the users need. The bottom line is, the sooner that user involvement in Web development takes place, the lower the cost.

Project Management Techniques

It's important to note that traditional project management techniques are still appropriate in the User-Centered Web Development Life Cycle. These techniques are useful, regardless of the client development scenario. For instance, the client could be an outside organization or a group within an organization where the Web developer works. Because the client requiring the Web site development and the developer creating it may come from different backgrounds and organizational cultures and use different terminology, it's always important to use good project management techniques. Good project management techniques ensure that the data collection effort translates into development changes, with the end goal being a better Web site for the user.

Clear Objectives

At the beginning of the Web development project, there should be a clear objective (see Web site mission and targeted users in Chapter 2) as well as an estimated timeline and cost for the project. The client should be clear about these objectives and timeliness, and there should be a written agreement to these facts because if the client changes the project objectives, the time and cost needed to complete the Web development will most certainly increase.

Specific Responsibilities

Responsibilities for the Web development project should be broken down with specific tasks assigned to specific members of the Web development team. Web developers must also expect and prepare for political situations within the client organization. For instance, the Web development team may hear different viewpoints stated as "fact" from different members of the client organization, which may cloud an understanding of responsibilities.

Documentation

As in any type of systems development or project, all stages of the process should be well documented. Nothing is more frustrating than trying to remember what occurred or what was decided at an earlier stage of development and not being able to remember or to find the documentation. Documentation of the user requirements is especially important if there are conflicts between the client and user needs. Upon completion of each stage of the life cycle, the client should be presented with the documentation and asked to provide written approval.

Progress Reports

Regular scheduled progress reports are also useful to inform the client of the progress toward the project goal. If the client later says that "this isn't what we wanted!" or that the development timeline isn't what was expected, the development team can show the client the signed documentation. Thorough documentation and timely progress reports can assist in clarifying what was agreed to and what was supposed to be achieved.

Chapter Wrap-Up

When designing an informational system such as a Web site, it is important to get the user involved in the design process.

- User-centered Web development methods can assist in making a Web site that users find both useful and easy to use.

- This book is geared toward developing Web sites with a user-centered Web development process.

- Regardless of whether a site is being designed for the first time (which is becoming less likely) or redesigned (which is becoming more likely), and regardless of whether a site is informational, e-commerce, entertainment, community-based, or an intranet, these techniques can help you produce a site that provides a positive user experience.

- Techniques for user-centered design, such as the requirements gathering and the usability testing, can be used to incorporate user feedback into designing any Web site, of any size, with any purpose.

- Just remember that the user is the most important part of development!

Discussion Questions

1. How is Web site design different from traditional software design?
2. Why is user-centered design for a Web site important?
3. What two factors greatly influence users to use a Web site?
4. How is Web development similar to developing a system using the traditional Systems Development Life Cycle (SDLC)?
5. What are some of the challenges in Web development that make it more difficult than developing a traditional information system?
6. Why is it important to define your target user population?
7. What project management techniques can help designers manage Web development projects?

Design Exercise

Imagine that you are a Web development team working inside the computer division of Choco-Cookie, a large company that bakes and sells chocolate chip cookies to distributors. You have been asked to develop a Web site for the Choco-Cookie Company. The three main user populations are the employees of Choco-Cookie, the distributors who purchase and sell the product, and the customers who purchase the product from the distributors. Your Web development team indicates that it wants to include users from all three populations in the Web site development, but management says that there is no time to involve the users. How would you justify the need to involve the users? What benefit will user involvement have? What metrics could you use to prove your point?

Suggested Reading

Bias, R., & Mayhew, D. (Eds.). (2005). *Cost-Justifying Usability: An update for the Internet Age.* San Francisco: Morgan Kaufmann Publishers.

Burdman, J. (1999). *Collaborative Web Development.* Reading, MA: Addison-Wesley.

Bush, V. (1945). "As We May Think." *The Atlantic Monthly*, 176, 101–108.

Carroll, J., Chin, G., Rosson, M., Neale, D., Dunlap, D., & Isenhour, P. (2002). "Building Educational Technology Partnerships Through Participatory Design." In J. Lazar (Ed.), *Managing IT/Community Partnerships in the 21st Century* (pp. 88–115). Hershey, PA: Idea Group Publishing.

Ceaparu, I. (2003a). "Governmental Statistical Data on the Web: A Case Study of FedStats." *IT and Society*, 1(3), 1–17.

Ceaparu, I., Lazar, J., Bessiere, K., Robinson, J., & Shneiderman, B. (2004a). "Determining Causes and Severity of End-User Frustration." *International Journal of Human-Computer Interaction*, 17(3), 333–356.

Ceaparu, I., & Shneiderman, B. (2004b). "Finding governmental statistical data on the web: A study of categorically-organized links for the FedStats Topics page." *Journal of the American Society of Information Science & Technology*, 55(11), 1008–1015.

Ellis, R. D., & Kurniawan, S. (2000). "Increasing the Usability of Online Information for Older Users: A Case Study in Participatory Design." *International Journal of Human-Computer Interaction*, 12(2), 263–276.

Gido, J., & Clements, J. (1999). *Successful Project Management.* Cincinnati: South-Western College Publishing.

Jacko, J., Salvendy, G., Sainfort, F., Emery, K., Akoumianakis, D., Duffy, V., Ellison, J., Gant, D., Gill, Z., Ji, G., Jones, P., Karsh, B., Karshmer, A., Lazar, J., Peacock, B., Resnick, M., Sears, A., Smith, M., Stephanidis, C., & Ziegler, J. (2002). "Intranets and Organizational Learning: A Research and Development Agenda." *International Journal of Human-Computer Interaction*, 14(1), 95–130.

Kemp, T. (2001, November 28, 2001). "Macy's Doubles Conversion Rate." *InternetWeek.com*. Available at: http://www.internetwek.com/story/ INW20011128S20010004.

Lazar, J. (2003a). "The World Wide Web." In J. Jacko & A. Sears (Eds.), *The Handbook of Human-Computer Interaction* (pp. 714–730). Mahwah, NJ: Lawrence Erlbaum Associates.

Lazar, J., Jones, A., & Shneiderman, B. (2005a). "User Frustration with Technology in the Workplace: An Exploratory Study." To appear in *Behaviour and Information Technology*.

Lazar, J., & Norcio, A. (2001). "User Considerations in E-Commerce Transactions." In Q. Chen (Ed.), *Human-Computer Interaction: Issues and Challenges* (pp. 185–195). Hershey, PA: Idea Group Publishing.

Lazar, J., & Norcio, A. (2003b). "Training Novice Users in Developing Strategies for Responding to Errors When Browsing the Web." *International Journal of Human-Computer Interaction*, 15(3), 361–377.

Lazar, J., Ratner, J., Jacko, J., & Sears, A. (2004). "User Involvement in the Web Development Process: Methods and Cost-Justification." Proceedings of the 10th International Conference on Industry, Engineering, and Management Systems, 223–232.

Lazar, J., & Sears, A. (2005b). "Design of E-Business Web Sites." In G. Salvendy (Ed.), *Handbook of Human Factors and Ergonomics*. Hoboken, NJ: John Wiley & Sons.

Marcus, A. (2002). "Return on Investment for Usable UI Design." *User Experience Magazine*, 2(1), 25–31.

Mayhew, D., & Bias, R. (2003). "Cost-Justifying Web Usability." In J. Ratner (Ed.), *Human Factors and Web Development* (2nd ed., pp. 63–87). Mahwah, NJ: Lawrence Erlbaum Associates.

Nielsen, J. (2000). *Why Doc Searls Doesn't Sell Any Books*. Available at: http://www.useit.com.

Pew Internet and American Life Project. (2003). "The Ever-shifting Internet Population: A New Look at Internet Access and the Digital Divide." Available at: http://www.pewinternet.org.

Preece, J. (2000). *Online Communities: Designing Usability, Supporting Sociability*. New York: John Wiley & Sons.

Roberts-Witt, S. (September 25, 2001). "A Singular Focus." *PC Magazine*.

Schuler, D., & Namioka, A. (Eds.). (1993). *Participatory Design: Principles and Practices*. Hillsdale, NJ: Lawrence Erlbaum Associates.

Shneiderman, B. (2000). "Universal Usability: Pushing Human-Computer Interaction Research to Empower Every Citizen." *Communications of the ACM*, 43(5), 84–91.

Shneiderman, B. (2002). *Leonardo's Laptop: Human Needs and the New Computing Technologies.* Cambridge, MA: MIT Press.

Tedeschi, B. (August 30, 1999). "Good Web Site Design Can Lead to Healthy Sales." *The New York Times.*

chapter 2

Defining the Mission and Target User Population

After reading this chapter, you will be able to:

- Define a Web site mission.
- Define a target user population.
- Determine typical measurable goals for a Web site.
- Understand the needs of diverse user populations.
- Understand the needs of international user populations.
- Use the audience splitting technique.
- Understand what considerations are important for site redesign.

Introduction

It all starts here. The Web development life cycle begins when you are contacted to design or redesign a Web site. You might be a member of a consulting firm that has been formally hired to develop a Web site. You might be an individual who has been asked by a colleague or friend to develop a small Web site. You might be an employee in the information technology division (or MIS department, user services, or Web development team) of a client organization that requires a Web site design or redesign. You might be asked to develop a site for a community organization or you might be required to develop a site as a class project. Maybe you might think: "Hey, I would really like to design a Web site about my favorite hobby, folk guitar music." In any event, you are about to design a Web site, either independently or as a part of a development team. The first steps in developing or redesigning a Web site are to determine the mission of the site and determine the target user population.

Mission of the Web Site

User-centered design activities are only successful if you are clear about your audience and your mission. Web sites are built to fulfill a purpose—to meet the needs of certain people and to achieve organizational goals. People spend money developing a Web site—they expect a return on their investment. Even if the return on investment is hard to measure, the Web site is meant to serve a purpose.

Consider consumer products, such as cars or kitchen tools. Most products are designed to meet the needs of certain groups of consumers. Although it's true that some companies are happy to sell products to anyone willing to pay—you can't build a product with the idea that "someone will want to buy this." You build a product with a certain target consumer group in mind. You include them, determine their needs, involve them in product development, and hope that your product is successful. When those consumers purchase your product, your organizational goals of increasing revenues and making a profit are realized. This is exactly what a Web site should do—it should help to meet organizational goals by meeting the needs of its users. Different types of Web sites have different organizational goals. The next section details some of these potential goals.

Typical Organizational Goals of Different Web Sites

Typical Informational Web Site Goals
- Replace paper-based information distribution
- Provide quicker response to frequently asked questions
- Increase name recognition
- Increase organization membership
- Increase donations (for a nonprofit)
- Decrease phone inquiries

Typical E-commerce Web Site Goals

- Sell products
- Provide alternate form of customer service
- Advertise brick-and-mortar store
- Provide a service
- Provide transactions (which can be profitable)

Typical Entertainment Web Site Goals

- Profit through subscriptions
- Profit through advertising
- Support another medium of entertainment (e.g., a Web version of newspaper comics)
- Support a cause through entertainment

Typical Community Web Site Goals

- Provide resources for members
- Increase attendance at events or meetings
- Provide emotional support
- Help to create a sense of community

Typical Intranet Goals

- Improve communication between employees and organizational members
- Increase productivity of distributed teams
- Improve the collection, storage, and access of organizational data

Process of Determining the Site Mission

A Web site's mission should be defined by the client organization. When a client asks for a Web site design, they have a general idea of what the site should accomplish. A definite mission may not be determined in advance; more likely, the client will have an inkling of what the site should do, but will need some assistance in clarifying the mission. It is also possible that a redesigned Web site might have a mission that differs from its previous mission.

Although the client might not have a clear vision of exactly what the Web site should do, the client should have a basic idea of its purpose. What type of Web site should it be? Informational, e-commerce, entertainment, community, or intranet? All of these support different types of organizations and organizational missions. How will the Web site support the organizational mission? There needs to be an initial strategy for deciding what constitutes "success" for the Web site in the future. What goals exist for the Web site as it relates to the mission of the organization? This is important to determine because launching a site is not the final step. A site requires continuous support even after it has "gone live." A Web site needs to relate closely to the mission of the organization, as time (i.e., money) is required to maintain the site properly, provide upgrades, update information, answer questions, and process transactions. What will the Web site do for the organization?

Once the general mission of the Web site is stated by the client, you or your development team can use it as a guide to determine exactly what type of content the users want. An essential task for the development team is to understand the mission and history of the client organization, as well as current issues it might be grappling with. If the team is not familiar with the client organization itself, this is a good time to read as much as possible about the group. It would also be helpful to examine any organizational documentation, such as press releases, brochures, catalogs, and annual reports. It's possible that separate divisions of the organization have different missions and users in mind (Eschenfelder '04). As background information, you might even ask if there were previous plans to develop or redevelop a Web site, and if so, why those plans did not come to fruition. Such information can highlight problems to avoid during the current Web development effort.

The mission of the Web site is decided by the sponsoring organization. The organization funds the project, evaluates its success, and therefore, decides its mission. However, the client organization only defines the mission of the Web site— ultimately the users should define the content of the site because they are the ones who determine success. It is the action of the user, whether learning about an organization, purchasing a product, or calling the organization to schedule an appointment, that the sponsoring organization is most interested in. Without the user, a Web site cannot be successful or meet the established mission. Without user involvement in development, the Web site will not meet the content or usability needs of the user, thereby giving the user a reason not to visit or return to the site, which in turn, prevents the site from succeeding. Organizations can choose to ignore what users want in a Web site, but they do so at their own risk.

Clients may give their perceptions of what users want and need, but only the targeted users can actually tell you what they want and need. Unfortunately, sometimes the wants of the users and clients will conflict. For instance, the users might be interested in a quick download time, but the clients want a large number of graphics on the site. There might be other conflicts between what the users have indicated that they want, and what the clients have indicated that they want. Sometimes, there can even be a conflict within the client organization, over who the primary users should be. For the Web developer, this presents a tricky tightrope to walk. You don't want to counter your client's request nor do you want to ignore the wishes of the users. The best approach is to show the clients the results of your requirements gathering with users. At a later stage, you can show the clients the results of the usability testing. This way you can convince the client that you have their best interest at heart, since you are trying to satisfy the client's users. Another possibility is to allow the client to see users actually attempting to navigate through their Web site, but struggling. This is one of the most effective ways to convince a client of the importance of satisfying the users. In short, the client establishes the mission of the Web site and the users decide what content will be offered.

While it is very important to listen to the users and understand their desires for Web site development, at the same time, the mission of the Web site is useful because it can help to define the boundaries of the requirements gathering activities. A project scope is important so that you understand what the mission of the Web site is and what it is not. Without a defined scope, a project can easily lose focus by attempting to do everything without limits on time and cost. Most Web development projects are not large-scale e-commerce projects, with tens of thousands of pages, offering entertainment, information, chat rooms, products, and so on. A Web development project for a local church, synagogue, or mosque is not equivalent to developing a competitor Web site for amazon.com or yahoo.com. A sure way for a project to fail is to allow the project to include anything and everything under the sun. Therefore, a clear Web site mission must be established early on.

Writing a Mission Statement

Having a written mission statement for a Web site is a very good idea (Burdman '99). A short statement will help to clarify the overall organizational goal of the Web site. For instance, a mission statement might say: "Company X will develop a Web site to advertise our products, with the goal of increased sales" or "Community group Y will develop a Web site to keep our community members informed, with the hope that the attendance at community meetings will increase" or "Organization Z will develop a Web site to increase awareness about the need for recycling in our community." A good mission statement is short, easy to measure, and relates the Web site to the organizational mission.

Perhaps there are a number of different missions, related to different target user populations. If there are several separate targeted user populations, there might be a different mission for each one and you should have each mission described in the written statement. These statements can be very powerful, as they help to define the scope of the Web development project. In addition, these missions can be used to evaluate the Web site after a year or two, to determine if the site is really supporting the organization as defined in the Web site mission statement. For instance, a good question to ask the client would be: "A year after the Web site has launched, how do you expect it will improve your organization?" Make sure the client specifies how success will be measured. By page visits? By products sold? By satisfied customers? By larger turnouts at organizational meetings? By a higher public recognition of the organization? Although evaluation of the success of a Web site will not happen until after the Web site has actually been implemented, this is a good time to define what criteria will be used for evaluation and how "success" will be measured. Sometimes, even the activity of creating a Web site can be helpful, as it allows various members of the organization to openly discuss, describe, and argue about how success will be defined, which in the end, will help provide a clearer path for developers to follow.

What If There Isn't a Mission?

It is important to note that there should be a site mission. If the clients and Web development team cannot determine a clear site mission, it might mean that the Web site is not actually needed. It is also possible that the site is being developed only because the competitors have sites, or the client just wants to have a quick presence on the Web. This is a big mistake. Users form impressions of an organization when they visit a Web site, and those impressions are hard to change later. If a "preliminary" Web site is launched without sufficient planning, or is hard to use and doesn't meet the users' needs, they will likely get frustrated and not return to that site in the future. Developing a preliminary Web site without consideration for the users will hurt the client organization in the long run. If no one can define what the Web site should do for the organization, there will not be a

Mission of the Web Site Influences Redesign at OXO

OXO is a company that makes human-centered tools, for kitchen, garage, garden, and other tasks. What makes OXO tools different is that the tools are ergonomically designed so that they can be used by people with arthritis, carpal tunnel syndrome, or other special needs. This ease of use is a part of the corporate mission. However, OXO's previous Web site was not consistent with this mission, since the main Web page was unclear and confusing, as shown in Figure 2.1. In repeated tests, users could not correctly guess what the links on the homepage represented. If the mission of the Web site was to show that OXO products are

designed for ease of use, the old Web site would not have performed this mission.

OXO later redesigned the site's home-page with improved navigation, as shown in Figure 2.2. The navigational choices are now much easier to identify. Users know what the site is about, and what content is available to them.

Hands-On Example

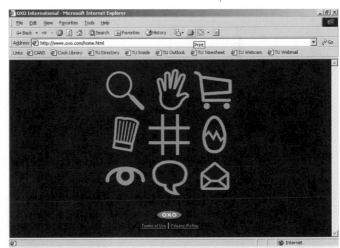

Figure 2.1 The previous homepage for oxo.com used icons that were hard to understand.

Figure 2.2 The new homepage for oxo.com is easier to use and showcases the organizational mission.

clear way to measure "success," which in turn means that most people won't define the site as successful. If a clear site mission and target user population can't be defined, this should raise a major "red flag." The bottom line is that if you don't know where you are going, you are not going to get there. At this point, you should ask three major questions:

1. What is the mission of the Web site?
2. What goals does the client have for user interaction on the Web site?
3. How will success be measured?

Targeted User Population

Once the mission of the Web site is defined, the next important question is: Who are the targeted users? This is sometimes hard to define because of the nature of the Web. Anyone can access a Web page from any geographic location, using multiple combinations of technology (connection speed, processor speed, monitor size, etc.). Since anyone can access the Web site (assuming that it's not password protected), some may ask, "What's the point of choosing a user population? Anyone can access it! The user population is everyone!" While it is true that anyone can access a site, it doesn't mean that the site is built specifically for them. Determining the target user population is sometimes known as "audience definition" (Fuccella '97). Only a few specific types of Web sites, such as multipurpose e-commerce sites (e.g., Amazon and Ebay), news sites (e.g., MSNBC and CNN), and search engines (e.g., Google and Yahoo!), are actually targeted toward the entire population of Web users.

Most other sites have a specific user targeted population. Another commonly used term is the "target market." Even though most organizations might not have a statement defining exactly who their site users are, and might not be able to identify their target user population, the fact remains that Web sites are built for a reason—to meet a specific organizational mission by attracting specific user populations to their site. These are known sets of users, with available demographic information and potential accessibility for requirements gathering. Web sites and their targeted user populations can be widely diverse. Some examples follow:

- The Association for Information Systems Web site (http://www.aisnet.org) is targeted toward researchers, teachers, and students who study information systems.

- The American Association of Retired People (AARP) Web site (http://www.aarp.org/) is targeted toward people who are 50 years of age or older.

- The INFORMS Web site (http://www.informs.org/) is targeted toward people who are interested in operations research and management science.

- The National Academic Quiz Tournaments Web site (http://www.naqt.com/) is targeted toward high school and college students who play a sport called quiz bowl.

- The Stash Tea Web site (http://www.stashtea.com/) is targeted toward consumers of tea in the United States who want to purchase tea products online or find a local retailer.

- The Cancernet Web site (http://www.cancer.gov) is targeted toward cancer patients, researchers, medical professionals, and health policy decision makers who are searching for information about cancer (see Case Study C: CancerNet).

- The PlayFootball Web site (http://www.playfootball.com) is targeted toward 8- to 14-year-olds who are interested in playing or watching football (see Case Study D: PlayFootball.com).

- The Institute of Notre Dame Web site (http://www.indofmd.org) is targeted toward faculty and staff, current students, parents of current students, alumni, and prospective students of IND.

Advantages of Knowing a Targeted Population

Without defining your targeted user population, there is no way to develop a successful site because if you don't know who the targeted users are, you cannot meet their needs. As discussed in the Introduction, if you don't know who will use a Web site, how can you develop a site that is both easy to use and helpful? As stated earlier, the focus in information systems is on designing for functionality/content (the ability to perform tasks that are needed) and usability (ease of use). If you don't know who your users are, it is impossible to determine their content and usability needs. You might think of a Web site as a consumer product. If you don't know who your targeted users are, how do you advertise your site? Most companies would not develop a product without first determining the target consumers. Products are not developed with the idea that someone will eventually purchase them. Business plans must specify the target consumers for the products or services sold by the business. This methodology should apply to Web sites. Even if you have general information about what type of people will be visiting your site, this can help with appropriate design efforts. Different guidelines should be followed for designing sites for younger children, older children, and mature adults. Connection speeds can determine how people experience a Web site. More information about how different user populations and computing environments can impact a site's usability is available in Chapter 3.

Targeting Different User Groups

A targeted population does not need to be one group of people only. It's possible that a Web site could be targeted to three or four specific, well-defined groups of people. If there are different user groups that constitute the target population, it is best to determine them at the beginning of development. For example, most university Web sites are targeted to a few different groups of people: current students, alumni, potential students, parents/siblings, and faculty and staff. Current students will probably want to know about courses, registration, and campus organizations and events. Faculty and staff might want to know about campus events, health insurance, and room and equipment reservations. Prospective students might want to know about dorms, tuition costs, and campus organizations. Some of the informational needs might be the same, and some might be different.

Another consideration is the technology: students, faculty, and staff on campus might have fast connections to the WWW, but prospective students and alumni, who are off campus, may have slow dial-up speeds. All of these groups and their respective needs must be considered. When there are multiple user groups within the target user population, it is important to involve them all in the development process. However, it's possible that while there are multiple user groups, some of them are higher priority (or will be more frequent users) than others. If there are, for instance, 10 different user groups, it should be noted which user groups are higher priority, and therefore, which groups will need to be included in the development process (see Case Study B: ASHA).

Developing User Profiles and Audience Splitting: Implications for the Development Process

In situations where there are different user groups within the target user population, it is necessary to determine what all of the different sets of users need.

Requirements Gathering with Multiple User Populations at Indiana University

The top levels of the Indiana University (Bloomington) Web site were going to be redesigned. For the redesign, they considered their "target audiences to be prospective students and their parents, as well as students currently enrolled, faculty and staff who are employed at IAB, and alumni." To help with the requirements analysis from these multi- ple user populations, past Web usage stats and questions sent to the Webmaster by users were analyzed. Thirty-three offices on the IAB campus, which dealt with all of the defined user populations, were interviewed by the development team. This indirect approach to collecting information was very appropriate, since one of the missions of the new Web site was to reduce the number of phone requests for information received by each of these offices. Based on the data collected, six general areas of information were identified (Corry '97).

Sometimes it's helpful to start out by developing user profiles for each user group in the target user population (Mayhew '99). These profiles should contain as much information as is currently known about each user group. That will assist in determining what information about the characteristics of the users will still need to be collected during requirements gathering. If requirements gathering is done with only one of the user groups that comprise the target population, then the results of the requirements gathering will be biased and not representative of the complete target population.

Planning at this stage can have major implications for later stages of the Web design. If there are different groups of users within the target population for a Web site, information on the site can be presented for the different groups using a technique called audience splitting. But that also means that requirements gathering must take place with all or most of these user populations. Some important questions to ask at this point include:

1. To whom is the Web site targeted?
2. Are there different user groups within the target population?
3. Can we develop separate user profiles?
4. Can we contact all of these different user groups?

An example of audience splitting is shown in Figure 2.3. On the homepage of cdwg.com, a company that sells computing equipment to government agencies,

Figure 2.3 The CDWG Web site, showing audience splitting for three different user populations (federal, state and local, and educational customers).

there are separate links for three different types of government customers: federal government customers, state and local government customers, and educational customers (which are primarily government funded). These links take different user groups to Web pages that are specifically tailored to their interests.

Hands-On Example

Multiple User Populations for a Digital Library on the Environment

A project took place at UC Berkeley to build an online digital library of public information about the environment. Much of this information was formatted as color images and related data from the California Department of Water Resources. For developing this Web-based digital library, there were five distinct populations of users identified: film library staff, publications staff, information officers, engineers, and lawyers. The distinctions between the user populations were important. For instance, film library staff were able to perform quick and appropriate searches, but other user populations did not have the same level of need and did not have similar search capabilities (Van House '96).

Diverse User Populations

There are a number of user groups that have been defined to have special needs related to Web design. It is important to determine if your targeted user population includes any of these well-defined user groups. These groups include younger users (14 and under), older users (65 and older), users with sensory disabilities (e.g., visual impairment), users with motor impairments (e.g., limited hand use), and users with low levels of computer experience (Shneiderman '00). Children as young as five are involved with computers, and despite the popular notion that children know everything about computers, they also find technology frustrating to use (Stellin '02). For Web design purposes, children can be split into separate age-related groups: preschool (<six years old), elementary school (6–10 years old), and middle school (11–14 years old), each having varied interface needs (Hanna '97). Children older than 14 years of age have interaction needs similar to those of adults. In general, younger children like interfaces with lots of color and animation, rather than large blocks of text (Clarke '01; Sullivan '00), even though this may not necessarily improve their task success.

Older users are increasingly using the Internet and finding the technology difficult to use. Older users tend to have more trouble finding information on Web sites and dealing with multiple application windows (Ellis '00; Mead '97). For instance, older users tend to make errors more frequently and have stronger negative reactions to making them (Birdi '97). Improvements in assistive technology, as well as initiatives in the programming and design community such as the World Wide Web Consortium's Web Accessibility Initiative, have made more Web content accessible for users with sensory or motor disabilities (Paciello '00; Slatin '03). But these Web sites can be used by people with disabilities only if the sites are designed with accessibility in mind. More information about universal design for the Web is available in Chapter 7.

It's possible that the targeted user population may include users from countries outside the country where the Web site is built. This can also influence the development process. It's important to determine whether users from different countries can use the same Web site. If the site is small and primarily informational, then it is probable that with relatively minor changes, it can be used by people from different countries. For instance, it might be necessary to provide translations from miles to meters and Fahrenheit to Celsius. Additionally, care must be taken to provide clear date formats (e.g., 02-09-05 is not a clear date because it means different things in different countries). This process is called internationalization. There is also the question of language. While English is the primary language for the Web, if there are large numbers of users for whom English is not their primary language, it might be useful to offer information in other languages, such as Spanish, French, or Chinese. While some search engines, such as Google, provide basic translation services, they tend to be imperfect. Even providing limited information in multiple languages can be helpful. For instance, L.L. Bean's Web site offers help in four languages (French, Spanish, German, and Japanese). See Figure 2.4.

For large informational and e-business sites with well-defined populations in multiple countries, it might not be sufficient to make a site international by simply providing multiple date and measurement formats. It might be necessary to set up multiple Web sites for each country served. Creating multiple versions of a Web site and modifying them to meet the needs of specific user populations is known as localization (Alvarez '98). Each Web site can be tailored to the local standards, icons, and especially, acceptable content. Different icons, such as mailboxes, hand gestures, and body symbols can be customized (Russo '93; Sears '00). Additionally, local Web sites make it easier to address the various cur-

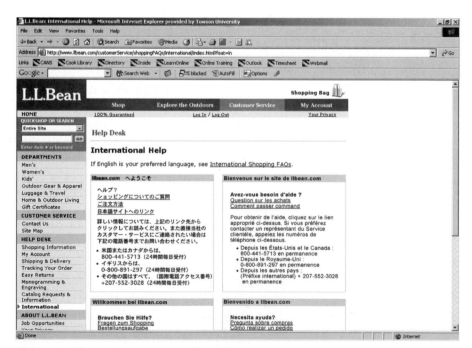

Figure 2.4 The L.L. Bean Web site offers help information in four languages: French, Spanish, German, and Japanese.

rencies, taxes, transaction costs, and shipping policies of different countries. In later stages of development, usability testing should be conducted with users from the different countries identified as part of the target user population. An example of a localized Web site is Twinings Tea, which offers separate Web sites for their customers in Australia, the United Kingdom, and the United States (see Figure 2.5).

Additional Considerations for Web Site Redesign

When designing a Web site from scratch, there are a number of issues to be decided, such as the target user population and the Web site mission. However, redesigning a Web site with the user-centered approach is a little different from designing a new site. If you are redesigning a currently existing Web site, the site mission and the target population should be well established. The client should easily be able to identify the Web site mission and the target user population. Feedback from users, whether formal or informal, might help to drive the

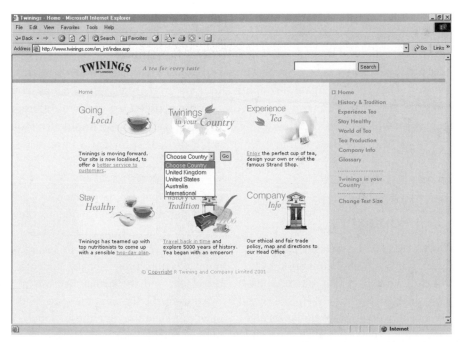

Figure 2.5 Twinings of London, a specialty tea company, offers multiple Web sites for customers from different countries.

changes that take place as part of the site redesign. It is possible that the client wants to keep the site mission and user population the same, and is only interested in changing the design to increase usability. It is also possible that with a site redesign, the client might be interested in changing the mission of the site, for example, by providing new services and broadening the target user population. A site should be redesigned only if there is a pressing need to do so. A site should be redesigned if the site usability is a problem, if the target user population or mission has significantly changed, or if so much information has been added to the site that the overall information structure is no longer appropriate. Changing a Web site design just for a "fresh look" is not a sufficient reason for a redesign. The IBM Ease of Use Web site is an example of a site where the mission and target user population changed (see Hands-On Example below).

Web Site Logs: Tracking Where Users Have Been

When redesigning a site, the Web site logs from the current site are a good resource for examining recent site users. Web site logs track information about requested pages and are usually stored on the Web server. Think of them as a sign-in book, except that when users visit a site, they do not need to record any information about themselves. The Web server automatically tracks information about their actions. The Web site logs provide information such as which Web pages are viewed most often, which domains request Web pages, and what paths users follow as they navigate through a site. As you analyze Web site logs, you might discover that the target population and the actual users are two different groups of people. If you are redesigning an existing Web site, you might also look at the logs from the site's search engine, which provide information about fre-

Hands-On Example

IBM Broadens the Target User Population

The IBM Ease of Use Web site provides a great example of site redesign. In 1996, the site, known as the HCI (Human-Computer Interaction) Web site, was developed with software designers and developers in mind. However, as the site grew, the target user population broadened. The name was changed to the "Ease of Use" Web site and the target user population was expanded to include human factors professionals, students, professors, and the media. Because of this growth, the site was redesigned and new considerations for these populations were taken into account (Lisle '98).

quently searched topics, and can indicate information that users have trouble finding. Additionally, comments left in the Web site "guest book," or informal comments sent to the Webmaster, can provide guidance for Web site redesign. More information about Web site logs is available in Chapter 11.

Research Prior Relationships

When you redesign a currently existing Web site, it is important to examine who developed the site in the first place (for example, a consulting firm or an in-house MIS group) to determine whether or not the relationship between the client organization and the original Web site development team is still positive. If the relationship is good, it might be useful to ask the designer(s) for documentation from the original Web site development. In some cases, the client organization might be dissatisfied with the Web site that was originally developed—that, in fact, may be the reason for the redesign. If so, the relationship might be less than positive, and it might be best not to contact the original site designer(s). In extreme cases, the person or firm who developed the original Web site might still have password access to the HTML files, causing a particularly awkward situation, and political issues might arise. As part of the new development team, the best approach is to work through the client organization.

If a Web site is being redesigned, there are a number of important questions to ask:

1. Should the target user population stay the same or change?
2. Should the mission of the Web site stay the same or change?
3. Should the site structure change? Will the current information structure support the new user population and/or new content?
4. Should the page layout stay the same?
5. Does documentation exist from the original Web site design?
6. Can the original design team be contacted?
7. Are there any political or organizational issues that could affect the successful redevelopment and implementation of the Web site?

Chapter Wrap-Up

Before Web site development takes place, two decisions must be made:

1. What is the Web site mission?
2. Who is the targeted user population(s)?

Unless the client has defined these issues, the rest of the Web development process will be fruitless. Without knowing the users and the Web site's mission, it will be impossible to

- collect user requirements (because you don't know who your users are)
- meet functionality and usability needs (because you don't know what users want)
- perform usability testing (because you don't know whom to have participate)
- advertise (because you don't know who to target)

These initial decisions in Web site development are important steps to ensure that the following phases of the Web development life cycle are not misguided activities.

Discussion Questions

1. Who should you talk with to determine the mission of a Web site?
2. What are the five main types of Web sites?
3. What type of documentation can be useful in determining the mission of a Web site?
4. What is audience splitting?
5. What is a Web site mission statement, and how does it relate to evaluation goals?
6. What is a user profile, and why might it be useful?
7. Give an example of a Web site that has multiple targeted user populations.
8. When you are redesigning a Web site, can the targeted user population change from that of the previous site?
9. What techniques for gathering information can be used when redesigning a Web site that cannot be used when designing a new site?

Design Exercise

Imagine that a new health club is opening in your area. The indoor club will consist of a pool, tennis courts, workout equipment, basketball courts, and aerobic classes. You have been hired to build a Web site for the new club. Because the managers are busy planning the grand opening, they have simply indicated that they want a Web site that will bring customers to the club. How would you define the mission statement of the health club Web site? Who is the target user population? What challenges do you anticipate in the development of the Web site?

Suggested Reading

Alvarez, M., Kasday, L., & Todd, S. (1998). "How We Made the Web Site International and Accessible: A Case Study." *Proceedings of the 1998 Human Factors and the Web Conference.* Available at: http://www.research.att.com/conf/hfweb/proceedings /alvarez/.

Birdi, K., & Zapf, D. (1997). "Age Differences in Reactions to Errors in Computer-Based Work." *Behaviour and Information Technology*, 16(6), 309–319.

Burdman, J. (1999). *Collaborative Web Development.* Reading, MA: Addison-Wesley.

Clarke, J. (2001). "Key Factors in Developing a Positive User Experience for Children on the Web: A Case Study." *Proceedings of the Human Factors and the Web 2001.* Available at: http://www.optavia.com/hfweb/index.htm.

Corry, M., Frick, T., & Hansen, L. (1997). "User-Centered Design and Usability Testing of a Web Site: An Illustrative Case Study." *Educational Technology Research and Development*, 45(4), 65–76.

Ellis, R. D., & Kurniawan, S. (2000). "Increasing the Usability of Online Information for Older Users: A Case Study in Participatory Design." *International Journal of Human-Computer Interaction*, 12(2), 263–276.

Eschenfelder, K. (2004). "The Customer Is Always Right, but Whose Customer Is More Important? Conflict and Web Site Classification Schemes." *Information Technology and People*, 16(4), 419–439.

Fleming, J. (1998). *Web Navigation: Designing the User Experience.* Sebastopol, CA: O'Reilly and Associates.

Fuccella, J. (1997). "Using User-Centered Design Methods to Create and Design Usable Web Sites." *Proceedings of the 1997 ACM Conference on Systems Documentation*, 69–77.

Gido, J., & Clements, J. (1999). *Successful Project Management.* Cincinnati: South-Western College Publishing.

Goodwin, N. (1987). "Functionality and Usability." *Communications of the ACM*, 30(3), 229–233.

Hanna, L., Risden, K., & Alexander, K. (1997). "Guidelines for Usability Testing with Children." *Interactions*, 4(5), 9–14.

Lazar, J., Beere, P., Greenidge, K., & Nagappa, Y. (2003). "Web Accessibility in the Mid-Atlantic United States: A Study of 50 Web Sites." *Universal Access in the Information Society*, 2(4), 331–341.

Lazar, J., Ratner, J., Jacko, J., & Sears, A. (2004). "User Involvement in the Web Development Process: Methods and Cost-Justification." Proceedings of the 10th International Conference on Industry, Engineering and Management Systems, 223–232.

Lazar, J., & Sears, A. (2005). *Design of E-Business Web Sites*. In G. Salvendy (Ed.), Handbook of Human Factors and Ergonomics. Hoboken, NJ: John Wiley & Sons.

Lisle, L., Dong, J., & Isensee, S. (1998). "Case Study of Development of an Ease of Use Web Site." Proceedings of the 1998 Human Factors and the Web Conference. Available at: http://www.research.att.com/conf/hfweb/.

Mayhew, D. (1999). *The Usability Engineering Lifecycle*. San Francisco: Morgan Kaufmann Publishers.

Mead, S., Spaulding, V., Sit, R., Meyer, B., & Walker, N. (1997). "Effects of Age and Training on World Wide Web Navigation Strategies." Proceedings of the Human Factors and Ergonomics Society Annual Meeting, 152–156.

Navarro, A., & Khan, T. (1998). *Effective Web Design*. San Francisco: Sybex.

Nielsen, J. (1996). "International Usability Engineering." In E. DelGaldo & J. Nielsen (Eds.), *International User Iinterfaces* (pp. 1–19). New York: John Wiley & Sons.

Nielsen, J. (2000, April 2, 2000). The Mud-Throwing Theory of Usability. Available at: http://www.useit.com/alertbox/20000402.html.

Paciello, M. (2000). *Web Accessibility for People with Disabilities*. Lawrence, KS: CMP Books.

Powell, T., Jones, D., & Cutts, D. (1998). *Web Site Engineering: Beyond Web Page Design*. Upper Saddle River, NJ: Prentice Hall.

Russo, P., & Boor, S. (1993). "How Fluent Is Your Interface? Designing for International Users." Proceedings of the InterCHI 1993, 342–347.

Sears, A., Jacko, J., & Dubach, E. (2000). "International Aspects of WWW Usability and the Role of High-End Graphical Enhancements." *International Journal of Human-Computer Interaction*, 12(2), 243–263.

Shneiderman, B. (2000). "Universal Usability: Pushing Human-Computer Interaction Research to Empower Every Citizen." *Communications of the ACM*, 43(5), 84–91.

Slatin, J., & Rush, S. (2003). *Maximum Accessibility*. New York: Addison-Wesley.

Stellin, S. (2002, April 22, 2002). "Seems Computers Baffle 10-Year-Olds, Too." *The New York Times*. Available at: http://www.nytimes.com/2002/2004/2022/technology /2022WEB.html.

Stout, R. (1997). *Web Site Stats*. Berkeley, California: Osborne McGraw Hill.

Sullivan, T., Norris, C., Peet, M., & Soloway, E. (2000). "When Kids Use the Web: A Naturalistic Comparison of Children's Navigation Behavior and Subjective Preferences on Two WWW Sites." Proceedings of the 2000 Conference on Human Factors and the Web. Available at: http://www.pantos.org/ts/papers/wkutw/.

Van House, N., Butler, M., Ogle, V., & Schiff, L. (1996). "User-Centered Iterative Design for Digital Libraries: The Cypress Experience." *D-Lib Magazine*, 2(2). Available at: http://www.dlib.org/dlib/february96/02vanhouse.html.

Requirements Gathering—What Information Is Needed?

After reading this chapter, you will be able to:

- Gather general user demographic information.
- Determine user domain knowledge.
- Understand user computing experience.
- Understand user computing environment.
- Define task analysis and content.
- Use benchmarking.
- Understand methods for requirements gathering for site redesign.

Introduction

The next phase of the Web development life cycle is requirements gathering—learning about your target users. You'll learn who they are, what they want, their computer experience, and their computing environment. We'll discuss the requirements gathering stage in two chapters. Chapter 3 defines the types of information you must collect from users and Chapter 4 covers methods for collecting the information. Requirements gathering is known by different names in different fields—information requirements, requirements determination, and needs analysis. The common goal is to learn as much as possible about what users require—what they need and what they want in order to have a successful interaction experience. There are many different types of information that must be collected from users, including general demographic information, domain knowledge, user computing experience, user computing environment, content, and benchmarking. We'll discuss each type of information in detail in the following sections.

General User Demographic Information

The process begins with gathering general demographic information about your users. For example: What are the respective ages of your target population? Is your target population mostly male or female? What is the respective educational level of your target users? Only relevant types of demographic information should be requested. Asking inappropriate questions in a survey, interview, or focus group lessens the likelihood that users will respond. Also, if too many questions are asked, users are less likely to respond.

Some basic demographic information may be provided by the client organization. If the client organization has previous demographic information about its users, then the responses to demographic information questions in the requirements gathering ensures that the responses represent the target user population. If your target population is 15- to 21-year-old males and most of the responses you receive are from females, then your inquiries do not represent the target population and your collected information is biased. Or perhaps your Web site is not targeted to a specific gender, but all of your information gathering responses are from men; then you might suspect that your responses do not accurately represent the target population.

If the sponsoring organization does not have much demographic information about the targeted users, the demographic information collected during requirements gathering can be used to establish a baseline. This is not ideal because it might be harder to determine if actual members of the target user population are being reached, but this situation occurs. Sometimes, by just eyeballing the demographic data, employees at the client organization can get a sense if the responses to user requirements gathering are from people who would typically represent the target user population.

Other demographic questions might relate to current employment status, job position, and salary. Asking users about their salary might be more appropriate for sites that attempt to sell products or solicit donations; otherwise, it is questionable whether users would be comfortable providing information about their salaries. It might be appropriate to ask about primary and secondary languages spoken, especially if the site is expected to draw users from outside the country of origin. If the Web site is for an organization such as a preschool, it might be appropriate to ask questions about the number and age of children in the family. The type of Web site being developed or redesigned determines which questions are appropriate. For a Web site sponsored by a stamp collecting club, asking about the marital status of users or asking how many children they have might seem inappropriate. However, it's very appropriate for understanding the user needs for a church, synagogue, or mosque, where child care and programs for singles are offered. Some important questions to ask, related to demographic information, include:

- What is your age?
- What is your gender?
- What is your educational experience?
- What is your current job?
- What is your primary language?
- Are you married?

Domain Knowledge

When we are involved in jobs, tasks, or other responsibilities, we bring a certain amount of previous knowledge and experience that is required to effectively complete the task. This previous knowledge related to a specific task or area, is known as domain knowledge. For instance, most adults know how to complete a banking task because they are familiar with checks, credit cards, bank accounts, and the processes involved; but most children under the age of 13 do not. Many job openings require that candidates have previous job experience; this prior experience serves as knowledge of the job domain.

Sometimes previous domain knowledge is required in order to use a Web site effectively. This might be the case if there is highly specialized information on the site, and the target population is specialized. For instance, a Web site about anesthesiology would likely include a lot of medical terminology, and this would be

Hands-On Example

Confusing Terminology for the General Public at the Fedstats Web Site

A number of studies have been done to examine the usability of the Fedstats Web site (http://www.fedstats.gov), as shown in Figure 3.1. The Web site is a central gateway to statistics provided by more than 100 U.S. federal agencies to serve both statisticians and the general public. The link titles under which data could be found were very confusing, and nonstatisticians (who make up a large share of users) were unable to find the data they were looking for. By changing the categories that the links are organized under, and by adding keywords that more accurately represent the terminology that most users are familiar with, the task success rate jumped from 15 percent to 42 percent. One example of confusing terminology on the site was the phrase "metropolitan areas"—users were looking for the word "cities." The biggest usability problem was not the layout or the navigation, but rather the terminology. Typical users did not have the domain knowledge in statistics that the developers assumed (Ceaparu '04).

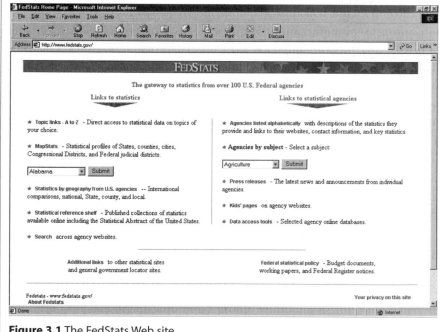

Figure 3.1 The FedStats Web site.

Unclear Terminology at the Quiz Bowl Web Site

Hands-On Example

When a Web site was developed for the Quiz Bowl community, it was important to note what terminology was frequently used in the community and therefore would need to be used on the site.

Despite using standard terms from the domain knowledge, usability testing revealed that a majority of users had problems understanding the terminology. Changes were made to clarify the meaning of the content, providing definitions of the various acronyms (Lazar '99).

Examples of Quiz Bowl terminology that was confusing to users:

- NAQT
- CBI
- ACF
- Toss-up
- Buzz
- Neg 5
- Chain bonus

appropriate if the target population is anesthesiologists. However, technical terminology about anesthesiology would be inappropriate if the Web site is targeted to nonmedical personnel who want to learn about anesthesiology. It is important to determine what terminology is most appropriate for the target user population. Surprisingly, this is a major problem. Sometimes the major usability problem of a Web site isn't a technical or coding issue, but one related to terminology. Sometimes, different user populations use different terminology. For instance, in Case Study C: CancerNet, we see that cancer can also be described as sarcoma or carcinoma. In other cases, terminology can be unclear and therefore interpreted in different ways (see the Hands-On Example above and on the previous page).

If domain knowledge is required for effective Web site use, the Web development team should query the targeted user population to determine what level of domain knowledge the users have. It would be a mistake for clients to assume that "everyone knows about X and Y." This assumption is as silly as saying, "We don't need to provide driving directions on our Web site. Everyone already knows how to get to our organizational headquarters." A Web site with a lot of technical jargon may limit effective use to those users with a large amount of domain knowledge. Limitations to user domain knowledge that could affect how material is presented on a Web site needs to be discovered at an early stage in the development process. It is much easier to learn about the terminology of users early on, rather than discovering it later in the process.

User Computing Experience

The amount of user computing experience can have a great impact on the success of interaction with a Web site. Novice users (people with little computing or Web experience), may interact with a Web site very differently from expert users. In human-computer interaction research, there has always been a major focus on the novice-expert continuum of users. Although definitions of novices and experts can differ, novice users are usually considered people who do not know much about the interface and the computer system and may use computer interfaces infrequently, whereas experts use computer interfaces frequently and are very familiar with the interaction required to complete their tasks. In between the novice and the expert is the intermittent user, who may have a broad knowledge of interface concepts, but uses a specific interface irregularly or may use a number of different interface systems.

When traditional information systems are designed, one of the most important considerations is the computing knowledge level of the target users. It would be inappropriate to force novice users to use a command language such as UNIX, which requires detailed knowledge to perform tasks. On the other hand, UNIX may be a natural choice for computer scientists or engineers. Novice users and expert users have different experiences, and therefore have different needs. Frequently, interface designers will allow for multiple paths for reaching a goal. For instance, in a desktop application, novice users might be able to go through a series of menus to reach their task goals. For experts, this might be tedious and time-consuming. Keyboard shortcuts (e.g., Control-G) and command languages support expert users in their tasks. In addition, some interfaces have a form of user modeling, where different user experience settings (novice, intermediate, expert) have different interaction methods best suited to their needs.

Most systems developers really do not understand what it's like to be a novice user. For most expert users, nothing is too frustrating, error messages are understandable, and system problems are considered challenges that can be overcome with relative ease. But for novice users, the world of computing is very different and can be very frustrating. In fact, the Web itself can be frustrating. For instance, many situations that users experience daily, such as long downloads, pop-ups, and unclear dialog boxes, are considered errors by novice users. In all of these situations the computer system is operating correctly as planned; however, novices perceive that the system is in an error state. Figure 3.2 is a perfect example of why users get frustrated. When users access a university intranet, there is a link for

Figure 3.2 A dialog box displayed when users click on a university intranet "help" link.

"help." When users click the link, they are told "help not found." It is easy to see how a user can get frustrated with that! There is a relationship between user experience levels and emotional levels of frustration; the more experienced users do not suffer as much of an emotional toll when they get frustrated. However, even experienced users can suffer frustration, especially when a system keeps them from completing important tasks or wastes a lot of their time.

Frustration with the computer is not a minor thing. It can even impact human physiological measures, such as muscle tightening and blood pressure (Riseberg '98; Hazlett '03). These high levels of frustration partially explain why many users eventually stop using the Web. In a recent study by the Pew Internet and American Life Project, 42 percent of Americans reported that they currently do not go online. While some of these people have never been online, many of them have gone online and found the experience to be so frustrating and confusing that they decide the Web just isn't worth the trouble (see Figure 3.3). This is a troubling finding, especially for businesses that hope to sell their products or services online. It definitely highlights the need to make the Web browsing experience as positive and easy as possible.

Because the level of user computer experience can greatly impact how a user interacts with a Web site, it is important to learn as much as possible about user experience with computers in general, and specifically, with the Web. It's possible that a user might be experienced with word processing, but not much else. It's possible that a user might use the Web often, but only check three favorite Web sites each time, and not use any other computer applications. It's possible that a user in the targeted user population may never have used a computer before. As Web developers, we are interested in knowing all of this information, because the more detailed a user profile we can create, the better off we are.

Users are often *very* frustrated by problems they encounter on computers.

The most common feeling users experience after a frustrating computer experience is anger.

Many users feel helpless and resigned after a frustrating computer experience.

Figure 3.3 The effects of frustration on users.

It's important to understand the level of user experience with computers in general, software applications such as word processing, databases and spreadsheets, Web browsing, and different types of Web sites. Within these categories, there are important determinations that relate to the frequency of use (how many hours per week, or how many weeks between usage) and the satisfaction of use. It might also be beneficial to ask users whether they use a computer in their workplace, and if so, whether that experience is enjoyable. It might be important to ascertain user typing skills. If it is expected that the target user population is not experienced with computers, you might ask how they feel about working with computers: whether they strongly like computers, like computers, dislike computers, or strongly dislike computers. This information might alert the Web development team (as well as the client organization) if they can expect resistance from the targeted user population to using the Web site. If there are several user groups within the target user population, the information collected related to user computing experience can help you gain a better understanding of how the user groups differ, and what design elements need to be placed on the Web site to meet these user needs.

Using Interface Metaphors

Some Web developers might ask, "Why is it important to determine all of this information from users? What difference does it make if users are familiar with spreadsheets? We are designing a Web site, not a spreadsheet." More information about users is always better than less information. For instance, if all of the user population is familiar with spreadsheets, you might be able to adapt spreadsheet concepts or terminology in your site design. The more you know about the users, the more you can use that information to design an interface that the users can relate to. If you find that your users are familiar with other software applications, those concepts can be included in the interface design. For instance, in many e-commerce sites, shopping cart and checkout metaphors are used. Other metaphors frequently used in interface design include the trash can and file folders. Simple metaphors based on the physical world are frequently used regardless of user computing experience. For instance, the New Hampshire Fall Foliage Web site uses the metaphor of a falling leaf, which can be adjusted to see the current level of foliage (see Figure 3.4). While these are basic metaphors, metaphors adopted from other applications (e.g., sheets and tabs from spreadsheets or saved queries from database programs), can be used if the data collected suggests that users will understand them.

Adapting to Past Experiences

Other types of information about user computing experience can be used to tailor your Web site to the users. For instance, if most users have never browsed the Web before, then it would be inappropriate to require plug-in applications (such as Adobe Acrobat) to view some of the site documents. The Web site for ISWORLD (http://www.isworld.org) requires using Adobe Acrobat to view some documents, but this is acceptable because ISWORLD is a resource used by teachers, researchers, and students of information systems, all of whom would be comfortable using Adobe Acrobat. On the other hand, if the target population for a Web site is preschool teachers, it might be unreasonable to assume that all

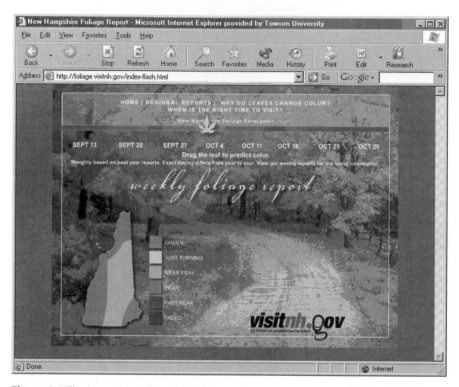

Figure 3.4 The New Hampshire Fall Foliage Web site uses the metaphor of a falling leaf to display fall foliage on various dates. Users adjust the position of the leaf to see what the foliage looks like on different dates.

preschool teachers are familiar with and comfortable using Adobe Acrobat. Plug-ins tend to crash and the dialog boxes can cause confusion for novice users. Therefore, a plug-in should be avoided, if possible, for novice user populations unless it is clear that most users in the target user population are familiar with the plug-in.

Asking questions about user satisfaction with their previous computing experiences can yield useful information. Understanding their past frustrations is just as important. For instance, if the most frequent frustration for a large number of users is slow download speed, then a primary design goal for your Web site should be quick download time, which means you should avoid graphics and large documents. If a sore point for users is confusing terminology, then you should take extra care to ensure that the terminology used on your site is clear and easy to understand. Determining the positive and negative computing expe-

that are used across the spectrum of Web users, this can be helpful. For instance, Google provides data on the operating systems and Web browser versions of users who visit their site (http://www.google.com/press/zeitgeist.html). Other sites that provide various types of data about Web usage include http://www.w3schools.com/browsers/browsers_stats.asp, http://www.netfactual.com/, and http://www.clickz.com/stats/.

Some important questions to ask, related to user computing environment, include:

1. What browser are you using? (Internet Explorer, Netscape Navigator, Neoplanet, Mozilla, AOL, Lynx, Firefox)

2. What version of the browser are you using? (version 4, 5, 6, etc.)

3. What platform are you using? (Windows, MacOS, Linux)

4. What screen resolution are you using? (800×600, 1024×768, etc.)

5. What is your Internet connection speed? (28.8, 56k, cable modem, DSL, etc.)

6. What plug-ins do you have? (Abobe Acrobat, RealAudio, Windows Media Player, etc.)

Task Analysis and Content

While most of the requirements gathering relates to who the users are and how they get to the Web site, tasks analysis and content relate to *why* users visit a site. A Web site can be 100 percent usable and accessible, but if it doesn't offer content that users want, then users either will not come to the Web site initially, or will not return to the Web site after one visit. Task analysis and content are closely related concepts. One way to define task analysis is simply what users want to achieve (Redish '03). This is different from determining the users, their technology, or their previous computing experience. Content is the information available on Web sites. Whether that content is static information on a Web page, data that is updated often (e.g., weather information or sports scores), or data accessed via searching a Web database, that content (information) is the primary reason that users visit Web sites.

Depending on the type of Web site, the tasks can be complex or simple. For instance, the task of using a search engine is a relatively simple task structure, and is well defined over years of experience with user searches. Small Web sites with information about a nonprofit organization are also relatively simple task structures, although the content that users want can be unclear and may need to be defined. For other types of Web sites, the task structures are far more complex. There are Web sites (such as an intranet or a complex B2B e-commerce site) where tasks are complex and based on the tasks in the workplace. These types of task structures might involve multiple people, processes, and accounts. For these sites, a thorough task analysis and examination of the workflow from person to person in the organization and organizational processes must occur (Redish '03). These sites tend to be transaction-oriented; in fact, they are closer to Web-based applications than Web sites (Hilberg '03). Frequently, these sites involve the transfer of money, products, services, or materials. Other references that can provide useful information on building complex e-business sites include (Norris '01; Turban '00; Nelson '02; Chan '01).

For other types of Web sites, such as community sites, a thorough understanding of the tasks must first take place. These tasks include reading and posting messages to the computer-mediated communication tool (list server, bulletin board, newsgroup), joining and unjoining the community, and searching for shared information resources (Preece '00). But for most strictly informational Web sites, the task structure is relatively simple: users want to find information. Primarily, users will use the built-in site navigation, but as a site structure grows or when users cannot immediately find what they are looking for, they will use a search engine (Proctor '02). The main question in these situations is what information (content), the users want to access. The different user groups that make up a target user population might have different ideas regarding what content might be useful to them; this should be taken into consideration.

Determining Content Preferences

Web development teams should try to determine whether users are interested in content such as: news about the client organization, a list of phone numbers, links to other sites, downloadable forms, pictures of events, or perhaps a "spotlight of the month." Other possibilities include FAQs, success stories, and file downloads. Would the users like to purchase certain products? Would the users be interested in video clips of events? What about educational materials? The content should draw users to the Web site. For instance, simply placing an electronic version of a paper brochure on the Web will probably not be sufficient to draw users to a site.

Determining the content that users are interested in can be challenging. The Web development team can discuss content with the client to come up with a list of possibilities. However, creating a list of possible content can be tricky. The Web development team and the client may not always be able to guess what the users are interested in. It might be necessary to do an exploratory study first, by interviewing users, creating a focus group (see Chapter 4 for more information on focus groups), or conducting a survey to determine what types of resources the users would be interested in. Another possible source of content ideas can be defined if the client organization describes recent problems. For instance, if the client organization describes a large number of requests for a certain document, maybe that document can be made available on the Web. Or if the organization has to repeatedly give the same information over the phone, this information would be a good candidate for content on the Web site. Although a content topic might be appropriate, generally it will need to be rewritten for the site. Paragraphs will need to be shorter and easier to scan, and graphics, or color may need to be added to make the content more attractive. Additionally, benchmarking can provide possible content ideas (see the benchmarking section later in this chapter).

Although the client usually has a good understanding of what they want the Web site to do, the users actually use the site, so their comments regarding content are very important. Users can rank a list of possible resources using a scale (1 = most interested, 9 = least interested). Users can select whether content is needed, wanted, or not wanted, or rank each choice in terms of importance (1 = first most important content, 2 = second most important content, etc.). Client suggestions of appropriate content are not enough; users should also be encouraged to suggest new content ideas.

Indirectly Collecting User Requirements at Indiana University

One way to determine content is by indirectly collecting content requirements from users. When Indiana University redesigned their Web site, they consulted 35 campus departments. Each department was queried about what questions were asked of them most frequently. These questions came through phone calls, visits, mail, and e-mail. A list of these questions and appropriate responses was developed and included as part of the Web site content. Although users were not contacted directly, their feedback and content requirements were considered in the design process (Corry '97).

It's possible that there might be a disagreement between what content users need on the Web site and what the client wants on the Web site. In the case of a disagreement, the best strategy is to show the clients the responses from the users, and encourage them to strike a compromise. If the content is not what users want, then the Web site will not meet the organizational goals; however, clients will be unhappy if their requested content is not in place. While user requests for content are more important, client requests for content cannot be ignored.

Assessing Existing Content

When the needed user content is defined, it's important to determine whether any of the content exists in paper or electronic form. Other resources might exist in photo, artwork, or video format. The Web development team should ascertain whether some of the content needs to be developed from scratch, or whether the resources already exist in a format that can be easily transformed into a Web page. It is useful to examine existing materials (such as brochures, reports, advertisements, press releases, newsletters, and forms) to see if there is any useful content that can be included on the Web site. Much content that users want may not be currently available in any type of electronic format. And of course, all existing content should not necessarily be placed on the Web, without regard to whether it is useful or appropriate to the electronic medium . In many cases, some of the needed content, such as frequently asked questions, may already exist in paper format, and other content resources will need to be developed.

Responsibility for Developing Content

It is the client organization's responsibility to develop and provide the content. The client organization is the entity with the expertise to develop the needed content. Although the Web development team might be responsible for determining what content is needed, and then adding that content to the Web site, the Web development team does not usually have expertise in the content area. Therefore, the responsibility of developing and providing the content (in paper, electronic, or other format) should be the responsibility of the client organization. Of course, it doesn't always work out perfectly. If the Web development team becomes responsible for any content development, the time required to do so should be considered when discussing project timelines. Even if the client agrees to develop the content completely, a project timeline might have to be reworked if the client organization does not provide the promised content in the promised time frame. On the other hand, the Web development team may take responsibility for structuring the content; that is, understanding how users structure the information in their mental models, and therefore, how the content should be presented on the Web site (Proctor '02).

The following list provides ideas for content sources:

- User responses to requirements gathering
- Frequently asked questions of the client organization (by phone, e-mail, or in-person)
- The client organization itself
- Existing content
- Easily developed content (assuming that it has value to the users)
- Benchmark Web sites

Benchmarking

The final part of requirements gathering is determining benchmark sites that can serve as a comparison to the site that you are developing. Ask the target users which Web sites they currently visit, and which sites might be topically related to the site being developed. If you learn what other Web sites the target user population is interested in, you can create a set of benchmarks to compare the new site to. The site in development can be compared to other sites with a similar mission; you might find good suggestions for the new site, as well as ideas of what not to do. A frequently used term in the Web industry is "gap analysis" or "competitive analysis," which refers to the gap between what other sites (e.g., the competition) offer and what the client organization's site offers. Benchmark Web sites are important for determining important interface design features, as well as content.

Benchmark sites are not necessarily your competition. Think of them as the neighborhood in which your site will live. You need to understand the "standards" for that neighborhood. This is useful information for a number of reasons. If you know which sites users in your target user population visit, you can determine which interface features are appropriate and which ones are not. Sometimes, understanding the usability features of related sites can give you feedback on site usability that users may not comment on. For example, if other sites use a specific plug-in, then maybe that plug-in is appropriate for your site. If other sites use a similar page layout, then it might be a good way to approach your page design. If other sites use certain terminology, then it might be terminology that is appropriate to use.

If you are developing an informational Web site, you can provide a list of links to benchmark sites. In return, those sites can provide links to your site. This can assist in marketing your Web site (see Chapter 10). When developing an e-commerce Web site, you would not want to provide links to your competitors' sites, nor is it expected that your competitors would want to provide links to your site. However, when developing an e-commerce site, determining benchmark Web sites can assist in ascertaining your competition. Using a search engine to find other Web sites on related topics can also be helpful.

If you ask targeted users what type of Web sites they are generally interested in, the Web development team and the client organization will gain an understanding of what external links would be useful. In addition, the Web development team or the client organization might find Web sites that users are unaware of, but that may be interesting to them. A final possibility is that the Web development team or the client organization might be a source for benchmark Web sites. For instance, if you are designing a site for a Lutheran congregation, it might be useful to look at the Web sites for other Lutheran congregations in that geographic area to see what types of resources they offer. This ensures that the Web site being developed does not provide the exact same content as an existing site. Some important questions to ask, related to benchmarking, include:

1. What other Web sites do you frequently visit?
2. What other categories of Web sites are you interested in?
3. What features of those sites do you like?

These areas of requirements gathering directly translate into design. For instance, if users have slow connections and slow computers, then the downloaded file size should be minimized. If user computing experience is low, then the Web site should be designed with absolute layout simplicity in mind. Terminology can be modified based on domain knowledge from requirements gathering.

Additional Considerations for Web Site Redesign

For developers who are redesigning an existing Web site, there is more information available to assist in requirements gathering than is available to developers who are creating a new site. Information about who visited the Web site in the past can assist in requirements gathering. More important, if a site is being redesigned, there should be some form of feedback about what users liked and did not like about the original site. There should be some sense of whether the site was successful or not.

It's possible that there might be previously collected information about visitors to the Web site. This demographic data might have been collected in the process of other data collection, and can assist with determining demographic information, domain knowledge, and user computing experience.

There might be a number of resources available for knowing what content users are interested in. Sometimes users leave messages in Web site guest books; these messages can suggest possible directions for new content. Sometimes users send e-mails to Webmasters with problems or suggestions.

If a Web site has already existed and is being redesigned, the Web site logs are very important informational tools. The Web site logs can provide information about what sites users visited before coming to the site. This may help to establish benchmark Web sites. Web site logs can also provide information about the user computing environment. For instance, logs can provide information on what browser and what browser version the user is using to request the Web page. Also, if most of the Web page requests are coming from a specific domain on the Internet (such as a school or organization), it might be possible to determine what the connection speeds, processor speeds, and monitor sizes are at that organization. Web site logs can assist in identifying which Web pages are most frequently and least frequently visited. More information on Web site logs is available in Chapter 11.

It's possible that usability testing was previously performed. The results of the usability tests can indicate possible usability pitfalls to avoid. Additionally, if usability testing has not been performed on an existing Web site, usability testing with a few users might be useful to uncover usability problems that currently exist. Users may not be able to describe the usability problems in a survey, but these problems may be clearly identified when the Web development team watches users attempting to find information on a site and failing miserably. See Chapter 9 for more information about performing usability tests.

Chapter Wrap-Up

When collecting user requirements, there are several different types of information that are important to collect.

- It is important for the Web development team to learn about general demographic information, domain knowledge, user computing experience, user computing environment, content, and benchmarking. This information can assist the Web development team in determining what the users need.

- There are a number of techniques for gathering these requirements, such as paper surveys, electronic surveys, focus groups, and interviews. These will be discussed in detail in Chapter 4.

Design Exercise

Consider building a Web site for the Happy Hills Pre-School and Kindergarten. The parents of children enrolled in the school (as well as parents of potential enrollees) are very busy people who do not have the time to answer questions about every area of requirements gathering. Considering the need to prioritize the requirements gathering, what specific areas of requirements gathering are most important? Come up with 10 questions that address the most important areas of requirements gathering for the Happy Hills Pre-School and Kindergarten. Explain why these questions are important and justify why you decided to leave out other questions.

Discussion Questions

1. Why is it important to determine what domain knowledge the users have?

2. What questions related to user computing experience might be important?

3. What are metaphors, and how are they used on Web sites?

4. What are five important factors in the user computing environment related to usability?

5. Why is it impossible to make statistical statements about the entire population of Web users?

6. What are seven examples of content?

7. What are some different sources for possible content ideas? What are the advantages and disadvantages of each?

8. Where does Web site content physically come from?

9. What is benchmarking? How is it different for informational Web sites versus e-commerce Web sites?

10. What are three requirements gathering areas that can be used when redesigning existing Web sites?

11. How and when does usability testing fit into the requirements gathering process for existing Web sites?

Suggested Reading

Allwood, C. (1986). "Novices on the Computer: A Review of the Literature." *International Journal of Man-Machine Studies*, 25(6), 633–658.

Barfield, W. (1986). "Expert-Novice Differences for Software: Implications for Problem-Solving and Knowledge Acquisition." *Behaviour and Information Technology*, 5(1), 15–29.

Bikson, T., & Panis, C. (1997). "Computers and Connectivity: Current Trends." In S. Kiesler (Ed.), *Culture of the Internet* (pp. 407–430). Mahwah, N.J.: Lawrence Erlbaum Associates.

Ceaparu, I., & Shneiderman, B., (2004). "Finding governmental statistical data on the web: A study of categorically-organized links for the FedStats Topics page." *Journal of the American Society of Information Science & Technology*, 55(11), 1008–1015.

Chan, H., Lee, R., Dillon, T., & Chang, E. (2001). *E-commerce: Fundamentals and Applications*. Chichester, England: John Wiley and Sons.

Corry, M., Frick, T., & Hansen, L. (1997). "User-Centered Design and Usability Testing of a Web Site: An Illustrative Case Study." *Educational Technology Research and Development*, 45(4), 65–76.

Fuccella, J., & Pittolato, J. (1999). "Giving People What They Want: How to Involve Users in Site Design." *IBM DeveloperWorks*. Available at: http://www4.ibm.com/software/developer/library/design-by-feedback/expectations.html.

Hazlett, R. (2003). "Measurement of User Frustration: A Biologic Approach." Proceedings of the ACM Conference on Human Factors in Computing Systems, 734–735.

Hilberg, S., & Lazar, J. (2003). "Developing and Testing a Set of Usability Heuristics for Web-Based Applications." Proceedings of the 2003 International Conference on Industry, Engineering, and Management Systems, 317–323.

Lazar, J., Jones, A., Hackley, M., & Shneiderman, B. (2005, in press). "Social and Psychological Issues in User Frustration: A Comparison of Novice and Workplace Users." To appear in *Interacting with Computers.*

Lazar, J., Meiselwitz, G., & Norcio, A. (2004). "A Taxonomy of Novice User Perception of Error on the Web." *Universal Access in the Information Society*, 3(3/4), 202–208.

Lazar, J., & Norcio, A. (2001). "User Considerations in E-commerce Transactions." In Q. Chen (Ed.), *Human-Computer Interaction: Issues and Challenges* (pp. 185–195). Hershey, PA: Idea Group Publishing.

Lazar, J., & Sears, A. (2005, in press). "Design of E-Business Web Sites." In G. Salvendy (Ed.), *Handbook of Human Factors and Ergonomics.* Hoboken, NJ: John Wiley & Sons.

Lazar, J., Tsao, R., & Preece, J. (1999). "One Foot in Cyberspace and the Other on the Ground: A Case Study of Analysis and Design Issues in a Hybrid Virtual and Physical Community." *WebNet Journal: Internet Technologies, Applications, and Issues*, 1(3), 49–57.

Mayhew, D. (1999). *The Usability Engineering Lifecycle.* San Francisco: Morgan Kaufmann Publishers.

Nelson, A., & Nelson, W. (2002). *Building Electronic Commerce with Web Database Constructions.* Boston: Addison-Wesley.

Norris, M., & West, S. (2001). *ebusiness Essentials: Technology and Network Requirements for Mobile and Online Markets.* Chichester, England: John Wiley & Sons.

Pew Internet and American Life Project. (2003). "The Ever-Shifting Internet Population: A New Look at Internet Access and the Digital Divide." Available at: http://www.pewinternet.org.

Pitkow, J., & Kehoe, C. (1996). "Emerging Trends in the WWW Population." *Communications of the ACM*, 39(6), 106–110.

Powell, T., Jones, D., & Cutts, D. (1998). *Web Site Engineering: Beyond Web Page Design.* Upper Saddle River, NJ: Prentice Hall.

Preece, J. (2000). *Online Communities: Designing Usability, Supporting Sociability.* New York: John Wiley & Sons.

Proctor, R., Vu, K., Salvendy, G., et al. (2002). "Content Preparation and Management for Web Design: Eliciting, Structuring, Searching, and Displaying Information." *International Journal of Human-Computer Interaction*, 14(1), 25–92.

Redish, J., & Wixon, D. (2003). "Task Analysis." In J. Jacko & A. Sears (Eds.), *The Handbook of Human-Computer Interaction* (Vol. 922–940). Mahwah, NJ: Lawrence Erlbaum Associates.

Riseberg, J., Klein, J., Fernandez, R., & Picard, R. (1998). "Frustrating the User on Purpose: Using Biosignals in a Pilot Study to Detect the User's Emotional State." Proceedings of the CHI 1998: ACM Conference on Human Factors in Computing Systems, 227–228.

Sears, A., & Jacko, J. (2000). "Understanding the Relation between Network Quality of Service and the Usability of Distributed Multimedia Documents." *Human-Computer Interaction*, 15(1), 43–68.

Shneiderman, B., & Plaisant, C. (2005). *Designing the User Interface: Strategies for Effective Human-Computer Interaction* (4th ed.). Boston: Addison-Wesley.

Turban, E., Lee, J., King, D., & Chung, H. (2000). *Electronic Commerce: A Managerial Perspective*. Upper Saddle River, NJ: Prentice Hall.

4

Methods for Requirements Gathering

After reading this chapter, you will be able to:

- Understand how to access users.
- Create and implement electronic and paper surveys.
- Run successful requirements gathering interviews.
- Run successful focus groups, both in person and electronically.
- Create and implement a card sorting activity.
- Understand how scenarios can be used in requirements gathering.
- Understand how paper prototyping can be used in requirements gathering.

Introduction

Once it is determined what type of information should be collected from the users, the next step is to collect the information. There are a number of different techniques for collecting information, including paper surveys, electronic surveys, focus groups, interviews, and electronic focus groups, with the resulting information evaluated through more interviews and card sorting. The method (or methods) chosen depend on what type of access to users the Web development team has. This chapter will discuss:

- different methods of collecting requirements
- when those different methods are appropriate
- how to implement the technical portion of the data collection method

It's important to note that each method of requirements gathering (surveys, focus groups, interviews, and so on) can be considered a field of its own. Each has its own terminology, such as a respondent (for a survey), an interviewee (for an interview), and a participant (for a focus group). Each of these terms refers to the same type of person: a member of the target user population. During the process of requirements gathering, it's possible that specific users can participate in different requirements gathering activities, and therefore, can have more than one of these terms attached to them.

Determining Access to Users

One of the deciding factors regarding which information gathering methods to use is the type of access you have to the target users. Are all of the targeted users in a specific geographic location, or are they geographically dispersed? Do you have e-mail addresses for the users? Do you have postal addresses for them? Do the users surf an existing Web site frequently? Are there frequent face-to-face meetings of the users? The client organization should be able to provide this information to you. Additionally, the client organization should have defined the target users in the early stages of the life cycle and should be able to provide ideas about how you can access them. If the client organization does not have an actual list of potential users to contact, see if there are any places or organizations where potential users congregate or communicate. Sometimes, community-based organizations can provide mailing lists or face-to-face meetings where requirements gathering can take place, or at a minimum, where information about the project can be distributed on paper. While a site redesign usually means that you have a clear idea who the users are and how to contact them, the client organization should reconfirm the target user population for the Web site. It's possible that over time, the target user population has changed.

The type of access to targeted users will, in part, determine what type of information gathering technique you can use. For instance, if there are face-to-face meetings of potential users, the Web development team can attend the meetings and lead focus groups, perform interviews, or conduct surveys. If you have a list of home or work addresses for potential users, the Web development team can mail paper surveys. If there are no face-to-face meetings with potential users who are geographically distributed, but there is a list of e-mail addresses, the Web development team can e-mail electronic surveys. Each type of requirements gathering technique collects different types of information. Surveys are good methods to gain shallow data from large numbers of respondents. Interviews are good means to gain deep data from a small number of respondents.

The methodologies for collecting user requirements are endless, and there are no right or wrong methods. There is also no limit to the number of information gathering techniques that can be used together. If it's feasible, you can use paper surveys and electronic surveys and focus groups along with interviews and card sorting. The more information collected, the better. However, it's unlikely that the Web development team will be able to use all of these techniques, as the user's time is limited. If there are multiple distinct target user populations, it's very possible that different methods will be appropriate for each different user group. This is acceptable. Similarly, it's very unlikely that all members of the target user population (i.e., a census) will be available to take part in requirements gathering. So it's important to ensure that those who participate represent the target user population. The development team should attempt to find users who are representative and can provide useful feedback. As always, perfection is elusive.

Various combinations of methods can be used. For example, if the target population of users consists of different user groups, it's important to get a representative sampling of responses from each group. The Hands-On Example, "Contacting Hard-to-Reach User Populations," on the following page shows how multiple information gathering techniques can be used.

Guidelines for Choosing Access Techniques

In general, the following guidelines apply: When the Web development team can access users face-to-face (at a workplace, meeting, or monthly gathering), interviews and focus groups are appropriate. If there are a large number of users at these meetings, surveys are also useful. If the Web development team has access to postal addresses for targeted users, paper surveys are appropriate. If the Web development team has access to the phone numbers of targeted users, phone surveys might be appropriate. If the Web development team has e-mail addresses for targeted users, or it's known that all targeted users are reachable via some type of

Contacting Hard-to-Reach User Populations

In Quiz Bowl, university teams compete against each other on knowledge-related questions. The game is similar to a team version of "Jeopardy!" or "Who Wants to Be a Millionaire?" The Web development team collecting user requirements for a Quiz Bowl Web site discovered that there were some face-to-face meetings of potential users (at tournaments); however, the people who attended the meetings comprised only a small portion of those potentially interested in the Web site (who were geographically distributed). There were also a number of targeted users who did not attend any of the face-to-face meetings. Therefore, Web-based surveys were used to collect requirements from those who were geographically distributed, and paper versions of the survey were passed out at face-to-face meetings. By using this hybrid approach, potential users who responded to the surveys represented users who attended face-to-face meetings and those who were located across the country and did not attend face-to-face events (Lazar '99).

Another example was the development of the Web site for the Down Syndrome Online Advocacy Group. It was determined that the only way to access the targeted users (who were geographically distributed) was through a list of e-mail addresses. Therefore, an e-mail survey was sent to targeted users (Lazar '00a).

For the Web site for St. John's Lutheran Church of Blenheim (located at http://www.stjohnslcms.org/), targeted users were mainly current church members. It was determined that the best way to access these users was by visiting the Sunday services and passing out paper surveys. After the surveys had been collected and analyzed, the development team led focus groups to help clarify the information collected (Lazar '00b).

electronic forum (such as a list server, USENET newsgroup, or groupware package), e-mail surveys might be appropriate. If a Web site already exists, it may be appropriate to place a Web-based survey on the Web site. A recent survey of 149 Web development projects highlights the most popular types of user involvement in Web development projects. For requirements gathering, 72 out of 149 projects incorporated interviews with users and 65 out of 149 projects incorporated user surveys (in paper, electronic, or phone format) (Lazar '04).

Introducing Surveys

A popular technique for gathering information from people is the survey. Surveys allow data to be collected from large numbers of people in a brief time.

Someone who responds to a survey is called a respondent. For the purposes of this book, a targeted user has the same meaning as a respondent. Surveys can consist of closed-ended questions (those requiring that respondents choose from a list of choices), open-ended questions (where respondents answer however they like), and other types of questions, such as ranking and Likert scales (Fowler '93). Examples of the different types of questions follow:

Closed-Ended Question

Have you ever visited the Web site of Towson University at http://www.towson.edu? (Please select one answer only.)

A. Yes   B. No

Open-Ended Question

What types of resources would you like to see available on the Web site?

I would purchase products from the Sneaker Incorporated Web site if …

Ranking Question

Please rank the following Web resources in order of importance (5 = most important, 1 = least important):

___ calendar of events

___ online phone directory

___ history of the company

___ merchandise available

___ pictures from previous events

Likert Scale Question

Finding information on the Towson University Web site is easy.

1. Strongly disagree
2. Somewhat disagree
3. Undecided
4. Somewhat agree
5. Strongly agree

There are some commonalities that apply to all surveys, including paper surveys, e-mail surveys, Web-based surveys, and phone surveys. Questions must be well

Hands-On Example

WEB-STAR: A Survey Tool for Requirements Gathering

Because the same survey questions need to be asked in the requirements gathering phase of many different Web development projects, a survey tool has been developed and tested, covering many of the usability and content-related issues discussed in Chapter 3. The WEB Survey Tool for Analyzing Requirements (WEB-STAR) is split into three sections. Section A includes questions that are useful for both new Web sites and existing Web sites, such as user computing experience and demographic information. Section B includes questions for new Web sites, and Section C includes questions for existing Web sites. It's important to note that the WEB-STAR questions are primarily related to the user computing experience, user computing environment, demographics, and benchmarking because these topics are relatively standard across all Web sites. The types of questions that are directly related to specific Web sites, such as domain knowledge and content, will need to be added by the development team. These questions can be asked in paper, Web-based, or e-mail format. A copy of WEB-STAR is available at http://www.aw.com/webusability.

written and unambiguous. It's important to test your survey questions with a few users (respondents) before unleashing the survey on the general population of respondents. This test is called a pretest or a pilot study. A pilot study ensures that survey questions are well written, unbiased, and appropriate, and that the respondents are able to understand the questions. Next, respondents (or people you hope will respond to the survey) must be aware of the purpose of the survey. The survey team (in this instance, the Web development team) should attempt to get as high a response rate as possible. These same issues relate to all types of surveys (paper, phone, e-mail, Web-based).

Paper Surveys

A traditional technique for collecting information is the paper survey. Paper surveys have been used in the requirements gathering stage of systems analysis and design for many years. These surveys are distributed to the targeted user population, either in person, or via traditional mail. Hopefully, a large percentage of the users contacted will fill out and return the survey. Paper surveys can include the types of requirements gathering questions that were discussed in Chapter 3.

As with all surveys, the questions must be pilot tested with a few users before being used with the entire target user population. With paper surveys, there are a number of time-tested techniques for increasing response rates. An introductory letter should be mailed prior to the survey, letting respondents know the purpose and importance of the survey and the qualifications of those conducting it (in this case, the Web development team). Without an advanced notice, users may be reluctant to respond because they do not know why the survey is being performed, nor do they know or trust those who are conducting it. During the survey period, the targeted users should be reminded about the deadline and method for turning in the surveys. Reminders can be handled through announcements at meetings or through postcards. Once surveys have been collected, the data should be entered into a spreadsheet or database for easy data analysis.

Electronic Surveys

There are many advantages to using electronic surveys. It's possible that targeted users will respond more quickly to electronic surveys than to paper surveys (because they do not have to worry about finding a stamp and a mailbox). Web developers using electronic surveys do not have to worry about the costs of copying and printing the surveys. In many cases, it's possible to configure an electronic survey to enter responses directly into a spreadsheet or database program, eliminating the need for data entry and avoiding human error that can occur during data entry (Bertot '96). However, using electronic surveys exclusively is appropriate only if the entire targeted user population can be easily reached through electronic means. Otherwise, the Web development team should distribute identical paper surveys and electronic surveys. When redesigning a Web site, it's very possible that there are users who are not using the existing site, so it can be challenging to reach these potential users through electronic surveys.

There are two different types of electronic surveys: e-mail surveys and Web-based surveys. E-mail surveys are sent as part of an e-mail message or as a file attachment. Web-based surveys exist as a Web page, and users can answer survey questions online. E-mail surveys and Web-based surveys each have their advantages and disadvantages. E-mail surveys require that users have an e-mail account that they check; users do not need to have an e-mail account to respond to a Web-based survey. If a Web site is being redesigned, Web-based surveys can be used on the site itself, so that users can respond to the survey while browsing the site (see the Hands-On Example, "Online Surveys for User Feedback at iVillage.com," on the next page). Web-based surveys can provide assistance to the user in filling out surveys by means of help screens or additional information. This is not possible with an e-mail survey. One odd fact is that users completing

Online Surveys for User Feedback at iVillage.com

One example of a Web-based survey used to gather user feedback on an existing Web site is iVillage.com. It was reported that many iVillage.com users sent e-mails complaining about the growing number of pop-up ads on the site. iVillage.com followed up on this unsolicited feedback by conducting a survey. The results of the survey revealed that 92 percent of respondents did not like the pop-up ads and found them very frustrating. iVillage.com removed all pop-up ads from the site and replaced them with other types of advertising, such as sponsored quizzes (Walker '02).

an e-mail survey can actually change the wording of the survey if they are not happy with the questions (Witmer '99). Users cannot modify the survey instrument on a Web-based survey. An e-mail survey, by means of the e-mail addresses acquired, may provide more demographic information about the respondents. Although Web-based survey respondents may choose to identify themselves, this doesn't automatically happen as it does with e-mail surveys. E-mail addresses (or other identification information) can assist in determining whether the survey responses are representative of the target user population. The basic steps for implementing an electronic survey are:

- Create the survey on paper.
- Pretest the survey questions.
- Develop the paper survey into an electronic survey.
- Perform usability testing on the electronic survey.
- Inform the target user population about the survey.

Regardless of whether an electronic survey is an e-mail survey or a Web-based survey, there are a number of preliminary steps that must take place before the survey can be distributed. The survey should first be designed on paper. As with any other type of survey, questions must be clear, easy to understand, and unbiased. After writing the survey questions, they need to be pre-tested with a few respondents who represent the target user population.

E-Mail Surveys

After the written survey instrument has been created, it can be developed into an electronic survey. If the Web development team has decided to use an e-mail survey, this stage is simple. The team needs only to copy and paste the survey into an e-mail message. Alternatively, the survey can be attached to an e-mail message, which can help to maintain survey formatting and allow for clarity. It's important to note that users are more likely to fill out a survey that is embedded in an e-mail message than they are to fill out a survey that is sent as a file attachment (Dommeyer '00). Users might not want to respond to a survey as a file attachment because they are worried about viruses, they don't have a word processor that can read the file, or they don't want to deal with the extra steps involved with opening a file attachment.

The nature of the population of interest may affect the decision to use an e-mail survey instead of a Web-based survey. For instance, if there is a well-defined user population and corresponding e-mail addresses are available (such as in a professional organization), it may make more sense to conduct an e-mail survey than a Web-based survey.

Web-Based Surveys

Alternatively, the Web development team can develop a paper survey into a Web-based survey. There are a number of different possibilities for creating this type of survey. The process requires a basic knowledge of Web programming. The Web development team can use the form controls in HTML, which is a relatively simple task. The harder part is to create the code to do something when the user hits the submit button to respond to the survey.

Creating a Web-Based Survey. The Web development team can use a Common Gateway Interface (CGI) script that can process the form and send an e-mail response to the Web development team. CGI scripts can be written in different programming languages, such as Perl and C++. However, the Web development team does not necessarily need to write a CGI script from scratch. A number of Web sites offer free downloadable scripts that can be easily modified and used to activate an HTML form. For instance, it's possible to download, customize, and install the FormMail script from Matt's Script Archive in approximately 15–20 minutes. (This Web site provides instructions on how to download and install the script.) The FormMail script processes the HTML form and sends the survey responses to an e-mail address. The following is a partial list of Web sites that offer free CGI scripts:

- CGI Resource Index (http://cgi.resourceindex.com)
- Developer's Daily (http://www.devdaily.com/)
- Freescripts.com (http://www.freescripts.com/)

- Free-Scripts.net (http://www.free-scripts.net/)
- Matt's Script Archive (http://www.worldwidemart.com/scripts/)

It's also important to check with the Internet service provider that is being used because some Internet service providers do not allow users to run CGI scripts. Other Internet service providers provide a set of commonly needed CGI scripts for use by their customers, so downloading and modifying a CGI script might be unnecessary.

A second possibility for creating a Web-based survey is to use a Web site that allows developers to create surveys without doing any coding. A number of Web sites guide the user through developing a Web survey, host the survey at no cost, and then tabulate the results. It's important to note that the popular term for Web surveys is a poll, so many of the Web sites that offer free surveys refer to them that way. The following is a list of several sites that offer free Web-based surveys:

- FreePolls (http://www.freepolls.com/)
- GigaPoll (http://www.gigapoll.com/)
- Pollcat (http://www.pollcat.com/)

Web development software, such as Microsoft FrontPage, offers tools for developing surveys (forms). Usually, these applications require only a minimum amount of programming (see Chapter 8 for more information on Web development software). Most Web-based surveys are relatively simple and can be developed quickly.

Usability Testing a Web-Based Survey. Once the electronic survey is developed, usability testing must be performed. Usability testing a survey is different from pre-testing. Pre-testing focuses on whether the questions are well written and easy to understand, whereas usability testing focuses on whether the interface is easy for the user to understand. In the case of a Web-based survey, usability refers to issues such as whether the text is large enough to read, the page layout is easy to follow, the color scheme is appropriate, the graphics are appropriate, and the navigation is easy to understand. For instance, it would hurt usability if a survey was divided into five logical sections and users had to hit a submit button for each one of the five sections.

There are a number of different approaches to usability testing. However, when designing a Web-based survey, the most appropriate method is to ask a few of the targeted users (3–5 individuals) to fill out the Web-based survey. They should be encouraged to comment openly about problems or confusing aspects of the interface, either by speaking aloud or by commenting on paper or by e-mail. Additionally, the Web development team can ask specific questions of the users related to the interface design. Feedback from the testers should be used to clarify and improve the Web-based survey before the majority of users receive it. (More information about usability testing is available in Chapter 9.) If time is a critical factor, pre-testing the survey questions can be combined with the usability testing of the Web-based survey—as long as the Web development team ensures that both areas receive attention. Usability guidelines should be followed when developing a Web-based survey (Lazar '99).

Usability Guidelines for Web-Based Surveys

- Make the survey error-proof. If some questions require independent answers, and others are multiple choice, then these rules for answering should be enforced.

- If the Web development team wants only a numerical answer, then that rule should be enforced.

- If there are required responses to specific questions, then users should not be allowed to submit a Web-based survey without answering them.

- Users should receive an error message if they don't fill out the survey form correctly. However, it's not a good idea to require that users respond to all questions because they may be reluctant to comply, and it could decrease the likelihood that users would respond at all.

- Make the survey work with most common browsers. The Web development team should test to make sure that the Web-based survey appears correctly in Internet Explorer, Netscape Navigator, Firefox, and Lynx, as well as in different versions of those browsers. (Browser compatibility is an important goal; see Chapter 7 for more information.)

- Test the survey with different monitor sizes and screen resolutions. The Web development team should make sure that the Web-based survey is not difficult to use on a small monitor size or with low resolution.

Informing Users about the Electronic Survey

After designing and testing the electronic survey, the next step is to inform the target users about its existence. For an e-mail survey, this step is simply sending the e-mail that includes the survey to the targeted users. For a Web-based survey, informing the targeted users can be more challenging. The Web development team must contemplate how to contact the targeted users by using the available means. This might mean distributing fliers; making phone calls; announcing the URL at face-to-face meetings; posting an announcement to a related newsgroup, bulletin board, or list server; adding a login script (if users are required to log into a system somewhere); or creating a link to the survey on Web pages that are frequently visited by targeted users. Additionally, if there is a list of e-mail addresses available, but a Web-based survey is being used, the target user population can simply be e-mailed and asked to access the Web-based survey. Targeted e-mail lists can be purchased from marketing companies. The target user population can also be informed about the Web-based survey through the use of banner advertisements on Web sites that they frequent. Periodic reminders (with a deadline date by which all surveys must be submitted) can then be sent via the same medium used to advertise the Web-based survey, with the eventual goal of maximizing the number of respondents. If possible, it's helpful to offer a prize, randomly selected, to people who respond to the survey. The prize (or incentive) can be small, yet it's another reason that users will respond to a survey. For redesigned Web sites, Web-based surveys can simply be included on the current site, with a notice on the homepage requesting that users fill out the Web-based survey.

It's important to determine if the survey responses truly represent the target user population. It's rare that a Web site user population is defined so specifically that there is a list of all users (this might be true only if the site is password protected, such as an intranet). It's even rarer to have a list of users when a Web site has not yet been built, so user surveys cannot use traditional sampling methods. Instead, the survey responses need to be somewhat representative of the target user population. One way to determine if survey responses represent the target users is simply by asking demographic questions on the survey. These questions can relate to topics such as age, gender, computer experience, or domain knowledge, and can help to ensure that survey responses actually represent the target user population. Additionally, if a survey is submitted using a Web-based form, it's sometimes possible to learn more about the users from the domains from which the form is submitted (see Chapter 11 for information on Web site logs). In summary, here are some ways to get a good response to an electronic survey:

- Have trusted people introduce the survey.
- Advertise the existence of the survey.

- Send periodic reminders to targeted users.
- Offer a randomly selected prize or incentive.

Interviews

Interviews are useful tools for collecting information. If targeted users are available, face-to-face interviews can be used. Interviews are heavily used in traditional requirements gathering. These interviews involve an interviewer and an interviewee, but the level of structure varies. Some interviews are highly structured, in which a specific set of questions is asked of the interviewee. Other interviews are unstructured; there is a general interview goal, but there are no definitive questions and the interview is more exploratory. In reality, most interviews fall somewhere in the middle (semi-structured). Interview questions can be open-ended ("What do you think the Web site needs?") or closed-ended ("Does the Web site need a schedule of events?"). However, caution should be taken to ensure that the questions asked are not loaded so that the response is influenced.

Face-to-face interviews are very useful when there is little information available to the Web development team, and the team needs a foundation of understanding before continuing with the requirements gathering. Interviews can also assist in clarifying responses given by users in other requirements gathering activities (such as surveys). The interviewer can change the course of the discussion if it appears that there is an area of questioning that needs more attention. Based on the responses from the interviewee, the interviewer can explore different directions or can ask for more in-depth information about a certain area. This "drill-down" of information is not available when using a survey. Interviews also allow for in-depth discussions of issues, and can be good for collecting a lot of data.

There are a number of disadvantages to using interviews, however. Interviews can be very time-consuming for both the interviewer and the interviewee. Another disadvantage is that the quality of the information collected is directly related to the interviewer's experience in performing interviews. It's important that the interviewer makes the interviewee feel at ease by being friendly, non-threatening, and able to explain the nature and purpose of the interview. It's possible that in some cases, the interviewee may not feel comfortable revealing information face-to-face and may prefer anonymity.

Planning is very important for a successful interview. In advance, the interviewer should check whether tape recording the meeting is permissible. If it's not, then it's imperative to take detailed notes. There should be a general outline of how the interview will be performed. The interviewer should know what type of information is important to collect, and should have a list of possible questions to ask. The interviewee should be informed about the topic of the meeting and the approximate time that the interview will take. After the interview, the interviewee should be thanked for his or her time, especially if a follow-up interview might be necessary.

Phone Interviews

In a phone interview, researchers (i.e., the Web development team) call targeted users and ask them standardized questions. Some researchers call this technique a "phone survey." It's debatable whether this should be categorized as an interview or a survey, but one way of looking at it is that if the interviewer does not deviate from a prepared list of questions, it could be considered a survey. If the interviewer changes the questions or the depth of the questions based on responses from the interviewee, it could be considered an interview.

Phone interviews can be used if a list of phone numbers of targeted users is available. However, conducting phone interviews can be tricky. Many people do not respond to unsolicited phone calls. The popularity of government "do not call" lists illustrates that many people do not want to be bothered by unwanted phone calls. Therefore, phone interviews might be appropriate only if the targeted users comprise a small, focused population, are well aware of the development of the Web site, and are supportive of the Web site development. For instance, phone interviews were used in the requirements gathering phase for an online community for the neighborhoods of Lake Linganore (see the Hands-On Example).

Focus Groups

Focus groups are an additional resource for collecting user requirements. A focus group is a discussion among a group of people with similar interests. (In the case of requirements gathering, all participants in focus groups should be part of the target user population.) The discussion usually takes place in a room with all participants present. It's possible to have a one-way mirror through which researchers can watch the focus group, but this is not necessary, nor is this common practice. A focus group usually consists of 4 to 12 people. In a group of 15 or more, communication can become confusing, and the group should

Phone Surveys for the Lake Linganore Web Site

Lake Linganore is a planned community in Frederick County, Maryland. During Web site development, phone interviews were conducted with chairpersons of the villages in Lake Linganore (the clients) and citizens of Lake Linganore (the users). The Web development team felt that it was important to talk with representative individual users, but because of time constraints, it was not possible to meet with them face-to-face. The Web development effort was sponsored in part by the community association and community members (the users) were in favor of building a Web site, so people responded to the phone interviews. If there had not been a high of level of support for the Web site effort, the phone interviews might not have been successful. For more information on the Lake Linganore online development, please see http://www.ifsm.umbc.edu/onlinecommunities/.

break down into subgroups. Usually, a series of focus groups take place, which allows for diverse views to be heard but no single group's views to dominate. Some focus groups can have a "personality," either quiet, outspoken, or warlike (Krueger '94). Just as the survey response from one person isn't statistically significant, the response from one focus group can be biased. Therefore, when it's possible, it's preferable to hold a series of focus groups with different participants. For example, when the Kodak Web site was redesigned, three focus groups were held in different cities in order to determine what type of content (such as product information and photography tips) the users wanted (see Case Study A: kodak.com).

In comparison to an interview, in which specific, closed-ended questions might be asked, in a focus group, the questions are non-directive. There are neither specific answers nor a list of possible answers. The focus group participants are asked a number of general questions, and discussion among the participants is encouraged without any limitations regarding possible responses. A specific facet of the focus group is the creation of a permissive environment in which participants are encouraged to share their feelings openly. This is one of the main advantages of focus groups; participants can interact and share their thoughts, and in the process, stimulate new ideas and comments that would not come to the forefront in one-on-one interviews. Hoffer, George, and Valacich have described this aspect of a focus group as a synergy. Because of synergies, focus group participants might be reminded of additional examples or problems. As these topics come to the forefront for discussion, the development team can observe whether there is a majority agreement among participants, and they can ascertain the strength of any disagreement.

The Moderator's Role

Successful focus groups require an experienced focus group moderator who asks questions and helps to manage the group. The moderator must make sure that there is an environment of openness in which participants are encouraged to share their thoughts. A focus group moderator should not be someone who has power or influence over the participants in the focus group in any area outside of the focus group, such as in the workplace. The moderator should encourage participation, stimulate discussion, and help the group stay focused on the task when the participants start digressing onto unrelated topics. The moderator might also have to help keep in check any participant who dominates the discussion and does not allow others to speak, or who mocks the statements of others. The moderator should not be concerned with taking notes during the focus group. Instead, the focus group should be taped (either in audio or video), or additional people from the Web development team who are familiar with the project should be present to take detailed notes.

Challenges of Working with Focus Groups

There are a number of problems that can occur with focus groups. Some participants may hesitate to talk at all, while other participants might dominate the discussion and fail to allow others to speak. An experienced moderator will ameliorate this situation by saying something like, "John Doe has already given us a lot of wonderful feedback; who wants to add to his comments?" It's also possible that outside influences will affect candor in the focus group. If the participants know each other outside of the group, they probably have some type of shared experience or history, and there might be issues among them that would hinder the effectiveness of the focus group. For instance, if a church group plans a focus group, participants might hesitate to speak up until they hear the views of the priest, pastor, or deacon. The same might hold true for a group of people from the same workplace; the participants might hold back on their comments until they hear the viewpoints of their superiors. Because the participants might be likely to echo the views of their superiors, and not discuss their true feelings, it's better to hold a focus group of participants without those who lead or manage members of the group.

Electronic Focus Groups

An electronic focus group is similarly structured to a traditional focus group, in that there are a number of people involved, the focus group participants interact with each other and discuss ideas, and there is a moderator. However, focus groups need not be limited to a group of people sitting around a room, talking. Electronic tools can be used, which can either support decision making and discussion when users are in the same place, or support a focus group of users who are geographically dispersed.

One possibility is to hold a focus group using a technology called a group decision support system (GDSS), in which the discussion takes place using computers located in one room, and all comments and discussions are anonymous. There is a projection screen in the front of the room, for all participants to see, and idea generation, ranking, and categorization are supported by the system software. Additionally, since all of the communication is electronic, there is automatic recording of all comments made. The idea behind a GDSS is that since the originator of the comments and ideas is not identified, then only the idea is considered; the status of the person presenting the idea is not considered. By using a GDSS, information gathering can be improved because group hierarchy and political issues are "taken out of the equation." However, installing GDSS software or a GDSS room is expensive and feasible only for situations when the client organization can afford to pay for the installation. This is usually not possible. It's one of those "it would be wonderful if we had unlimited money, but we don't" situations.

Another possibility, for cases in which the target users are distributed geographically, is to have an electronic focus group. The focus group discussion can take place using groupware software that provides chat areas and shared tools, such as drawing tools. The electronic focus group can also take place using standard chat room software. If the users are geographically dispersed, the same types of group discussions can occur as with a traditional focus group, with the moderator playing the same role. An added benefit is that there are no travel costs incurred for participants to come to the focus group location. A drawback to the distributed approach is that the moderator and the participants might feel less at ease, since they cannot see each other, and therefore receive less communication feedback (whether people are smiling, frowning, bored, angry, or otherwise). Another challenge of electronic focus groups is that all users must have access to the specific chat room technology (some Web sites require that you download chat room software or groupware technology), and be experienced using it. And all participants must be available at the same time, even if they are physically located in different time zones. So, while electronic focus groups seem promising, they may not be appropriate in many cases.

Participatory Design

The ultimate level of user involvement is participatory design, where representative users are actually part of the development team. Users are not limited simply to requirements gathering or usability testing, but rather, as part of the team, they actually make the decisions that guide the progress of the Web site development. Participatory design takes a lot of time, both in terms of the users' time and in terms of development time; therefore, participatory design is traditionally used when the needs of the users are not well understood, and the users will be using a system for a large amount of time daily to perform critical job related responsibilities. For instance, participatory design has been used to design computer technology used by teachers in their instructional classes throughout the day (Carroll '02). More information about participatory design is available in Chapter 1.

For most Web sites, participatory design is not an appropriate user involvement method, because the costs of including the users in all stages of development outweigh the benefits when users expect to use a Web site for only a few minutes daily. However, participatory design is beneficial when users use Web-based applications, intranets, or other types of applications that are delivered through Web browsers and are full-fledged applications that users will use for job-critical tasks for long periods of time. Another example of the valuable use of the participatory design methods is for user populations with special needs, such as older users, younger users, or users with disabilities. The ezSIS site, designed using participatory design, is described in detail in Chapter 1.

It's important to remember that while requirements gathering takes place primarily with users, there is a still a role for the client during user requirements gathering. Most information from the client (such as the mission and target user population of the Web site) should be collected before the user requirements gathering, as the client information should help set the parameters for the user requirements gathering. But during user requirements gathering, clients can help to interpret some of the information collected from users, as well as provide feedback about how the user requests fit with the client's mission for the site. The Web site must meet the needs of the users, so that in the end, the Web site will

Advantages and Disadvantages of Each Method

Method	Advantages (+) and Disadvantages (−)
E-mail surveys	+ Arrive directly in user's inbox; users are more likely to respond
	− Must have a list of e-mail addresses to send to; hard for responses to be anonymous
Web-based surveys	+ Useful for an existing site; users can simply fill out the survey online
	− If a site doesn't already exist, it can be hard to contact users who are interested and will respond
Paper surveys	+ Easily distributed at face-to-face gatherings
	− Mailing paper surveys is time-consuming and costly; data entry usually must be done manually
In-person interviews	+ Provide deep knowledge about what users want
	− Conducting interviews is time-consuming; users may not be available
Phone interviews	+ Useful when phone numbers of the targeted users are available and data must be collected quickly
	− Most people don't want to be contacted by phone for interviews and won't respond
Focus groups (in person)	+ Stimulate discussion and lead to new ideas when users share their views
	− A few people can easily dominate the meeting
Focus groups (distributed electronically)	+ Users do not need to be located in the same physical place
	− Without physical presence cues, users may not feel free to comment openly
Participatory design	+ Provides the best understanding of users and their tasks
	− Too time-consuming for most Web development projects

meet the client organization's goals. As always, a happy medium between the users' wishes and needs and directives of the client will need to be found.

Other User Involvement Activities for Structuring Information

After basic user requirements have been gathered—whether by using surveys, interviews, or focus groups—the data now needs to be collected and interpreted. This data drives the design or redesign of the Web site. Additionally, there are other activities involving users that can take part at this time. These are usability engineering activities, which help structure or organize the basic data collected during requirements gathering. The activities can take place toward the end of requirements gathering or the early stages of conceptual design, and can bridge the gap between requirements gathering and later usability testing, once a full-fledged interface has been developed. These activities include card sorting, scenarios, and paper prototyping.

Card Sorting

Once the general Web site requirements have been collected, card sorting can be used to better understand the information that users have supplied (Fuccella '99). Card sorting can influence the navigation structure of a Web site because it reveals the users' mental models of how the information is organized. In card sorting, names of the different content areas are written on index cards. For instance, items such as a schedule of events, personnel lists, membership benefits, and so on, are listed on cards. The names on the cards should match the Web site content requirements (also called Web site objects) that were discovered during the main requirements gathering. The cards are given to the users in a random order. Targeted users (5–10 users is sufficient) are asked to organize the cards in a way that makes sense to them.

It's very frustrating when a user seeks content on a Web site, but doesn't look in the right place for it. By doing a card sorting activity, it is possible to see how a user views the site content and to visualize a user's mental model of how the content should be organized (Proctor '02). Users should be encouraged to describe why they organize the cards as they do and to suggest names for each group of cards. If there is a consensus among a few users of how the content should be organized, the Web development team can use this organizational scheme on the Web site itself, as a part of the information architecture.

Card sorting can help to ensure that the navigation and information architecture match the mental models of the users, so that users can find information using the site navigation, rather than search engines. While it's useful to have a site search engine, sometimes users have problems correctly forming searching syntax. Card sorting has been used as part of requirements gathering at a number of organizations, including IBM and Indiana University (Fuccella '99; Corry '97). The technique is used more frequently when a Web site already exists and the development team is looking for a better way to organize the existing content.

The United States National Institute of Standards and Technology (NIST) offers a free software tool to help with an electronic version of card sorting. The software, titled WebCat, is available at http://zing.ncsl.nist.gov/WebTools/WebCAT/overview.html.

Scenarios

Scenarios can be useful to help get a handle on how users want to interact with Web sites and what they want to achieve. A scenario is simply a story with a setting, character, sequence of actions, and outcome (Rosson '03). Scenarios concretely describe how people will interact with systems, in a way that various groups (users, designers, usability engineers, etc.) can understand. Usability scenarios help developers understand potential functionality, highlight possible problems, and bring attention to miscommunications. Someone might respond to a usability scenario by saying, "no—you totally misunderstood—that's not what we're trying to accomplish here." It's much more effective for this type of communication to be made early in the design phase. Scenarios can also help with clarifying user requirements (as with a prototype) and with planning for usability testing and other forms of evaluation. A sample usability scenario from the FedStats Web site (http://www.fedstats.gov) follows:

> *I'm a social activist in the Raleigh-Durham, North Carolina area and have become increasingly concerned about urban sprawls and the loss of rural areas for both farming and recreation. I need statistics to support my claim that significant differences occur when urban development occurs in rural and/or farming areas* (Ceaparu '04).

Paper Prototyping

Paper prototypes are simple representations of possible screen layouts. Paper prototypes are useful because they are quick and inexpensive to create. "Mock interfaces" can be drawn on paper or rendered with a computer drawing tool, such as PowerPoint. This technique presents interface ideas to users, who can give feedback about which mock interfaces are useful and what they like and don't like about them. Usually, paper prototyping takes place in the later stages of development, when the actual interface design is about to begin. However, it's sometimes possible, by presenting potential screen layouts to users, to help them explain what they want. Paper prototypes can deal with the "I don't know what I want, but I will know when I see it" syndrome. Developers tend not to be too dedicated or

Hands-On Example

Using Scenarios and Card Sorting at the University of Michigan Business School

The University of Michigan Business School redesigned their Web presence, which includes more than 3000 Web pages, with a user-centered design approach. User requirements analysis was done partially through interviews and focus groups. Scenarios were written, which helped to describe some of the tasks that users wanted to achieve.

Users performed a card sorting activity, where the cards identified Web pages in the top two or three levels of the site. Users grouped these cards and provided labels for each group. Based on the card sorting, page names and categories were changed in the new site design. Usability testing was also done with all four target user populations: current students, prospective students, faculty, and alumni/recruiters. With changes made, task success rates on the Web site increased from 61.7 percent (on the old Web site) to 92.5 percent (on the final version of the new site) (Brink '03).

protective of paper prototypes, since they usually have not invested much time developing them. An example of a paper prototype can be seen in Figure 4.1. This prototype, drawn by hand, is helpful when users give feedback. For instance, in this example, what does "people" refer to? Staff who work in the student union? Students who are leaders of organizations? What does "things" refer to?

Final Thoughts

In all requirements gathering techniques, targeted users should be notified that their responses will not be attributed to any of them personally. If users are worried that their identities will be displayed with their responses, they may hesitate to be as open or truthful as they might otherwise be. Users might worry that the Web development team will reveal that it was Joe Smith who said that "the system is hard to use, and whoever designed it is incompetent." Anonymity encourages targeted users to be open and honest and to provide useful comments and suggestions.

In a perfect world, the Web development team would be able to learn everything there is to know about the users and their needs. However, in reality, it's impossible to find out everything about the targeted users. A full-scale survey might

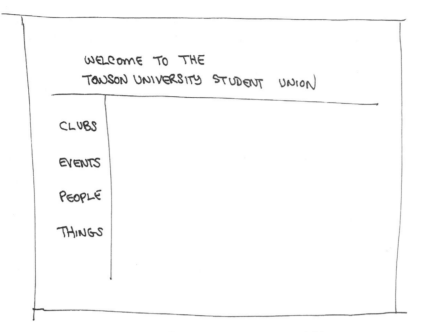

WELCOME TO THE
TOWSON UNIVERSITY STUDENT UNION

CLUBS

EVENTS

PEOPLE

THINGS

Figure 4.1 A prototype interface written on paper to quickly test ideas for the new Towson University Student Union Web site.

cover 10 pages, which most users would hesitate to fill out. Gathering user requirements from all users, on all possible topics, using all of the methods discussed, is simply not feasible; therefore, it's necessary to compromise. The Web development team should select and ask questions that are most important to the development of the site. The team should examine the methods that are most appropriate for collecting the requirements, and proceed with those methods. Targeted users are not willing to respond to two surveys, participate in an interview, take part in a focus group, and answer a phone survey. If extensive demand is put on users, they will feel intruded upon and may develop negative feelings toward the Web development team. Additionally, although a large number of users should take part in the requirements gathering, unless the target user population is very small (20–30 people), it's impossible to collect information from all users, or even a majority. Therefore, it's important to gather requirements from a representative sample of users.

Chapter Wrap-Up

Requirements gathering can be a long and detailed process; however, it's central to the concept of user-centered design.

- Through gathering user requirements, the Web development team discovers the characteristics a system or Web site must have in order to meet the needs of its users.

- Requirements gathering is more of an art than a science. There is no "one right way" to do requirements gathering.

- The methods chosen are influenced by how much and what type of access the Web development team has to the targeted users.

- Surveys, interviews, focus groups, scenarios, prototypes, and card sorting can all be used to help gather and sort user requirements.

- Obviously, the more information that can be gathered, the better. It's unrealistic however, to assume that all methods of requirements gathering will be used, just as it's unrealistic to assume that all users will be queried.

- The Web development team must determine when it has gathered enough information to understand the user requirements; only at that time should the requirements gathering stage be considered complete.

Discussion Questions

1. Why is access to users an important consideration in requirements gathering?

2. What are the different types of surveys? How do they differ and in what situations are they appropriate?

3. How is pretesting a survey different from usability testing a survey?

4. When might an interview be appropriate for requirements gathering? What are some steps involved in planning an interview?

5. What are three challenges in implementing a successful focus group?

6. Create a situation in which an electronic focus group might be appropriate. Describe the users involved and the technology used to implement the electronic focus group.

7. Why is card sorting frequently used when redesigning existing Web sites?

8. When are scenarios useful? Create a scenario of usage for a typical student using a university Web site.

Design Exercise

Imagine developing a new Web site for a vegetarian restaurant chain called Veggieland. There are currently three restaurant locations, all on the north side of Seattle. The restaurant chain wants to expand into the other areas of Seattle, including downtown and the suburbs. What is the best requirements gathering method to reach the targeted users near the existing restaurant locations? What about the targeted users near potential restaurant locations? Are there any community-based organizations that might be helpful with requirements gathering?

Suggested Reading

Bertot, J., & McClure, C. (1996). "Electronic Surveys: Methodological Implications for Using the World Wide Web to Collect Survey Data." Proceedings of the 59th Annual Meeting of the American Society for Information Science, 173–185.

Brink, T., Ha, S., Pritula, N., Lock, K., Speredelozzi, A., & Monan, M. (2003). "Making an iMpact: Redesigning a Business School Web Site around Performance Metrics." Proceedings of the 2003 Conference on Designing for User Experiences, 1–15.

Carroll, J., Chin, G., Rosson, M., Neale, D., Dunlap, D., & Isenhour, P. (2002). "Building Educational Technology Partnerships through Participatory Design." In J. Lazar (Ed.), *Managing IT/Community Partnerships in the 21st Century* (pp. 88–115). Hershey, PA: Idea Group Publishing.

Ceaparu, I., & Shneiderman, B., (2004). "Finding governmental statistical data on the web: A study of categorically-organized links for the FedStats Topics page." *Journal of the American Society of Information Science & Technology,* 55(11), 1008–1015.

Corry, M., Frick, T., & Hansen, L. (1997). "User-Centered Design and Usability Testing of a Web Site: An Illustrative Case Study." *Educational Technology Research and Development,* 45(4), 65–76.

Dix, A., Finlay, J., Abowd, G., & Beale, R. (2003). *Human-Computer Interaction* (3rd ed.). London: Prentice Hall England.

Dommeyer, C., & Moriarty, E. (2000). "Comparing Two Forms of an E-mail Survey: Embedded vs. Attached." *International Journal of Market Research,* 42(1), 39–50.

Fowler, F. (2001). *Survey Research Methods* (3rd ed.). Newbury Park, California: Sage Publications.

Fuccella, J., & Pittolato, J. (1999). "Giving People What They Want: How to Involve Users in Site Design." *IBM DeveloperWorks.* Available at: http://www-4.ibm.com/software/developer/library/design-by-feedback/expectations.html.

Hoffer, J., George, J., & Valacich, J. (2002). *Modern Systems Analysis and Design* (3rd ed.). Reading, MA: Addison-Wesley.

Krueger, R. (1994). *Focus Groups: A Practical Guide for Applied Research*. Thousand Oaks, California: Sage Publications.

Lazar, J. (2000b). "Teaching Web Design through Community Service Projects." *Journal of Informatics Education and Research*, 2(2), 69–73.

Lazar, J., Hanst, E., Buchwalter, J., & Preece, J. (2000a). "Collecting User Requirements in a Virtual Population: A Case Study." *WebNet Journal*, 2(4).

Lazar, J., Jones, A., & Greenidge, K. (2004). "Web-Star: Development of Survey Tools for use with Requirements Gathering in Web Site Development." In A. Sarmento (ed.) *Issues in Human–Computer Interaction*, Hershey, PA: Idea Group Publishing, 37–48.

Lazar, J., & Preece, J. (1999). "Designing and Implementing Web-Based Surveys." *Journal of Computer Information Systems*, 39(4), 63–67.

Lazar, J., & Preece, J. (2001). "Using Electronic Surveys to Evaluate Networked Resources: From Idea to Implementation." In C. McClure & J. Bertot (Eds.), *Evaluating Networked Information Services: Techniques, Policy, and Issues* (pp. 137–154). Medford, NJ: Information Today.

Lazar, J., Ratner, J., Jacko, J., & Sears, A. (2004). "User Involvement in the Web Development Process: Methods and Cost-Justification." Proceedings of the 10th International Conference on Industry, Engineering, and Management Systems, 223–232.

Lazar, J., Tsao, R., & Preece, J. (1999). "One Foot in Cyberspace and the Other on the Ground: A Case Study of Analysis and Design Issues in a Hybrid Virtual and Physical Community." *WebNet Journal: Internet Technologies, Applications, and Issues.*, 1(3), 49–57.

Lisle, L., Dong, J., & Isensee, S. (1998). "Case Study of Development of an Ease of Use Web Site." Proceedings of the 1998 Human Factors and the Web Conference. Available at: http://www.research.att.com/conf/hfweb/.

Marchionini, G. (1995). *Information Seeking in Electronic Environments*. Cambridge, England: Cambridge University Press.

Niederst, J. (1999). *Web Design in a Nutshell*. Sebastopol, CA: O'Reilly and Associates.

Proctor, R., Vu, K., Salvendy, G., et al. (2002). "Content Preparation and Management for Web Design: Eliciting, Structuring, Searching, and Displaying Information." *International Journal of Human-Computer Interaction*, 14(1), 25–92.

Rosson, M., & Carroll, J. (2003). "Scenario-Based Design." In J. Jacko & A. Sears (Eds.), *The Handbook of Human-Computer Interaction* (pp. 1032–1050). Mahwah, NJ: Lawrence Erlbaum Associates.

Schmidt, W. (1997). "World Wide Web Survey Research: Benefits, Potential Problems, and Solutions." *Behavior Research Methods, Instruments, & Computers*, 29(2), 274–279.

Turban, E. (1995). *Decision Support and Expert Systems: Management Support Systems.* Englewood Cliffs, NJ: Prentice-Hall.

Tuten, T., Bosnjak, M., & Bandilla, W. (2000). "Banner-Advertised Web Surveys." *Marketing Research*, 11(4), 17–21.

Walker, L. (August 4, 2002). "Pop Go the Pop-Ups." *The Washington Post*, H7.

Whitten, I., Bentley, L., & Dittman, K. (2003). *Systems Analysis and Design Methods.* Boston: Irwin McGraw-Hill.

Witmer, D., Colman, R., & Katzman, S. (1999). "From Paper-and-Pencil to Screen-and-Keyboard: Toward a Methodology for Survey Research on the Internet." In S. Jones (Ed.), *Doing Internet Research: Critical Issues and Methods for Examining the Net* (pp. 145–161). Thousand Oaks, California: Sage Publications.

chapter 5

Information Architecture and Site Navigation

After reading this chapter, you will be able to:

- Determine and organize Web site objects.
- Understand how information architecture relates to menu design.
- Design different types of site navigation.
- Ensure that users know where they have been, where they are, and where they can go.
- Properly label and present navigation choices.
- Design a sitemap.
- Design appropriate path analysis.
- Understand the minimum technological requirements for site navigation.

Introduction

After the user requirements have been collected, it's important to "do something" with them. Using the requirements, the Web development team should create a conceptual design plan for the Web site. Conceptual design involves figuring out what will be done to design the site; it does *not* mean coding the site. Conceptual design involves answering questions such as what content will be needed, how navigation will be provided, how pages will be laid out, what color scheme will be used, how user technological requirements will be addressed, and how browser compatibility will be ensured. These issues need to be resolved before coding begins. The next few chapters discuss in detail all of the decisions that must be made. As part of that discussion, this chapter begins with the important decisions concerning Web site objects, information architecture, and site navigation. Methods for presenting and locating navigation on the page, technical requirements for navigation, and navigation terminology are discussed in this chapter.

Information architecture and Web navigation deal with the structure of the Web site—how information is organized so that users can easily find it. How will the various pieces of content be organized and arranged? What approaches to site navigation will be taken? What titles will be used for navigation? Site navigation should make it easy for users to find the site content. Information architecture is the study of organizing large information spaces for optimal user interaction. Although information might be available on a site, users very often cannot find the information they are looking for. There is a popular lapel button distributed at human-computer interaction conferences that reads, "If the user can't find it, the function's not there." It's very problematic if users cannot find the content they are looking for. The site navigation is like a map through the Web site, providing guidance to users on how to get where they want to go.

Web Site Content Objects

Two concepts help to transition from the process of requirements gathering to the early stages of conceptual design. At this point, a Web site can be characterized as being either static (with a fixed number of Web pages), or database-driven. Requirements gathering can help to determine which Web content objects (content that was identified as important from the requirements gathering) should exist on the site.

A majority of small- to medium-size Web sites are static, meaning that there are a specific number of HTML files with fixed content. Fixed content is content that changes only when someone (such as the Web developer) changes the data in the files. In contrast, larger Web sites (including e-commerce sites) are database-driven. A database-driven site allows users to search for and request specific data, and most Web pages are created "on-the-fly" by the database. Templates, which are bare bones HTML pages that include layout and navigation information but no content, are used. When data is requested, the database supplies the content and a template page layout presents it. From an informational architecture point of view, the page, whether static or database-driven, still occupies the same place in the overall structure of the site. If a user clicks on a link one level down in a hierarchy, it doesn't make a difference if the page is a static page or a database-driven page.

Determining the Web Content Objects

To determine what content should be included on a Web site, a good way to start is to review the requirements gathered and the Web site mission as defined by the client and determine what Web content objects would be appropriate for the site. A content object is a well-defined piece of content. A content object can take up an entire Web page, or multiple, related content objects can share the same Web page. The data from the user requirements gathering should naturally lead to a list of potential content objects. The content object is simply the smallest granularity of content. It's possible for instance, that the content of "company employees" could be split further into three different types of employees (e.g., public information officers, sales staff, and internal employees). If there are plans to add database-driven sections to a Web site, they can be added to the list of potential content. For instance, if there is a database-driven portion of a Web site to respond to users' requests for information about staff members, the page layout will be the same, regardless of the user request. Only the data will change, and the combination of query requests and responses can be considered a category, or class, of content. On a list of content, this example could be listed as "staff information upon dynamic request."

When determining which Web content objects should be included in the new Web site, the data from the requirements gathering should be analyzed. Although it would be nice to include all Web content requested by users, in most cases, this is not a realistic goal. If there are many different content resources requested by users (and suggested by the clients), then these requests should be prioritized. One way to prioritize Web content objects is to count how often they were requested in the requirements gathering. The most requested objects should be included in the Web site plan. If the requirements gathering asked targeted users whether they would be interested in certain content objects, a threshold percentage can be used.

For instance, a Web site object might be included on the Web site if 50 percent or more of targeted users indicate that they are interested in the resource.

Based on the requirements gathering, possible Web content objects can be divided into three categories: mandatory, desirable, and optional. Mandatory content objects are those that are necessary for a successful Web site, desirable content objects are those that would be helpful and should be added as soon as possible, and optional content objects are those that might be useful, but will not affect the overall success of the site. Changes in time or money allocated for the Web development project might mean that more (or fewer) desirable and optional Web site objects will be included. If quantitative data is available about whether objects are perceived as mandatory, desirable, or optional, this data can be analyzed using decision-making models. Additionally, there might be some Web content objects requested by users that the clients are strictly against, and therefore, cannot be included in the actual Web site, at least at the present time. For instance, if users want chat rooms, content of a partisan nature, or information about competitors, the client might be strongly against including such content. Theoretically, all content desired by the users should be developed for a Web site. However, given time limits, resources, and conflicting design goals, this rarely happens. The content that appears on a Web site is usually a compromise of what users and the client organization wants. The process of deciding exactly what content will appear on a Web site can be challenging.

Organizing Web Content Objects

Once a list of content objects exists, it's important to determine how these various Web content objects are organized. The next step is to organize the content objects into Web pages. A list should be made of all of the Web pages that will need to be developed for the site. For a site redesign, a list of the Web pages on the current site should be made and modified. While a Web content object can take up an entire Web page, various Web content objects can be grouped together on a single Web page, especially if requirements gathering activities indicate that users tend to organize these content objects together. Making a list of all Web pages that should be on the site can help to ensure that nothing will be left out, and will determine who should develop the content. It might be helpful to develop a table that lists all of the Web pages to be developed, as well as the pertinent information about each Web page (where the content comes from, how often it's updated, etc.). An example is shown in Table 5.1. While this may seem like a small task, remember that many Web sites have hundreds or thousands of pages. It's important to understand how users organize information in their minds, because that's how information should be organized on the Web site. Techniques such as paper prototypes and card sorting (described in Chapter 4) can help to gain a better understanding of how information is organized in users' minds, and can determine what content should be organized together on a page, and how pages should be grouped. In summary, for each Web page, the Web development team needs to decide important issues such as:

- the title of the Web page
- the purpose of the Web page
- the content to be developed, and how it will be developed
- how often the data will need to be updated
- who will be responsible for updating the data
- how specific content relates to other content on the site

Table 5.1 Possible Web Content Objects for the Web site of the Towson University Leadership Honor Society (Omicron Delta Kappa)

Content	Source	Updated
History of the Towson ODK circle	From advisor	Once a year
Induction ceremony	From advisor	Once a semester
Downloadable application	From national office	Infrequently
Meeting dates/locations	From student officers	Monthly
Officers	From advisor	Once a semester
Pictures	From advisor	Infrequently
Membership list	From student officers	Once a semester

Information Architecture

A classic TV commercial asked, "How many licks does it take to get to the center of a Tootsie Roll Pop?" Mr. Owl found that it took three licks to get to the center of a Tootsie Roll Pop. When designing a Web site, an important question to consider is, "How many clicks does it take for users to get to the information they want?" Information architecture is the study of how users navigate (or travel)

Hands-On Example

Improving the Information Architecture of Health Information for Older Users

Kurniawan and Zaphiris performed an information architecture study using card sorting and category labeling for a health care Web site for older users. Participants were given 64 index cards, representing 64 Web site pages. The users categorized the data very differently from the way the Web site presented the data. The users found the content organization confusing because much of the content was organized by the geographical location of the research (e.g., France) rather than the purpose of the content (e.g., research centers on diabetes). Users also suggested less formal titles such as "active seniors" instead of "positive well-being" (Kurniawan '03).

through information spaces. When applied to the Web, information architecture is the study of how Web sites are structured. Information architecture covers issues such as: How many levels of pages will the Web site architecture contain? How many choices will be available on each level? What paths will exist for the user to travel through the structure? How many clicks will be required to get from the homepage to the content page of interest?

Although the hypertext that creates the foundation for the Web theoretically allows the user to click from any page to any other page, Web sites are generally set up in some type of organizational structure. This structure should be planned in advance, to allow for a clear structure that can help users find what they want. The best structure for Web sites is the hierarchy, a top-down approach similar to a family tree or an organizational chart, which users can readily understand (Rosenfeld '02). A hierarchical structure can be set up with a "top page" (homepage), "middleman pages" (for content areas or audiences), and content pages. A sample structure from a university is shown in Figure 5.1. The number of choices on each level (groupings), and the category titles, should be influenced by the requirements gathering activities such as card sorting. It's important to plan ahead, and sketch out the paths that a user can take through a Web site.

Theoretical Foundations/Relationship to Menu Design

The list of choices to click on a Web page is the means by which a user navigates up or down through levels in the site architecture. It's really a menu. There is a

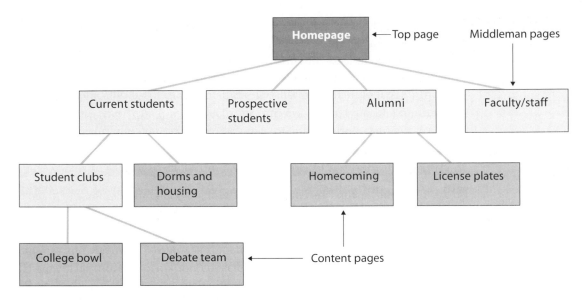

Figure 5.1 Most Web sites use a top-down hierarchy, with the homepage at the top, and middlemen pages, which help users find content pages.

great deal of research on menus related to designing links and the information hierarchy on a Web site. For instance, it's preferable to provide more choices on a single menu level, rather than to offer numerous menu levels with fewer choices. If you think of a menu structure as a tree, two aspects of the structure are the depth (the number of menu levels) and the breadth (the number of items on a menu) (Shneiderman '05). Given a static number of menu choices, as you increase the number of levels, you generally decrease the number of menu items per menu level. As the number of menu levels increase, users can lose sense of where they are in the overall information architecture of the site. The actual architecture of the site is rarely visible to users; therefore, they tend to form their own model of the site architecture (which may or may not match the actual architecture). However, the more levels that users must travel to get to the content that interests them, the less likely they will know where they are in the architecture, making it harder for them to find the content they were originally looking for, and also less likely to find other areas of the site.

How can the research on menu design be applied to designing Web sites? The fewer menu choices (hypertext links) per Web page, the more Web pages (and levels) users must go through, and the more clicks users will have to make.

Research findings indicate that users may give up if they are required to go through more than four or five clicks to get to the desired content (Rosenfeld '02). Too many choices can frustrate users by overwhelming human cognitive limits. A classic research article states that humans process information in chunks of 5–9 items (7±2) (Miller '56). There is some debate in academic circles about whether cognitively, this rule should apply to interface design, which deals with recognition, rather than recall (Preece '02). However, because most interfaces are already designed with this rule in mind, it has become an interface standard, which users expect. In most current interfaces, choices, menus, and links are organized, or chunked, into groups of 7–9 items. There can be a number of different groupings. However, having 50 links organized into 5 groups of 10 links each is far superior to a plain list of 50 items.

This is a balance between the need to limit the number of levels in the information hierarchy and the need to limit long lists of unorganized choices. Think of restaurant menus. If there were hundreds of options available for order, a simple list of 500 food items would be overwhelming and would not support the customer's goal of finding what he or she wants to order. At the same time, providing four or five separate menus, one for appetizers, wines, desserts, and entrees, where customers would have five separate menus on their table, could also be overwhelming. The preferable method is to provide one menu with all of the items, but with all of the food choices categorized and presented in logically ordered groupings (appetizers, salads, meat, seafood, dessert). This allows for the maximum number of food items per menu and the shortest time to find a particular item because all of the items are logically arranged. Similarly, on a Web site, the various factors must be balanced for a successful user experience. For Web sites, a broad, shallow hierarchy structure is superior to a narrow and deep hierarchy structure. A broad and shallow hierarchy structure provides more choices per level (with choices organized into groups, of course), and fewer levels in the overall information architecture. Providing more choices per level and fewer levels, requires fewer clicks by users and reduces the likelihood that they will be overwhelmed and lost in the structure.

Figure 5.2 shows a comparison of a narrow and deep hierarchy and a broad and shallow hierarchy. It takes fewer clicks to get from page A to page B in the broad and shallow structure than it does in the narrow and deep structure.

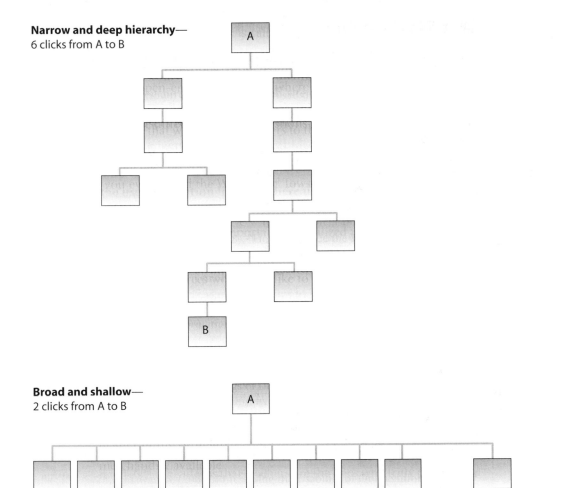

Figure 5.2 Comparison of two types of information architecture: narrow/deep and broad/shallow.

Web Navigation

There are three different types of Web navigation available to users: information on where they have been, information on where they are, and information on where they can go.

Knowing Where Users Have Been

Browsers have built-in features to tell users where they have recently been. For instance, Web browsers have a history feature, which allows users to see what sites they have recently visited. Most Web browsers provide this information in a pull-down menu in the address bar (see Figure 5.3). Users can also see where they have recently been by using the Back button. The default (unless developers change it) is to have visited links appear as different colors. While unvisited links appear as blue underlined text, visited links (links to sites that users have recently visited) appear as underlined red or purple links. It's important to remember that users frequently use the Forward and Back buttons to navigate through sites, and this can sometimes lead to results that the developer did not anticipate!

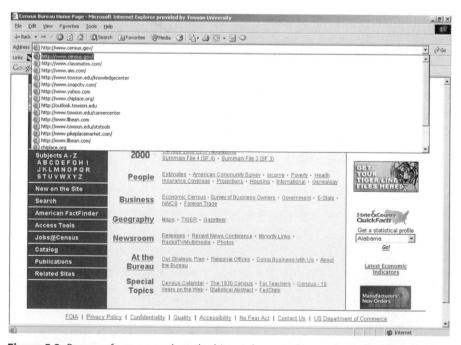

Figure 5.3 Browser features, such as the history, let users know where they have been.

Knowing Where Users Are

When you stop at a rest stop on a busy highway, or when you check out the map of stores in a shopping mall, you probably look for the phrase "You are here" on a map. Since Web site navigation provides a map of a site, navigation schemes must provide some way of telling the user "You are here". Users need to know where they are in the overall structure of a Web site. This is especially true if the user does not access the site starting from the homepage, but rather, links from another Web site and enters the site one or two levels down in the site hierarchy.

Thinking, "Well, when the user clicks on the link, it changes colors" is not enough. Usually, links change colors once users have clicked on them, to show that they have already clicked that link. However, this is not sufficient to show current location. Once the user has followed all navigation links on a Web site, the links are all the same color. And, depending on how users have set up their browser preferences, those links might be displayed in the same color for a long time. With all links displayed as "visited," users know where they have recently been, but they have no information about their current location.

Users need information about where they currently are in the overall structure of the Web site. This can be done in a number of different ways. If the navigation links are textual, then when the user is viewing a certain page, the link to that page should be deactivated. This serves two purposes: The user knows the current location and is unable to repeatedly click the link, which could cause confusion. An example of deactivation can be seen in the homepage for the ACM CHI (Human Factors in Computing) Conference 2001, as shown in Figure 5.4. When the user is on the homepage, the navigational link to the homepage is deactivated, and appears as plain text. Other ways to signify the current location of the user include small symbols or graphics, but it's important to ensure that users with assistive technology, who may be browsing with text-only or some other method, are able to determine where they are. Maybe a phrase such as "you are here" would meet the needs of all users.

Knowing Where Users Can Go

Site designers inform users about where they can go using site navigation. Site navigation is a description, most prominently displayed on the homepage, of where users can go within a Web site. Most users enter a site through the homepage, which serves as the front door of the site. The homepage provides information on how users should navigate through the site to find what they like.

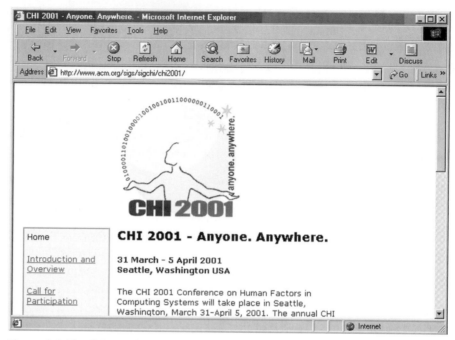

Figure 5.4 The CHI 2001 homepage has deactivated the "home" link so that users know where they are.

Navigation should be provided on all pages on the site, and should be at least somewhat consistent (if not totally consistent) with the homepage. When users access the homepage, they are usually greeted with a number of different options on where to find the content that interests them. Think about when you place a phone call to a company and get a voice mail menu, "If you want to place an order, press one; if you want to talk to the customer service department, press two; if you want to return an item, press three; if you are interested in a job at our company, press four." This is the same basic concept as the navigation on the homepage (and throughout) the site. The Web site is saying, "If you are interested in upcoming events, click here; if you want to learn more about our organization's history, click here; if you want to learn more about our officers, click here."

If card sorting was done during the requirements gathering phase (see Chapter 4), then the card sorting should strongly influence how the Web site navigation is presented. The navigation on the homepage can be organized using different types of schemes, which all help to logically organize the content available for navigation. On a homepage, the four most common types of navigation schemes are: topical, audience splitting, metaphor, and organizational structure.

Topical Navigation. One way to organize the homepage is based on similar topics. The homepage can be split into topics such as history, leadership, products, and so on. The most common type of site navigation is topical navigation based on the top-level sections of the site. Each of these top-level navigation topics should be defined based on the results of requirements gathering, including card sorting. Labels should be clear.

For a larger Web site, the main content areas provide information and links to Web pages in that topic area. For instance, top-level content areas on an art museum Web site might include exhibitions, permanent collections, calendars, volunteer and membership information, museum store, programs, and events. When the exhibitions link is selected, the user receives a list of the 10–15 pages that relate to different temporary exhibitions at the art museum. For a larger Web site, these middleman pages serve as gateways to the actual content pages. For a smaller Web site, these might be the only content pages out of perhaps 10–15 pages. CHIplace (http://www.chiplace.org), an online community for people who work in the field of human-computer interaction, provides topical navigation to help users find information among hundreds of Web pages (see Figure 5.5). The navigation is consistent throughout all pages on the site.

Regardless of the purpose of the Web site or the number of pages involved, some type of navigation must remain present on all pages of the site. Users need navigation choices in order to know where they can go. There shouldn't be dead-end pages without information about navigation choices. Navigation should not be provided back to the homepage only; rather, navigation should be provided to all major topic areas of the site, so that users don't need to return to the homepage every time they want to find other content. The worst navigation is no navigation; a dead-end page provides no help about what to do or where to go for more information. What if the user wants to learn general information about the organization by accessing other sections of the site? The skeptic will say, "The user only needs to click the Back button on the browser to get back to the homepage." This solution does not always work because it's possible that the user linked to the dead-end page from another Web site; clicking the Back button would not take the user to the homepage of the current site, but instead back to the Web site that initiated the link to the dead-end page.

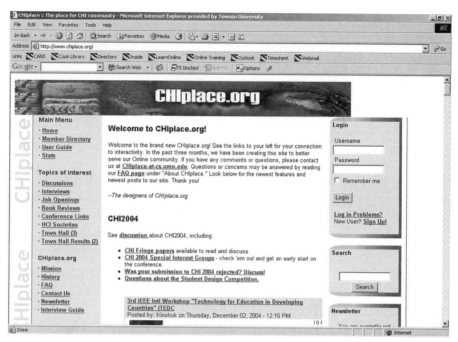

Figure 5.5 CHIplace.org uses a topical navigation scheme.

Audience-Splitting Navigation. Another way to organize the homepage is with a technique called audience splitting. Audience splitting is a good way to approach Web site navigation if there are a number of target user populations that are unique and well defined from the requirements gathering. When there are numerous user groups that might be looking for different types of information, you set up links and Web site sections for each unique user group. For instance, on many university Web sites, there are separate sections for faculty/staff, students, alumni, and prospective students. Even though some of the content might be the same for different user groups, each user group may define the content differently (using different terminology) or organize the content differently. Audience splitting, where content is presented or organized differently for each user population, is a good way to meet the needs of multiple user groups. An example of audience splitting is seen on the Towson University Web site shown in Figure 5.6, where information is provided for the different audiences: prospective students, current students, alumni, business, and faculty and staff.

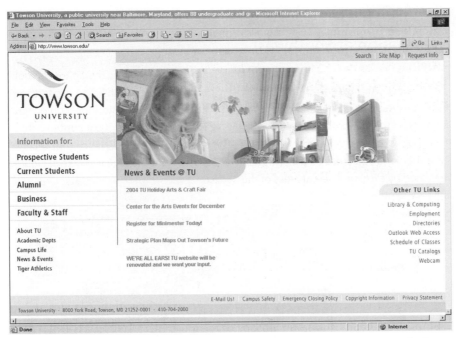

Figure 5.6 The Towson University Web site uses an audience splitting navigational scheme.

Metaphor Navigation. A third way to organize the homepage is to use metaphors. Metaphors relate the interface to objects and concepts in the user's everyday life, and they can sometimes assist the user with understanding the structure of a Web site. For example, a baseball team Web site could use the graphical metaphor of a stadium, where users click different graphical objects that represent content, such as a graphic of a seat to learn about purchasing tickets, a graphic of a dugout to learn about the team players, a graphic of the concession stand to learn what food and memorabilia are available, or a graphic of a parking lot to get directions to the stadium.

While metaphors are generally useful in interface design, they can be limiting for site navigation, since navigation must encompass an incredible amount of information and work well for all user populations. For instance, if an entire site structure is based on a baseball stadium metaphor, it might limit the future growth of the site or may hinder users from finding information. For example, where do you find information about the community service performed by baseball players if

Hands-On Example

Improving the Homepage Navigation at Southwest Airlines

Southwest Airlines used an airport check-in desk as a metaphor for their Web site navigation until 1999, when they decided to change the design. In the metaphor, all areas of the site were reached by clicking different areas of the check-in desk. As shown in Figure 5.7, flight schedules were represented by a book icon and news was represented by a newspaper icon. The metaphor was not intuitive and it was hard to expand the site, since the metaphor could not encompass the various content that needed to be added. The current topical navigation homepage is shown in Figure 5.8.

Also in the
Color Insert

 Also in the
Color Insert

Figure 5.7 The Southwest Airlines homepage as it appeared until 1999, using metaphor-based navigation.

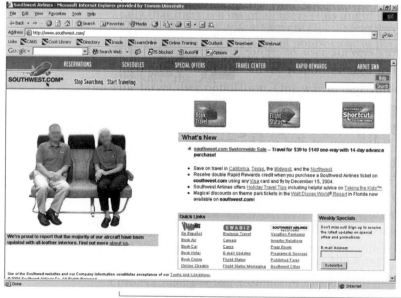

Figure 5.8 The Southwest Airlines homepage as it appears in 2005, using topical navigation.

the entire Web site is based on the baseball stadium metaphor? Where do you learn about stadium access for people with disabilities? Metaphor-based site navigation was popular in the past, however, today it's used infrequently. The Hands-On Example on the previous page shows an example of metaphor-based navigation that was once used on the Southwest Airlines Web site. A metaphor-based site is only good if the metaphor is appropriate, can be understood, and can accommodate all aspects of the site, including future growth. Additionally, if a graphical metaphor is used, there must be some way to translate the metaphor into appropriate usage methods for users with disabilities.

Organizational Structure Navigation. Some Web sites present navigation by using an organizational structure. Most organizations have an internal structure, where different tasks are broken down into departments, divisions, or offices. In some cases, each division has a figurehead (such as a vice president or chairperson). Organizational structure used for navigation only works if all users are familiar with the structure, which is rare. For instance, if the Web site is only used by employees within an organization (such as a password protected intranet), then using the organizational structure for navigation might be appropriate. However, for most external user populations (where the target user population does not consist solely of employees of an organization), using the organizational structure to present navigation is likely to fail. Users typically do not know the structure of the organization, and therefore cannot determine in which division or department the content they seek will appear. Studies of government Web sites have determined, for instance, that users perform better when the navigation is organized based on task (what the users want to accomplish) rather than by office or division.

Sitemaps. While not technically a form of site navigation, a sitemap can be helpful because it provides information to the user about how the site is structured. Essentially, a sitemap is a graphical or textual representation of the information architecture. A sitemap does not necessarily present information in a way that is most useful to the user, but it provides an alternative way to present the information and indicates how the information is structured on the site. It can also be helpful to users who know that a certain piece of content is available, but cannot find the appropriate link to that content. Listing links to all content on one page is not the best navigation method, but it may be helpful for users who use their browser to search for the content title that interests them. Cadbury's Web site, as shown in Figure 5.9, provides a sitemap of all content available on the site.

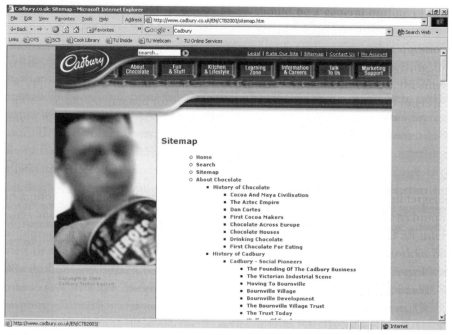

Figure 5.9 The sitemap for Cadbury's, which uses bullet points to show the level of various content in the information architecture.

Organizing and Labeling Navigation Choices

It's important to make sure that navigational choices are organized appropriately with informative labels. As stated earlier, too many unorganized choices can be overwhelming. However, the same number of choices, organized properly, can be helpful. This is apparent by examining the Web site of the University of North Carolina-Charlotte, before and after navigational changes. The older version of the site, as shown in Figure 5.10, offers too many links that are not coherently organized. There are links to the left of the picture, on top of the picture, below the picture, and to the right of the picture. There are nearly 40 links, not coherently organized. The groupings (below, above, and left of the picture) do not represent any meaningful organization. After a redesign, as shown in Figure 5.11, the navigation is much clearer. On the left, navigation is provided based on the organizational structure (athletics, academic affairs, business affairs, etc.). On the top, audience splitting provides links for current students, future students, faculty and staff, etc. Two columns of links highlight clear headings of university news and campus events. The redesign is a far better way to provide site navigation.

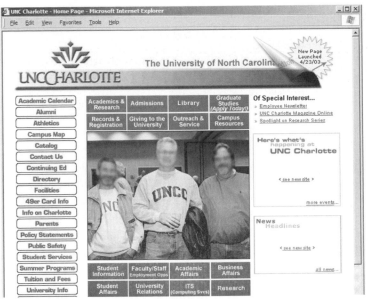

Also in the
Color Insert

Figure 5.10 The old version of the UNCC homepage.

Also in the
Color Insert

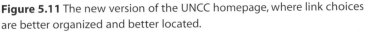

Figure 5.11 The new version of the UNCC homepage, where link choices
are better organized and better located.

Hands-On Example

Unclear Navigational Labels at a Mid-Atlantic University

Usability testing was performed on a Web site for a business school at a private university in the Mid-Atlantic United States. One of the tasks asked users to find information about a course during the current semester. The navigational links provided on the site were:

- Admissions
- Student Life
- Alumni
- MBA Program Calendar
- MBA Courses
- Student Organizations

- MBA Career Management
- Technology

The users who took part in the usability test looked for information about current courses under MBA Courses (which was logical). However, this was not where the current course information was located. Instead, the information appeared under Student Life, and was reached by following the link to Academics and then Spring 2002 MBA Courses. Instead of placing the information under MBA Courses, the site placed the information under the following confusing path:

Student Life → Academics → Spring 2002 MBA Courses.

Labeling site navigation appropriately is also important. Labels must be understood by the target user population and must accurately represent the content reached by following a labeled link. A discussion of the issue of domain knowledge and a target user population's understanding of terminology appears in Chapter 3. It's also important to make sure that site labels, even if they are clearly understood, accurately represent the content that they link to. One example where this wasn't the case is described in the Hands-On Example above.

Client Feedback

If a team outside of the client organization is developing a Web site, it might be useful to consult with the client about a list of Web pages, information architecture, and site navigation. The list can be a simple document sent to the client for approval. If the client signs off on the conceptual design of the Web site, a subsequent misunderstanding between the client and the development team can possibly be avoided. It's also possible that some content requested by users cannot be included (either because it's impossible or because the client is not in favor of it). Client approval of the high-level conceptual site design avoids possible future problems.

Breadcrumbs Navigation

While consistent navigation is traditionally provided throughout the Web site (using topical, audience-splitting, metaphor, or organizational structure), another way to provide navigation once users are immersed in the site is to show the user the path that was used to reach the current page being viewed. Instead of just letting users know what the main sections of the site are, path analysis navigation informs them how they arrived at the specific page within the site. This approach is called breadcrumbs navigation because users leave telltale breadcrumbs on their path to reaching a certain page. For instance, a path analysis on a university Web site might be the following:

www.towson.edu → Campus Life → Student Activities → Leadership Program

Path analysis shows the user the path to get to the page for the Towson University Leadership Program. The page listed on the left (the Towson University homepage) is the highest level, and as the user moves to the right, each arrow represents one level lower in the Web site hierarchy. Moving from left to right in the path analysis, the user moves from the homepage (broad) to the current Web page (specific) for the Leadership Program. Each Web page mentioned in the navigation (www.towson.edu, Campus Life, and Student Activities) should be a hypertext link, so that the user can click to return to that particular page. Additionally, if a user reaches the Leadership Program page from an outside site without having visited other Towson University Web pages, the path analysis provides navigation guidance about how to access information on student activities, campus life, and Towson University as a whole. Figure 5.12 is an example of path analysis provided by Yahoo! that shows the hierarchical path taken to reach the current Web page. Yahoo! also provides the path in the page title (see the title bar). Additionally, Yahoo! set up its directory structure so that users can determine the path taken from the URL of the Web page. The path analysis is displayed on the Web page, title bar, and URL.

To use path analysis effectively, the Web site must be organized hierarchically, with only one specific path to reach a certain Web page. For instance, if users could take 10 different paths to reach a certain Web page, then it would be hard to provide a trail of how they reached the page. If users could reach the Leadership Program page under Campus Life, Academics, Libraries, Faculty and Staff, and so on, what path would be presented? It could be confusing, since the user would read the path and say, "but that's not how I got here!"

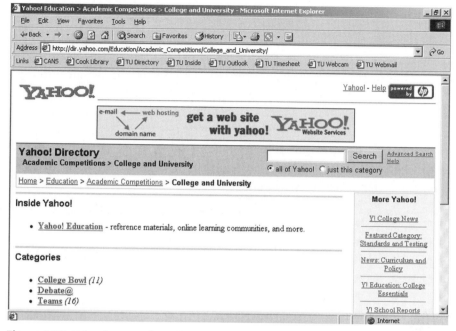

Figure 5.12 Yahoo! uses path navigation on the Web page, title bar, and URL. Reproduced with permission of Yahoo! Inc. © 2004 by Yahoo! Inc. YAHOO! and the YAHOO! logo are trademarks of Yahoo! Inc.

There are added benefits of path navigation. The path navigation can help users from getting lost. By seeing the path navigation, it reinforces the information architecture and helps users identify where they are in the overall site structure. Path navigation can sometimes cut down on the number of clicks required to move from one content page to another within a site. Figure 5.13 displays how path navigation can cut down on the number of clicks. Instead of having to use the Back button to return to the homepage, and then click forward to find new content, which takes four clicks, by using path navigation, the user can jump to the correct middleman page and access the content they want with only two clicks.

Search Engines for Navigation

Many Web sites offer search engines to help users find what they are looking for. There is no conflict between having a hierarchically structured Web site and including a search engine. However, remember that users typically have problems using search engines effectively. Forming queries correctly is a highly technical skill, and different search engines use different approaches, which can

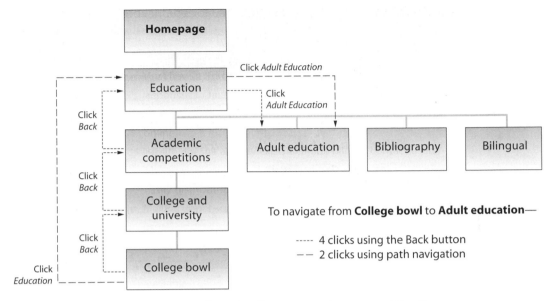

Figure 5.13 Path navigation on the Yahoo! site allows users to jump around the site easily, decreasing the number of clicks required.

confuse users more. A search engine should be considered as a secondary means of navigation if users cannot find what they want by using site navigation (Lee '99). It's also important to note that if users use the search engine to help them find the Web page they are looking for, the path analysis information is useful because it shows them where the page is in the hierarchy, and it provides context information about similar pages on the site.

It's important to note that navigation can be provided in multiple ways. A Web site can offer two navigation schemes: one displaying the main topic areas of the site and another offering a path analysis. They do not conflict. Users may have preferences for how information is presented and different mental models of a site. Therefore, providing multiple navigation options is a good idea. One possibility for providing both topical area navigation and path analysis navigation is to provide navigation links that expand and collapse. The Web site for L.L. Bean, as shown in Figure 5.14, provides this type of navigation. At first, the user is presented with a list of the main sections of the site (men's, women's, kids, and so forth). When the user clicks for more information on men's clothing, and then clicks for men's shirts, the navigation menu on the left expands to provide path information on how the user got to that point (see Figure 5.15).

Figure 5.14 The main Web page for men's apparel at L.L. Bean.

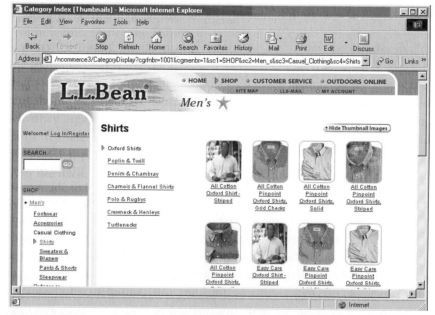

Figure 5.15 When a link is selected, the menu expands, providing both detailed navigation for shirts, as well as path navigation.

Location of Navigation

Navigation is important to the user and needs to be consistently present. The Web site developer has the challenge of not knowing how much screen space is available—users may have different monitor sizes and different screen resolutions. Complicating things further, users may resize the browser window to any size they like, and they may have their fonts set differently from how the Web developer desires. Navigation needs to be easily visible, regardless of the size of the monitor being used or how the browser window is sized. Navigation should be provided on either the top or left side of the page, or some combination of the two, because the left side and the top of the page are usually visible. In most western cultures, people read from left to right, and the navigation should always be the first thing they see. An example of navigation placed appropriately on the page is the Pike Place Market homepage, displayed in Figure 5.16. Navigation is located on both the left side and the top of the screen.

If navigation is placed on the right side or the bottom of the page, it's possible that the user might never see it and be confused as to how to navigate through

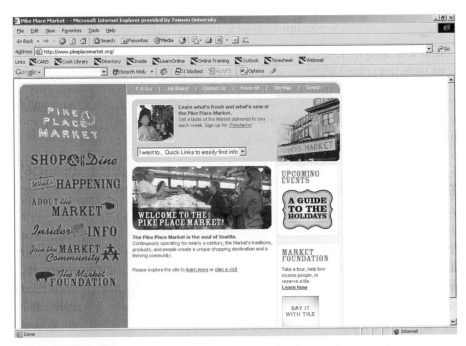

Figure 5.16 The Pike Place Market Web site has navigation on the top and left side of the page.

the site. The most valuable screen space is the space in the left and top of the page. For instance, on the American Recorder Society homepage shown in Figure 5.17, it's unclear where the navigation is. There is a lot of wasted valuable space that could be used for navigation or other important information. The navigation for Kevin's Candy Company's Web site is not visible, as shown in Figure 5.18, until the user scrolls down to the bottom of the screen (see Figure 5.19).

Technical Requirements for Navigation

Navigation should be available using text. Users may not want to wait for all graphics to load, they may not have the plug-ins required, or they may be using assistive technology. Users might be browsing the Web using an older browser that cannot handle advanced technology or they might be browsing with graphics, JavaScript, or Java applets turned off. This doesn't mean that navigation must be strictly textual, without any graphics or other adornment. It might be sufficient to have alternative text (see Chapter 7) on graphical navigation links. But

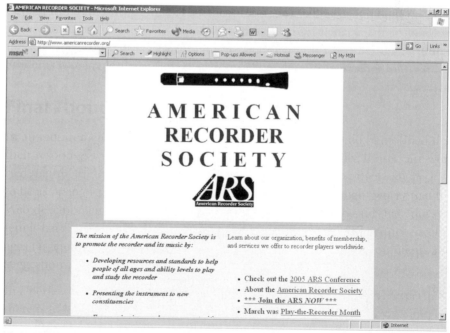

Figure 5.17 The homepage of the American Recorder Society wastes a lot of space and does not display the navigation clearly.

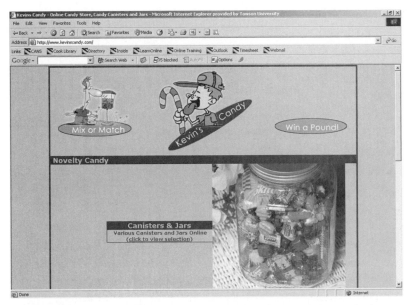

Figure 5.18 The homepage for Kevin's Candy has the navigation at the bottom of the page, which is not clearly apparent to users looking at the top.

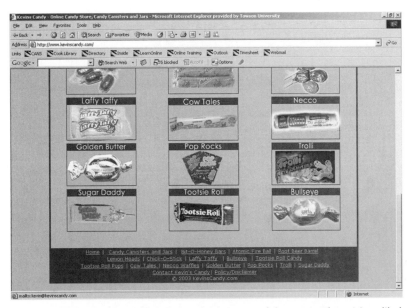

Figure 5.19 Navigation is located at the bottom of the page, where it's unlikely users will find it.

navigation should not be provided using Java applets or any other plug-ins, especially since plug-ins tend to crash the Web browser. Since navigation is a basic requirement for a successful user experience, navigation should be provided for the lowest common capability. Use of graphics for navigation is acceptable, as long as the graphics used (icons, buttons, or text bars) for navigation also have appropriate <alt> tags. These can help users who are browsing using text-only, slow connections, or assistive technology. It's not acceptable to require that users download a plug-in to use the site navigation. See Figure 5.20 for an example of a site that requires users to download a plug-in. If a Web site has textual navigation, or textual equivalents for the graphical navigation, and does not require any plug-ins, it can be used by different user populations, including those with disabilities. More information on designing for universal usability is available in Chapter 7.

Figure 5.20 The GooGoo Web site requires that users download a plug-in to use the site effectively.

When user requirements are collected, they serve as a rich base of information.

- This information should be used to create the conceptual requirements for the Web site, including the navigation.

- The Web development team has to consider which content should be included and how it should be displayed.

- Once the Web site objects are defined, the team must define the information architecture for the Web site and plan the navigation.

- A number of different approaches can be used for navigation, such as topical, audience-splitting, metaphor, or organizational structure. Topical and audience-splitting are the most appropriate.

- Path navigation can help users find where they are in the overall site structure.

- Appropriate terminology and groupings of navigational choices can help users find what they are looking for.

- Simple technical approaches for navigation ensures that everyone who wants to browse the site can.

Design Exercise

Imagine a Web site being developed for a nonprofit environmental policy organization concerned with air and water quality. Given the four main types of navigation schemes: topical, audience-splitting, metaphor, and organizational structure, come up with ideas for how you might provide navigation using each type of scheme. Of the four potential schemes, choose the one that seems to be most appropriate for the site, and justify your choice. Then create a site structure, using the navigation scheme, and show how various Web content objects (such as advocacy, local data on water/air quality, local chapters, impact on fish, impact on human health, etc.) can be organized within the site structure.

Discussion Questions

1. What is a Web site object?
2. Why is the information architecture of a Web site important? Why must it be planned in advance and how does it help users?

3. What is a broad and shallow navigational structure?

4. What are three questions, related to navigation, that users commonly ask? Which types are provided by the browser and which types are provided by the Web site?

5. What are the four most common Web site navigational schemes?

6. Why isn't it a good idea to show users where on a site they are with a colored graphical object?

7. In which limited situations would navigation based on organizational structure be appropriate?

8. Where should the labels for site navigation come from?

9. How can breadcrumbs navigation be used in conjunction with other site navigation?

10. Where should site navigation be displayed on a Web page?

11. Why shouldn't plug-ins be used to provide site navigation?

Suggested Reading

Cockburn, A., & Jones, S. (1996). "Which Way Now? Analyzing and Easing Inadequacies in WWW Navigation. *International Journal of Human-Computer Studies*, 45(1), 105–129.

Fuccella, J. (1997). "Using User-Centered Design Methods to Create and Design Usable Web Sites." Proceedings of the 1997 ACM Conference on Systems Documentation, 69–77.

Kurniawan, S., & Zaphiris, P. (2003). "Web Health Information Architecture for Older Users." *IT and Society*, 1(3), 42–63.

Lazar, J., Meiselwitz, G., & Norcio, A. (2004). "A Taxonomy of User Perception of Error on the Web." *Universal Access in the Information Society*, 3(3–4), 202–208.

Lee, A. (1999). "Web Usability: A Review of the Research." *SIGCHI Bulletin*, 31(1), 38–40.

Lynch, P., & Horton, S. (1999). *Web Style Guide: Basic Design Principles for Creating Web Sites*. New Haven: Yale University Press.

Miller, G. (1956). "The Magical Number Seven, Plus or Minus Two: Some Limits on Our Capacity for Processing Information." *Psychological Review*, 63(2), 81–96.

Navarro, A., & Khan, T. (1998). *Effective Web Design*. San Francisco: Sybex.

Newfield, D., Sethi, B., & Ryall, K. (1998). "Scratchpad: Mechanisms for Better Navigation in Directed Web Searching." Proceedings of the ACM UIST, 1–8.

Niederst, J. (1999). *Web Design in a Nutshell*. Sebastopol, CA: O'Reilly and Associates.

Nielsen, J. (2000). *Designing Web Usability: The Practice of Simplicity*. Indianapolis: New Riders Publishing.

Powell, T., Jones, D., & Cutts, D. (1998). *Web Site Engineering: Beyond Web Page Design*. Upper Saddle River, NJ: Prentice Hall.

Preece, J., Rogers, Y., & Sharp, H. (2002). *Interaction Design: Beyond Human-Computer Interaction*. New York: John Wiley & Sons.

Rosenfeld, L., & Morville, P. (2002). *Information Architecture for the World Wide Web* (2nd ed.). Sebastopol, CA: O'Reilly and Associates.

Shneiderman, B., & Plaisant, C. (2005). *Designing the User Interface: Strategies for Effective Human-Computer Interaction* (4th ed.). Boston: Addison-Wesley.

Page Design

After reading this chapter, you will be able to:

- Understand how download speed impacts user perception of Web content.
- Determine appropriate levels of animation and plug-ins.
- Understand how screen resolution affects Web page presentation.
- Design appropriate grids, layouts, and patterns.
- Identify appropriate font color and size.
- Identify and collect appropriate Web page content.

Introduction

A Web site is a series of interconnected and related Web pages, but the user only views a single Web page at a time. Even though there might be more than one document or file involved (e.g., frames, multiple graphics, or plug-ins), the user still perceives only one Web page. Therefore, the issues involved in page design can make or break the user experience.

The Web page is at the heart of the user experience. Developers must consider what content should go on a Web page, and how it should be presented. What page layout will allow the user to have a pleasant experience? Which add-ons (such as graphics, animations, or applets) will be helpful, and which ones will detract from the user experience? How will download speed impact the user's perception of the Web page?

Truthfully, there is no such thing as a perfect Web page. While download speed is of paramount importance, most other issues associated with page design are tradeoffs. For instance, bigger fonts make the text more readable, but require more scrolling, since less material can fit into a given amount of screen space. Graphics and animation can be useful in presenting Web material, but a high level of graphics is distracting and slows the download speed. The solution is usually to take a "middle of the road" approach.

This chapter discusses how to make a Web page that is easy to use and meets the needs of the user, delivering the information quickly and easily. It covers issues that can help or hurt the user experience when viewing a Web page. The first section discusses technical considerations, such as download speed, use of plug-ins, graphics and animation, and screen resolutions. The second section covers layout issues, such as background patterns, grid structure, font face and size, and color. The third section examines content-related issues, such as clear identification, context information, and page titles.

Technical Considerations

Download Speed

When requesting a Web page, the user wants it to appear quickly. The human-computer interaction research is clear on this; users want a speedy response to their request. Not only are users likely to give up if a Web page takes too long to download, but also the download speed can affect the perception of the quality and usefulness of the material (Ramsay '98; Sears '97). Download speed is the number one concern of Web users (Pitkow '96; Lightner '96; Nielsen '00).

The time it takes for a Web page to download is the product of a number of factors, including the user's connection speed to the Internet, the Internet service provider's capacity and speed, traffic coming to the site being requested, and the size of the Web files being requested (Sears '00a). Only one of these factors is under the control of the Web development team: the size of the files being requested. If the user has a slow computer processor, or if a plug-in must be "warmed-up," it can add to the user's perception of the download time, even though it's not directly related to the download. The user controls the connection speed to the Internet—depending on how much an individual is willing to pay, he or she can get a 28.8 dial-up all the way through to a broadband connection. The client organization decides which Internet service provider to use, which may determine the server response speed. Current traffic to the site being requested is a random unpredictable measure, but the Web development team determines the size of the Web files.

When users request a Web page, they are requesting the HTML document that contains the majority of the content and presentation, as well as any graphics, Java applets, sound files, or other objects. As more of these objects are requested, the download time increases. An HTML file that is 20K will not take long to download; however, the 2MB of graphics that comes along with the file take longer to download and the wait can frustrate users.

Long downloads are one of the top frustrations for users, but what is surprising is that a long download actually affects how users perceive a Web page. Downloading time has a large influence on the user experience because how a user perceives a document depends on how long the document takes to download. A long download time changes the user's perception of whether the content is interesting (Ramsay '98). It also changes the user's perception of the quality of the content (Jacko '00). The longer a Web page takes to download, the more likely that a user will feel lost (Sears '00b). The longer a Web page takes to download, the harder it is for the user to remember information about the context of the task and the overall site structure (Shubin '97). If a Web page takes longer to download than the user expects, the user is likely to perceive that an error has occurred (Lazar '04). When a user perceives that an error has occurred, he or she is likely to perform actions (such as repeatedly clicking "reload") that will cause an actual error to occur. The research on download time is very clear that users don't like long downloads, and long downloads change how people perceive the Web page being downloaded.

Web developers tend to believe that everyone has a high connection speed (broadband) to the Web. However, this is simply not the case. As discussed in Chapter 2, there is no database of all Web users, so it's impossible to know exact sampling estimates, but work in this area has been performed by the Pew Internet and American Life Project. For instance, in February 2004, only 39 percent of adult Internet users had high-speed access to the Internet at their residence, and only half of those with broadband were using cable modems (the rest were primarily using DSL) (Horrigan '04). Of all Americans, only 24 percent have broadband Internet access in their home, of any type. For a large percentage of users, they do have broadband access, but only in their workplace. For instance, by the end of 2004, 55% of *all* Web users in the United States had access to broadband, either at work or at home (see http://www.nielsen-netratings.com for current statistics). However, this is still a very select group. Unless a Web site is being targeted to such an elite group, it should not be designed with the idea that all of the target users have broadband access to the Web.

The download time should be minimized by limiting the amount of data being downloaded. Graphics are good, but too many can be overwhelming. The download time should be minimized by using appropriate amounts of graphics, sound, animation, and Java applets. If content can be presented without using these extra files, then it should be presented without them. If these extras are integral to the presentation of the Web page, users should be warned about the long download time, with an explanation why the large file downloads are necessary. This can help to avoid user perception of error, since the users won't perceive an error if they know that large files are being downloaded. Another approach is to offer different versions of a Web site, one for high-bandwidth users, and another for low-bandwidth users. A number of sites actually provide a graphical version of the site, as well as a text-only version. While the main goal of this action is usually to provide a separate version for users with disabilities,

Hands-On Example

Improving the Download Time at the Columbia House Web Site

Columbia House, a company that sells music and movie CDs and DVDs, wanted to improve the conversion rate of their site (the rate at which visitors to the site actually sign up to purchase items). Specifically, large numbers of people visited the Columbia House Web site, but relatively few joined as members to purchase CDs and DVDs. The results of user feedback showed that one of the biggest usability problems was that the pages were slow to download. Previously, the Columbia House site had graphic-inten-sive pages, which took a long time to load, regardless of the user's connection speed. Additionally, the wording was unclear to users and feedback was missing from the process. One of the main objectives of the redesigned Web site was to develop "lightweight" pages that were no more than 100k in size, and took no more than 10 seconds to download, even at slower connection speeds. In addition, wording was improved, and more feedback to users was added. After the site redesign, which included the "lightweight" pages, the conversion rate increased 180 percent, increasing the number of Columbia House club members and items sold (Fletcher '02).

the text-only site can also be used when a user has a very slow or unreliable connection (e.g., a wireless connection). Figure 6.1 shows a text-only version of the Medicare Web site. The text-only site is in addition to their main site.

Plug-Ins

Plug-in applications, or helper applications, such as PDF (Portable Document Format), RealAudio, and Flash, can assist in presenting data appropriately and usefully. However, plug-in applications are helpful only if the user has them installed. If the user does not have the plug-in application, then requiring it can become a hindrance to the user's browsing experience. The conventional (and incorrect) wisdom is that "as long as the plug-in is available for free, we can provide a link to download the plug-in application." The unconventional (and correct) wisdom is that requiring users to download a plug-in application will take a few minutes. This has the same effect as increasing the file size so that it takes a few minutes to download. There is also the possibility that the user will not want to download the plug-in application; will not be able to figure out how to

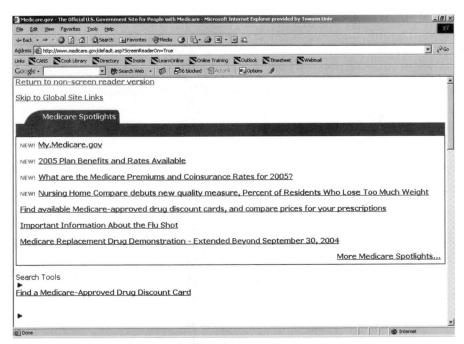

Figure 6.1 Text-only version of the Medicare Web site.

download the plug-in application; or will attempt to download the plug-in application and make an error. Perhaps the user's local area network at a workplace will not allow downloaded applications because of security reasons. Finally, many plug-ins cause the browser to crash, so based on previous experience, users may not want to use a plug-in.

When using a plug-in as a part of your Web page, there are two important questions to ask:

1. Does most of your target user population have the plug-in?
2. Is the plug-in really needed to present the content?

It's safe to require the use of a plug-in application only when you know that almost all of your targeted users have the plug-in application installed. For instance, it's relatively safe to assume that all Computer Science and Information Systems researchers have the Adobe Acrobat Reader (for PDF files) installed, or will feel comfortable installing it. A number of conference Web sites provide the call for papers and the papers themselves in PDF format. Based on the information gathered on the user computing environment during the requirements gathering, the Web development team might know for instance, that 90 percent of targeted users have RealAudio installed. It would then be safe to require the use of RealAudio on the Web site.

It's important to determine whether a plug-in is really needed to present the content. For instance, frequently, information is posted on the Web in PDF format, Word format, or Excel format, simply because the information was saved in that format originally. Because it was created in a certain format is not a reason to distribute it on the Web the same way. All information that the user will read or print should be created in HTML format. If a user needs to interact with the data or graphics on the page in a special way (e.g., performing calculations or viewing an object in 3D), then a plug-in might be appropriate.

Animation

Animation is appropriate only for a very limited number of Web sites. Animation can be very distracting to users and generally inappropriate for informational or e-commerce sites. Research shows that animation on Web pages decreases the performance of information retrieval (Zhang '00a). Animated characters can increase user anxiety and decrease user performance (Rickenberg '00). Imagine reading a book with pictures that move. It would be very distracting to read while there were moving pictures. Animation is no different. Animation distracts the user's attention from the current task. Think about an animated graphic that is serving as a banner advertisement at the top of a Web page. The purpose of the animated ad is to grab the user's attention. The movement from animation is great if you are the company sponsoring the advertisement, but not so great if you are the content provider because the attention has been grabbed away from the content and your message. Why would a Web designer want to distract users from their original purpose in coming to the site?

Despite its inappropriateness for basic information retrieval, animation can be appropriate for Web sites that will be primarily used by children because it helps to keep their attention and is preferred by young children (Sullivan '00). But above 14 years of age, Web usage tends to be similar to that of adults (Hanna '97). Even for children as old as 10, heavy use of animation might not be appropriate. Figure 6.2 shows the NASA Web site (the United States Space Agency) for children, which appropriately uses graphics and animation. Animation is appropriate on Web sites whose purpose is to entertain because the animation (the

Also in the
Color Insert

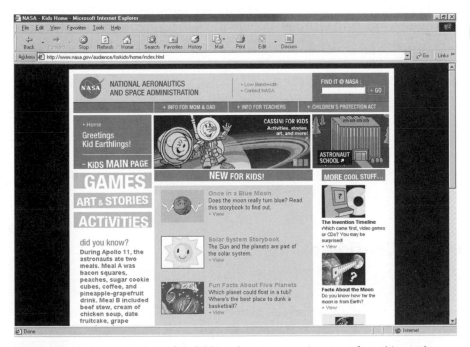

Figure 6.2 The NASA Web site for children shows appropriate use of graphics and animation for children.

entertainment) is the content itself. Animated graphics are not equivalent to video. Video is content that the user chooses to view as content. An animated picture is a picture that moves and changes shape or form, and unless users turn off all graphics, they cannot force the animation to stop moving.

Screen Resolution

A user's screen resolution affects how many pixels will fit on the screen. Monitors have built-in limits on resolution (1024×768 pixels are common for CRT monitors, and 1280×1024 pixels are common for newer LCD flat-panel monitors.). However, users can also choose to set their monitor to display information at a resolution less than the maximum that their monitor can handle. For instance, many users have monitors that can handle 1024×768, but set their monitor to display their screen at 800×600 pixels. This allows the screen, the text, and all screen components to appear larger and more readable.

Web pages should be tested with multiple screen resolutions, to ensure that the pages will appear appropriately in different resolutions. The Web page doesn't need to appear the same in all resolutions, just appropriately. Most users currently are using either 1024×768 or 800×600 for Web browsing (http://www.w3schools.com/browsers/browsers_stats.asp). Therefore, these are the resolutions that designers should design for. One way to address the issue of multiple screen resolutions is by using percentages instead of exact pixel descriptions in the coding. For instance, when coding, a description of 300 pixels will appear differently in 1024×768 and 800×600 resolution screens. However, a "30 percent" attribute will appear the same, regardless of screen resolution. Figures 6.3 and 6.4 show the difference between a Web site displayed in 1024×768 and 800×600 resolutions. One way to test a site at various screen resolutions is to use the screen size tester at http://www.anybrowser.com/ScreenSizeTest.html.

Layout Considerations

Cluttered Design

People think that it's better to add as many graphics, objects, and sounds to a Web page as possible—"more is better." However, overloading the page is simply not good Web page design. Based on what we know from human-computer

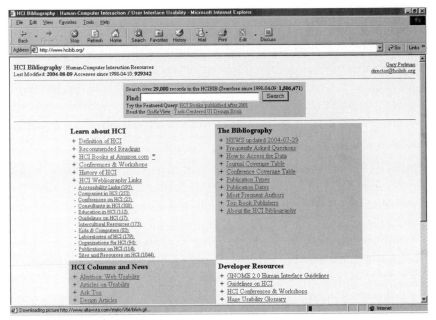

Figure 6.3 The HCI Bibliography Web site at 1024 × 768 screen resolution.

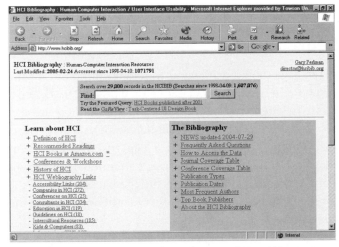

Figure 6.4 The HCI Bibliography Web site at 800 × 600 screen resolution.

interaction research about interface design and user reactions, we know that cluttering up a Web page decreases its usability. Think about going to an art museum. You don't see 50 paintings all closely displayed on one wall. Too many paintings presented together would be overwhelming to the museum visitor and would not enhance the viewing experience. When you are looking for directions at an airport, you don't see clustered images for 25 locations, such as restroom, gift shop, customs, and security because 25 icons of airport amenities would be overwhelming to the airport visitor.

Providing a cluttered screen of many graphics, all clamoring for attention, is just as much of a mistake. Human-computer interaction research finds that the related concepts of short-term memory and chunking give the physiological foundation to explain these phenomena. As humans take in data from their sensory environment, the data is processed in short-term memory. But humans have limits on how much data they can hold and process in short-term memory. Specifically, humans can process 7±2 chunks of data at a time. A chunk can be a letter, a word, a concept, or a category. If 30 choices are presented to the user, the entire grouping can be overwhelming, but if the 30 choices are chunked into six categories of five choices each, they are more easily processed. Organizing choices into categories assists users in finding what they want. Without the distraction of many cluttered items or graphics, the user can more easily process the information on the page. The goal of a Web page should be to deliver information to users in a quick and easy manner, rather than to "make a statement."

Background Patterns

The background on a Web page should be plain; it shouldn't "jump out" at the user and scream for attention. In most cases, a clear color should be used, and a background graphical pattern should not be used at all. However, there are certain circumstances where a background pattern, if subtle, can be visually appealing. For example, a background could be set in a papyrus-type document graphic. This could look stylish and not distract the user's attention. However, an obviously repeating graphic should not be used to tile the background. If the client organization is interested in placing a seal or other identifying mark on the Web page, such a graphic should be used only once. Repeatedly displaying the graphic does not improve user recognition of the Web page; it decreases the ability of the user to focus on the task, and in many cases, it hinders the user's ability to read the text. Figure 6.5 shows a Web page with a distracting background pattern.

Do this

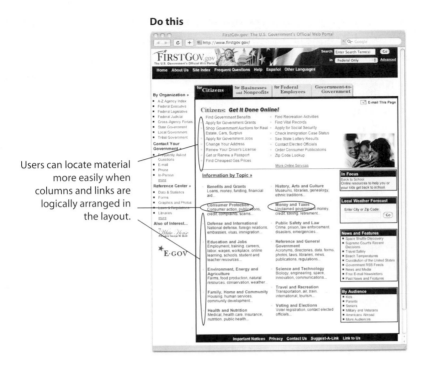

Also in the
Color Insert

Users can locate material
more easily when
columns and links are
logically arranged in
the layout.

Don't do this

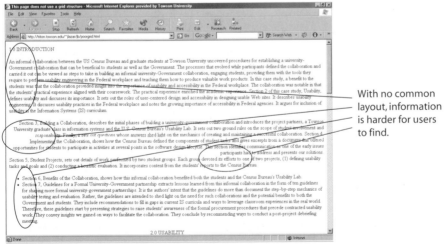

With no common
layout, information
is harder for users
to find.

Figure 6.6 A comparison of a page layout using grids and columns, and one not
using any type of standard layout.

While it would not be appropriate for design guidelines to demand the use of a specific color, it's important, regardless of which colors are used, that there is a contrast between the text color and the background. The color of text must have a planned contrast to the background color. Black text on a black background is obviously not perceptible, but combinations such as blue text on a black background or yellow text on a white background can also be difficult for users to discern. Figure 6.7 (see the color insert) displays various font colors on a white background. Even color pairings that seem to be appropriate (such as red and blue), strain the eye because they are on opposite ends of the color spectrum (Shneiderman '05). The PetBehave Web site, shown in Figure 6.8 (see the color insert), uses red text on a pink background, which is hard for the user to discern.

A good guideline is to use dark text (such as black) on a light background, or light text (such as white or yellow) on a dark background. Background page color should be neutral, such as black, white, gray, brown, and tan. Light background colors tend to have the least problems displaying primary text colors (red, blue, and black). Regardless of what color combination is used, it's important not to use too many different colors. Human factors guidelines suggest using no more than four colors on a single screen and seven colors on a set of screens, so as not to overwhelm the user (Shneiderman '05).

It's important to make sure that color is not the only method used to present content because some users may have various forms of color blindness. Estimates are that 8 percent of men, and 0.5 percent of women, have some form of color blindness (Badre '02). For them, color contrasts may be perceived differently, or not at all. Those who are limited in their ability to see red or green see gray instead. Figure 6.9 (see the color insert) illustrates how different colors are perceived by people with color blindness.

Font Size and Face

Font face and font size are interesting attributes. On one hand, Web developers can set any font face and size they prefer. The goal, of course, is to make the text as readable as possible. On the other hand, users can apply their own style sheets to a Web page, allowing the text to appear in the exact font face and size they desire. This is especially useful for a user with low vision or color blindness, when the designer's text presentation might be problematic (Slatin '03). While users can override the developer's text settings, they are rarely aware of this feature, and infrequently take advantage of it (Ellis '00). Given these complications, it still makes sense for the developer to use fonts that are agreeable to most user populations.

Generally, the font size should be consistent throughout a Web site. Larger font sizes can be used to emphasize certain sections, or for subheadings and titles. Different font sizes should not be used to indicate different topics. To differentiate sections, the Web developer should use techniques such as titles, subheadings, bullets, horizontal rules, and extra white space. Generally, a 12-point or larger font should be used throughout a Web site. While a 10-point font might be sufficient for some users, many older users prefer a larger font size.

Developers can design with various fonts, but the available font faces depend on the font sets installed on the user's computer (Niederst '99). Due to this reality, developers should only choose standard and common fonts that are found on most users' computers. For instance, Times New Roman, Arial, Helvetica, and Courier are common fonts.

Although font sizes can be mixed, font faces should not be mixed. One font face should be chosen and used throughout the Web page. According to the National Institute on Aging, sans serif fonts, such as Arial, Helvetica, and Verdana, are preferred to serif fonts, such as Times New Roman and Georgia, because serif fonts are condensed, which makes them harder for older users to read. Sans serif fonts, such as Verdana and Arial, were actually designed to display on computer screens; serif fonts, such as Times New Roman, were transferred from years of paper use (Boyarski '98).

Text Spacing

The text on a Web page should not be one continuous blob of words; it should be broken up into sections. This aspect of page layout comes from effective graphics design. The text that appears on a Web page should be easy for the user to scan. Most users do not read all the text on a Web page. Instead, they usually scan the content to find exactly what they are looking for. The denser the page, the longer it takes to find what they are looking for. Content scanning especially takes place on Web pages at the top of the information architecture, which tend to be topical pages, audience-splitting pages, or middleman pages. Users usually read more on the content pages, which are located lower in the information architecture. Designers should use appropriate spacing to support user text scanning.

Content Considerations

Content is at the heart of a Web page. Users visit a specific Web page because of the content (in most cases, the information) that it contains. Without content, users have little reason to come to a site. The requirements gathering should have determined what types of content the users want (for more information, see Chapter 3). At this point, the content to be included in the Web site will already have been determined. The content should be provided by the client or developed by the client with the assistance of the Web development team. In developing the content, the terminology and the writing style used in the content should be appropriate to the targeted user population. Writing for an audience of 10-year-olds is very different from writing for an audience of surgeons.

Users should perceive that the quality of the content is high. Content should be accurate, timely, grammatically correct, trustworthy, and believable. Out-of-date content (unless posted for historical purposes and clearly stated as such) can affect the user's perception of content quality. Research finds that when users are acquainted with the structure and navigation of a site, usability becomes less of a consideration (because it becomes habitual for the user), and the importance of quality content increases (Davern '00). Content is a factor in motivational quality, which determines why users return to Web sites. If content appears to be out-of-date, biased, or incorrect, it negatively affects the user's perception of the quality of the site, decreasing the chance that the user will return (Small '00). Content should be continuously updated and improved, providing a meaningful reason for a user to return to the site.

Identification

Let's compare various print media. When reading a typical book, people usually read from the beginning. It's rare for a reader to "jump into" the middle of a book. All of the book pages are contained within the physical book covers, so if the reader is reading a page, there are physical clues as to the overall layout of the book. The title page provides information about the author or editor and the date of publication. Compare a book with a newspaper. The newspaper has a new issue every day. Each article can be read individually; there is no need to read the articles in a certain order. Each newspaper article might be written by a different person and each article clearly identifies the specific writer. The top and bottom of a newspaper page include information such as the name of the newspaper, the date published, the newspaper section (sports, metro, arts, etc.) and the page.

In this example, a Web page is similar to a newspaper. Web users can jump from article to article, and there is no logical order necessary for comprehension. They can jump from another Web site directly into a Web page deep within a site. Because of these considerations, when viewing a Web page, users need to have context information about the origin of the content and when the information was last updated. Therefore, each Web page should include identifying information and be able to stand alone. Users should be aware of how current the information is. If the information is out of date, users may have a low opinion of the quality of the Web site. Furthermore, out of date information may not provide useful content for the user.

It's also important to clearly identify who is sponsoring the Web page. This can be as simple as a line at the bottom of the page, or a copyright statement. On the Web, the source of the information can sometimes be unclear. The source is directly related to the quality of the information. Data coming from the Department of Education will usually be reliable, whereas data coming from a sixth grader's science project might have questionable validity. If the users don't know who is supplying the information, how will they be able to trust it? In Figure 6.10, it's unclear what organization sponsors the Web site, or what they do. Compare it with Figure 6.11, where the sponsoring organization is clearly given at the top of the Web page. Additionally, a mailing address, phone and fax numbers, and an e-mail address, provide a clear indication of who sponsors the site. Contact information should be included on every Web page, if possible. At minimum, an e-mail address should be provided. The mailing address, phone number, and fax number of the organization should be provided somewhere on the Web site.

Credibility

Features such as up-to-date content, context information, and clear identification of who sponsors the site, can help establish the credibility of the Web site. A credible Web site is one which contains believable information that users feel can be relied upon for accuracy and correctness (Fogg '99). Users want to interact

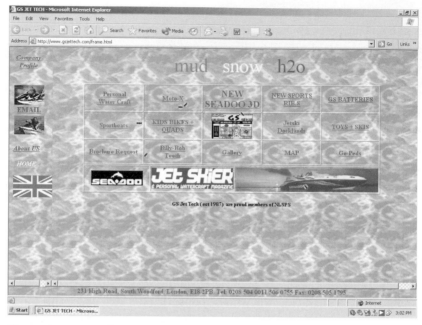

Figure 6.10 It's unclear what organization sponsors this Web site.

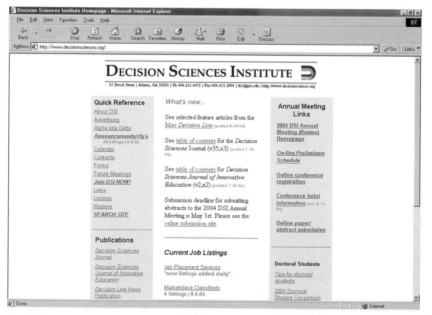

Figure 6.11 It's very clear that this Web site is sponsored by the Decision Sciences Institute.

with a credible Web site. They don't want to interact with a Web site that provides untrue or questionable information, and if they discover questionable content, chances are good that they will not return. This is especially true for e-commerce sites, where users must trust that the payment methods are secure, the company is credible, and when payment is made, the product or service will actually be provided.

An important way that sites can help establish their credibility is to provide a certification seal. Certification seals exist to certify that networks are secure (e.g., VeriSign and TrustE), that a company follows a code of ethics (e.g., BBBOnLine), and/or that health information is credible (URAC and Hi-Ethics). All of these seals can help provide external verification of a site's credibility. Offering a privacy policy on the site also helps establish credibility.

Fogg et al. provides a set of seven design heuristics for establishing that a Web site is trustworthy and credible:

1. Design Web sites to convey the real world aspect of the organization.
2. Make Web sites easy to use.
3. Include markers of expertise.
4. Include markers of trustworthiness.
5. Tailor the user experience.
6. Avoid overly commercial elements.
7. Avoid the pitfalls of amateurism.

The topic of Web credibility is a growing area in the research community. For current information on credibility-related projects, check out: http://www.ischool.washington.edu/credibility and http://credibility.stanford.edu.

Chapter Wrap-Up

Individual Web pages should be designed with a number of user considerations in mind; the most important of these considerations is a fast download speed. This is not to say that all plug-ins, graphics, and Java applets are bad; rather, before including any of these features, it's important to make sure that these extras will actually add value to the user experience.

- Clean, predictable page layouts ensure that users can find what they want with maximum speed.
- Good color combinations and readable fonts help users to avoid eye strain.
- Appropriate page titles, headings, and contact information identify the Web site and make it easy for users to find more information or contact the Web site sponsor.

Design Exercise

Imagine that you are designing two different Web pages for a local hospital about skin care protection from the sun. One page is geared toward 10–12-year-olds, and the other page is geared toward adults. How would the page design differ for the two pages? Specifically, address the appropriate use of plug-ins, graphics, and animation. What types of fonts and colors would be appropriate? How should the writing style be different for the two populations? Sketch a sample page layout for each page.

Discussion Questions

1. What is chunking and how does it relate to page layout on the Web?
2. What factors influence download speeds, and which of these factors can the Web development team control?
3. What are three factors that influence a user's perception of quality content?
4. Why is it not a good idea to require that users download a plug-in application?
5. Why might animation be distracting, and on what Web sites might animation be appropriate?
6. How can you test a Web page to determine how it will appear with various screen resolutions?

7. How is a Web page like a newspaper, and why do you need to provide identification and contact information on every page?

8. What are the default colors for unvisited and visited links on Web pages, and why should Web designers use the default colors?

9. What can Web designers do to ensure that the needs of color blind users are met?

10. When might a text-only (or low bandwidth) Web page be appropriate?

Suggested Readings

Axtell, R. (1991). *The Do's and Taboos of International Trade.* New York: John Wiley & Sons.

Badre, A. (2002). *Shaping Web Usability: Interaction Design in Context.* Boston: Addison-Wesley Publishers.

Boyarski, D., Neuwirth, C., Forlizzi, J., & Regli, S. (1998). "A Study of Fonts Designed for Screen Display." Proceedings of the CHI: ACM Conference on Human Factors in Computing Systems, 87–94.

Ceaparu, I., Lazar, J., Bessiere, K., Robinson, J., & Shneiderman, B. (2004). "Determining Causes and Severity of End-User Frustration." *International Journal of Human-Computer Interaction*, 17(3), 333–356.

Chen, G., & Starosta, W. (1998). *Foundations of Intercultural Communication.* Boston: Allyn and Bacon.

Davern, M., Te'eni, D., & Moon, J. (2000). "Content versus Structure in Information Environments: A Longitudinal Analysis of Website Preferences." Proceedings of the International Conference on Information Systems, 564–570.

DelGaldo, E., & Nielsen, J. (1996). *International User Interfaces.* New York: John Wiley & Sons.

Dix, A., Finlay, J., Abowd, G., & Beale, R. (2003). *Human-Computer Interaction* (3rd ed.). London: Prentice Hall England.

Ellis, R. D., & Kurniawan, S. (2000). "Increasing the Usability of Online Information for Older Users: A Case Study in Participatory Design." *International Journal of Human-Computer Interaction*, 12(2), 263–276.

Fletcher, D., & Brookman, A. (2002). "Making Joining Easy: Case of an Entertainment Club Website." Proceedings of the Conference on Human Factors in Computing Systems: Case Studies of the CHI2002/AIGA Experience Design Forum, 1–16.

Fogg, B., Marshall, J., Laraki, O., Osipovich, A., Varma, C., Fang, N., Paul, J., Rangnekar, A., Shon, J., Swani, P., & Treinen, M. (2001). "What Makes Web Sites Credible? A Report on a Large Quantitative Study." Proceedings of the CHI 2001: Human Factors in Computing, 61–68.

Fogg, B., & Tseng, H. (1999). "The elements of computer credibility." Proceedings of the 1999 ACM Conference on Human Factors in Computing Systems (CHI), 80-86,

Hanna, L., Risden, K., & Alexander, K. (1997). "Guidelines for Usability Testing with Children." *Interactions*, 4(5), 9–14.

Horrigan, J. (2004). *Pew Internet Project Data Memo*. Pew Internet and American Life Project. Available at: http://www.pewinternet.org/pdfs/PIP_Broadband04 .DataMemo.pdf.

Jacko, J., Sears, A., & Borella, M. (2000). "The Effect of Network Delay and Media on User Perceptions of Web Resources." *Behaviour and Information Technology*, 19(6), 427–439.

Lazar, J. (2005). "Tools and Technologies for Web Credibility." Proceedings of the Internet Credibility and User Symposium. Available at: http://www.ischool.washington.edu/credibility

Lazar, J., Meiselwitz, G., & Norcio, A. (2004)"A Taxonomy of User Perception of Error on the Web." *Universal Access in the Information Society*, 3(3-4), 202-208.

Lightner, N., Bose, I., & Salvendy, G. (1996). "What Is Wrong with the World Wide Web? A Diagnosis of Some Problems and Prescription of Some Remedies." *Ergonomics*, 39(8), 995–1004.

Luo, W. & Najdawi, M. (2004). "Trust building measures: a review of consumer health portals." *Communications of the ACM*, 47(1), 109-113.

National Institute on Aging (2002). "Making Your Web Site Senior-Friendly." Available at: http://www.nlm.nih.gov/pubs/checklist.pdf.

Niederst, J. (1999). *Web Design in a Nutshell*. Sebastopol, CA: O'Reilly and Associates.

Nielsen, J. (2000). *Designing Web Usability: The Practice of Simplicity*. Indianapolis: New Riders Publishing.

Parush, A., Nadir, R., & Shtub, A. (1998). "Evaluating the Layout of Graphical User Interface Screens: Validation of a Numerical Computerized Model." *International Journal of Human-Computer Interaction*, 10(4), 343–360.

Pitkow, J., & Kehoe, C. (1996). "Emerging Trends in the WWW Population." *Communications of the ACM*, 39(6), 106–110.

Ramsay, J., Barbesi, A., & Preece, J. (1998). "A Psychological Investigation of Long Retrieval Times on the World Wide Web." *Interacting with Computers*, 10(1), 77–86.

Rickenberg, R., & Reeves, B. (2000). "The Effects of Animated Characters on Anxiety, Task Performance, and Evaluations of User Interfaces." Proceedings of the CHI: ACM Conference on Human Factors in Computing Systems, 49–56.

Sears, A., & Jacko, J. (2000a). "Understanding the Relation between Network Quality of Service and the Usability of Distributed Multimedia Documents." *Human-Computer Interaction*, 15(1), 43–68.

Sears, A., Jacko, J., & Borella, M. (1997). "Internet Delay Effects: How Users Perceive Quality, Organization, and Ease of Use of Information." Proceedings of the CHI 97: Human Factors in Computing, 353–354.

Sears, A., Jacko, J., & Dubach, E. (2000b). "International Aspects of WWW Usability and the Role of High-End Graphical Enhancements." *International Journal of Human-Computer Interaction*, 12(2), 243–263.

Shneiderman, B., & Plaisant, C. (2005). *Designing the User Interface: Strategies for Effective Human-Computer Interaction* (4th ed.). Boston: Addison-Wesley.

Shubin, H., & Meehan, M. (1997). "Navigation in Web Applications." *Interactions*, 4(6), 13–17.

Slatin, J., & Rush, S. (2003). *Maximum Accessibility*. New York: Addison-Wesley.

Small, R., & Arnone, M. (2000). "Evaluating the Effectiveness of Web Sites." In B. Clarke & S. Lehaney (Eds.), *Human-Centered Methods in Information Systems: Current Research and Practice* (pp. 91–101). Hershey, PA: Idea Group Publishing.

Sullivan, T., Norris, C., Peet, M., & Soloway, E. (2000). "When Kids Use the Web: A Naturalistic Comparison of Children's Navigation Behavior and Subjective Preferences on Two WWW Sites." Proceedings of the 2000 Conference on Human Factors and the Web. Available at: http://www.pantos.org/ts/papers/ wkutw/.

Tullis, T., Boynton, J., & Hersh, H. (1995). "Readability of Fonts in the Windows Environment." Proceedings of the CHI: ACM Conference on Human Factors in Computing Systems, 127–128.

Zhang, P. (2000a). "The Effects of Animation on Information Seeking Performance on the World Wide Web: Securing Attention or Interfering with Primary Tasks?" *Journal of the Association for Information Systems*, 1(1). Available at: http://jais.aisnet.org/.

Zhang, X., Keeling, K., & Pavur, R. (2000b). "Information Quality of Commercial Web Site Home Pages: An Explorative Analysis." Proceedings of the International Conference on Information Systems, 164–175.

Designing for Universal Usability

After reading this chapter, you will be able to:

- Understand the concept of universal usability.
- Design appropriate Web pages for older users.
- Design appropriate Web pages for younger users.
- Design appropriate Web pages for users with disabilities.
- Write a universal usability statement.
- Understand what causes Web pages to appear differently in different browsers.
- Design solutions to ensure that Web pages will appear appropriately in all browsers.

Introduction

One of the biggest challenges for designers is the need to design Web sites for universal usability. Universal usability includes two different, but related topics—technology diversity and user diversity. Technology diversity includes different Web browser brands, versions, and platforms, as well as screen resolutions and connection speeds. User diversity includes users with perceptual, motor, and cognitive disabilities, older users, and younger users. It is important to design a Web site that is as universally usable as possible. At the same time, if a large portion of the target user population is one of these special user populations, then guidelines for those populations should be followed as closely as possible. Following appropriate design guidelines and testing ensures that a maximum number of people are able to use your Web site.

Universal usability means designing information systems that can be used by anyone, from any platform, screen size, browser, location, and with any disability (Shneiderman '00). As the population of Web users has expanded over the last few years, no group of people has remained untouched by the Web. Web users now include children as young as five years old, mature users (65+ years), users with various disabilities (motor impairment, perceptual impairment, cognitive impairment), users with limited computer experience, and people new to computers. There is also the subject of technology diversity. Users view Web sites using different browser brands, platforms, and versions. Users check out the Web while traveling, on different screen sizes, and with wireless connections, including handheld devices. Web site design for all browsers and locations is an increasingly important challenge. Universal usability is an area of study that encompasses all types of information systems, not only the Web. Background information on universal usability can be found at http://www.universalusability.org/ and http://www.otal.umd.edu/uupractice/.

User Diversity

There are many diverse user groups on the Web and sites should be designed for everyone to use. Given that, interface design is not influenced by someone's being Catholic or Protestant, brown-haired or light-haired, or short or tall. A few Web user groups, however, represent large numbers of people and specific needs related to interface design. These special groups include older users, younger users, and users with disabilities.

Older Users

Older users, also known as senior users or mature users, are over the age of 65. Typically, this group is not what most computer developers picture as their user population, but in reality, there are a large number of older users on the Web. For instance, in the United States, a recent statistic reveals that 22 percent of people 65 years and older use the Internet (Fox '04).

Tasks and interface needs can differ for older users. E-mail is a very popular application for older users, who communicate to stay connected with friends and family, especially if their mobility is limited. Finding health and hobby information are also popular pursuits, as are news and weather information. The number of older users purchasing products, making travel arrangements, and banking online is increasing.

Some older users may have declining motor and cognitive skills, therefore, interface needs of older users can be different. There is research evidence that older users have more trouble finding information on Web sites and dealing with multiple application windows (Mead '97; Ellis '00) and that they find pointing devices (used heavily in the graphical user interface) to be challenging to use accurately (Worden '97). Therefore, both the tasks utilized by older users, as well as their interaction needs, may differ from younger users. Errors can be especially problematic for older users, who may make them more frequently and have stronger negative reactions when they do (Birdi '97). Small type sizes can be problematic for older users (see Chapter 6 for more information about font sizes). One way that a Web site can adapt is by providing a link that users can click to receive the same Web page with larger fonts. For instance, Figure 7.1 displays the Pew Internet and American Life Project Web site, where users can adjust the font sizes simply by clicking a link to make the font bigger or smaller. Due to these specific concerns, the U.S. National Institutes on Aging has developed a set of design guidelines that specifically address the needs of older users (see the

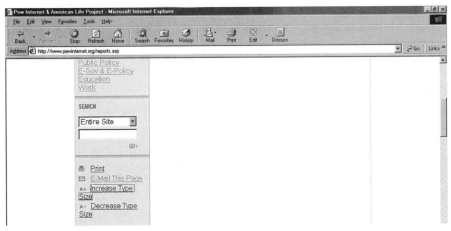

Figure 7.1 The Pew Internet and American Life Web site allows users to increase or decrease the font size easily.

Hands-On Example

Guidelines for Making Your Web Site Easy to Use by Older Users

From http://www.nlm.nih.gov/pubs/checklist.pdf

Designing Readable Text for Older Adults

- Use a sans serif typeface, such as Helvetica, that is not condensed. Avoid serif, novelty, and display fonts.
- Use 12 point or 14 point type size for body text.
- Use a medium or bold fonts.
- Present body text in uppercase and lowercase letters. Use all capital letters and italics in headlines only. Reserve underlining for links.
- Double space all body text.
- Use left-justified text, which is optimal for older adults.
- Avoid yellow, blue, and green in close proximity. These colors and juxtapositions are difficult for some older adults to discriminate. Ensure that text and graphics are understandable when viewed on a black and white monitor.
- Use dark type or graphics against a light background, or white type on a black or dark-colored background. Avoid patterned backgrounds.

Presenting Information to Older Adults

- Present information in a clear and familiar way to reduce the number of inferences that must be made. Use positive statements.
- Use the active voice.
- Write the text in simple language. Provide an online glossary of technical terms.
- Organize the content in a standard format. Break lengthy documents into short sections.

Hands-On Example above). While it's always a good idea to design with senior users in mind, it's especially important to follow these guidelines if a Web site is expected to draw a lot of older users (such as a Web site for health information or pension plans). In addition, Chapter 9 discusses an automated software program ("Dottie") that utilizes these guidelines.

Younger Users

Many governments have made it a priority to get schools connected to the information resources of the Web. Partially because of this, the young Web user population has exploded in the last few years. For Web design purposes, children can be split into separate age-related groups: preschool (< six years old), ele

Incorporating Other Media
- Use text-relevant images only.
- Use short segments to reduce download time on older computers.
- Provide text alternatives such as open-captioning or access to a static version of the text for all animation, video, and audio.

Increasing the Ease of Navigation
- The organization of the Web site should be simple and straightforward. Use explicit step-by-step navigation procedures whenever possible to ensure that people understand what follows next. Carefully label links.
- Use single mouse clicks to access information.
- Use a standard page design and the same symbols and icons throughout. Use the same set of navigation buttons in the same place on each page to move from one Web page or section of the Web site to another. Label each page in the same location with the name of the Web site.
- Incorporate text with each icon if possible, and use large buttons that do not require precise mouse movements for activation.
- Use pull-down menus sparingly.
- Avoid automatically scrolling text. If manual scrolling is required, use specific scrolling icons on each page.
- Incorporate buttons such as Previous Page and Next Page to allow the reader to review or move forward.
- Provide a sitemap to show how the site is organized.
- Use icons with text as hyperlinks.
- Offer a telephone number for users who prefer to talk to a person or provide an e-mail address for questions or comments.

mentary school (6–10 years old), and middle school (11–14 years old), each of which has different interface needs (Hanna '97). Above 14 years of age, interaction needs are similar to those of adults. In general, younger children like interfaces with lots of color and animation, rather than large blocks of text (Clarke '01), even though this may not necessarily improve their task success (Sullivan '00b). Some aspects of user interaction remain the same, regardless of age. For instance, children, like adults, perform well with point-and-click interaction (Inkpen '01) and they dislike long download times (Nielsen '02; Sullivan '00b). However, the fine motor skills of young children might not be equal to that of adults, so clickable targets should be bigger, and drag-and-drop tasks could be challenging. For more information on designing Web sites for younger users, see Case Study D: PlayFootball.com.

Users with Disabilities

An accessible Web site is a site that can be successfully used by people with disabilities. While Web accessibility has been an important topic in the past, more attention has been paid to Web accessibility since new provisions went into effect for many governments around the world. For instance, countries such as Canada, Australia, and Portugal all require certain government information on the Web to be accessible for people with disabilities (for more information, go to http://www.w3.org/WAI/Policy/). In the United States, these provisions are known as Section 508 (for more information, go to http://www.section508.gov/). Section 508 of the Rehabilitation Act was amended in 1998, went into effect in mid-2001, and specifically requires that the U.S. Federal Government only purchases information technology that incorporates accessibility features. Furthermore, Section 508 requires that U.S. Federal Web sites and certain related categories of sites (primarily federally funded) are accessible. Section 508 guide-

---

Hands-On Example

Web Content Accessibility Guidelines for Users with Disabilities

Priority Level 1 checkpoints are available at http://www.w3.org/TR/WCAG10/full-checklist.html. Copyright © 2002. World Wide Web Consortium. All Rights Reserved.

- Provide a text equivalent for every nontext element (e.g., via "alt," "longest," or in element content). This includes: images, graphical representations of text (including symbols), image map regions, animations (e.g., animated GIFs), applets and programmatic objects, ascii art, frames, scripts, images used as list bullets, spacers, graphical buttons, sounds (played with or without user interaction), stand-alone audio files, audio tracks of video, and video.

- Ensure that all information conveyed with color is also available without color, for example from context or markup.
- Clearly identify changes in the natural language of a document's text and any text equivalents (e.g., captions).
- Organize documents so they may be read without style sheets. For example, when an HTML document is rendered without associated style sheets, it must still be possible to read the document.
- Ensure that equivalents for dynamic content are updated when the dynamic content changes.
- Until user agents allow users to control flickering, avoid causing the screen to flicker.
- Use the clearest and simplest language appropriate for a site's content.

lines do not currently apply to company or private Web sites, although there are efforts underway to expand the scope of these laws.

Web accessibility is an important topic because it affects a lot of people. In the United States it's estimated that there are more than 50 million people with some type of disability (Slatin '03; Paciello '00). At least six million people have some form of visual impairment that hinders the use of traditional displays, and nearly nine million people have motor impairments that interfere with the use of traditional keyboard and mouse-based interfaces (Ghaoiu '01). One estimate is that in the United States, nearly 13.1 million people use some type of assistive technology (Paciello '00). Internationally, it's estimated that 10–20 percent of the world population has some type of disability (Paciello '00). As more people with disabilities enter the workforce, and as more children with disabilities are included in regular classrooms, assistive technology can help bridge the gap. However, assistive technology can only assist with Web sites if sites are designed to be accessible!

- Provide redundant text links for each active region of a server-side image map.
- Provide client-side image maps instead of server-side image maps except where the regions cannot be defined with an available geometric shape.
- For data tables, identify row and column headers.
- For data tables that have two or more logical levels of row or column headers, use markup to associate data cells and header cells.
- Title each frame to facilitate frame identification and navigation.
- Ensure that pages are usable when scripts, applets, or other programmatic objects are turned off or not supported. If this is not possible, provide equivalent information on an alternative accessible page.
- Until user agents can automatically read aloud the text equivalent of a visual track, provide an auditory description of the important information of the visual track of a multimedia presentation.
- For any time-based multimedia presentation (e.g., a movie or animation), synchronize equivalent alternatives (e.g., captions or auditory descriptions of the visual track) with the presentation.
- If, after best efforts, you cannot create an accessible page, provide a link to an alternative page that uses W3C technologies, is accessible, has equivalent information (or functionality), and is updated as often as the inaccessible (original) page.

Web accessibility does not happen by accident. Rather, accessibility happens by design, when Web pages are specifically designed to be usable by people with assistive technology. A Web page should be flexible enough so that someone with assistive technology, such as a screen reader that reads text on the screen in computer-synthesized speech, is able to fully use a Web page. Assistive technologies, such as screen readers, Braille displays, adaptive pointing devices, and adaptive keyboards, are used by people with sensory or motor disabilities, such as hearing impairment, visual impairment, color blindness, and motor impairment (e.g., difficulty with use of the hands). At this point, there is limited research on how to design computers for people with cognitive impairments. Accessibility can be thought of as a subset of usability because it deals with ease of use. Because making a Web site accessible is achieved by the ability to interface successfully with assistive hardware and software, the problem can be solved with programming. A set of Web accessibility guidelines can provide suggestions and examples for how to make a Web site accessible.

There are two well-known sets of accessibility guidelines. One is the Web Content Accessibility Guidelines version 1.0 (http://www.w3.org/TR/WCAG10/), spon-

---

Hands-On Example

Section 508 Web Site Guidelines for Users with Disabilities

Rules from Section 508, Subpart B—Technical Standards, 1194.22 Web-based intranet and Internet information and appliances are available at http://www.section508.gov.

A. A text equivalent for every nontext element shall be provided (e.g., via "alt," "longdesc," or in element content).

B. Equivalent alternatives for any multimedia presentation shall be synchronized with the presentation.

C. Web pages shall be designed so that all information conveyed with color is also available without color, for example, from context or markup.

D. Documents shall be organized so they are readable without requiring an associated style sheet.

E. Redundant text links shall be provided for each active region of a server-side image map.

F. Client-side image maps shall be provided instead of server-side image maps except where the regions cannot be defined with an available geometric shape.

G. Row and column headers shall be identified for data tables.

H. Markup shall be used to associate data cells and header cells for data tables that have two or more logical levels of row or column headers.

I. Frames shall be titled with text that facilitates frame identification and navigation.

sored by the Web Accessibility Initiative of the WWW Consortium. These guidelines are divided into three priority levels, with Level 3 being the most stringent. Priority Level 1 guidelines must be satisfied (see the Hands-On Example on the preceding pages for Level 1 checkpoints), otherwise a Web site is inaccessible. Priority Level 2 guidelines should be satisfied if possible, and Priority Level 3 guidelines are optimal. The most serious accessibility infractions fall under Priority Level 1. Note that a working draft of Web Content Accessibility Guidelines version 2.0 is currently under development at http://www.w3.org/TR/ WCAG20. While these are not yet official guidelines, Web developers should monitor the site for updates. Another set of accessibility guidelines are those the U.S. government's Section 508. Section 508 guidelines are very similar to those from the Web Content Accessibility Guidelines Priority Level 1, but there are some differences.

One of the most important aspects of accessibility is simply to include alternative text for any multimedia, graphics, audio, or animation. For instance, all graphics should have alternative text. Any multimedia, animation, or video should include an alternate text format that can be used with assistive technology. Textual transcripts should be provided for streaming audio. In addition,

J. Pages shall be designed to avoid causing the screen to flicker with a frequency greater than 2Hz and lower than 55Hz.

K. A text-only page, with equivalent information or functionality, shall be provided to make a Web site comply with the provisions of this part, when compliance cannot be accomplished in any other way. The content of the text-only page shall be updated whenever the primary page changes.

L. When pages utilize scripting languages to display content, or to create interface elements, the information provided by the script shall be identified with functional text that can be read by assistive technology.

M. When a Web page requires that an applet, plug-in, or other application be present on the client system to interpret page content, the page must provide a link to a plug-in or applet that complies with §1194.21(a) through (l).

N. When electronic forms are designed to be completed online, the form shall allow people using assistive technology to access the information, field elements, and functionality required for completion and submission of the form, including all directions and cues.

O. A method shall be provided that permits users to skip repetitive navigation links.

P. When a timed response is required, the user shall be alerted and given sufficient time to indicate that more time is required.

Web site navigation should be text-based. No applets, graphics, or other techniques should be required for site navigation, since they may cause problems for those using assistive technologies. That is not to say that a visual interface with graphics is not appealing and can't be used, it's just that alternative content for nonvisual users must exist behind the scenes. If the Web site navigation is not accessible, users with disabilities may not be able to get past the homepage.

There are a number of other challenges when creating accessible Web sites. For instance, information should not be presented with color alone, because it will then be inaccessible for users with color blindness. For instance, if there is a colored pie chart, then the corresponding data should also be presented in textual format. Interfaces should not attempt to provide status information with color only. For instance, if a link is blue and underlined, then it will appear as a link, even to someone who cannot discern blue. However, it's problematic if underlining is turned off, so that the only way to determine that it's a link is through the blue text (shown here as gray).

Not good: More information on apple pie is available.

Better: More information on <u>apple pie</u> is available.

Users must be able to navigate a Web site without using a pointing device, or with an alternative pointing device or alternative keyboard. So providing graphical interaction only is not sufficient for accessibility. A Web site can have a visually appealing interface and include graphics; but again, there must be equivalent methods of interaction for users who are using alternative keyboards, pointing devices, or different output devices.

Design guidelines are not the only resource for developers who want to make a Web site accessible. A number of software tools can assist with Web site accessibility. Development tools such as FrontPage and Dreamweaver, have accessibility features. They are discussed in more detail in Chapter 8. For existing sites, stand-alone tools such as InFocus, A-Prompt, and RAMP can examine a Web site, compare it to the design guidelines, and provide assistance in making the site accessible. In some cases, tools can automatically make the changes, greatly decreasing the time and expertise needed to make a site accessible. More information on automated testing tools is available in Chapter 9.

Web pages should be created with a minimum number of tables and frames. These tools to control graphical layouts can be problematic when linearized. When they are used, they should be clearly identified through appropriate headers and titles. For instance, frame names such as "top," "bottom," and "left" will not help a nonvisual user browse through a Web site. However, frame names such as "navigation," "main content," and "searchbox," allow nonvisual users to browse the frames easily. Web pages should also be tested to determine if they appear appropriately when style sheets are turned off. This is not to say that the page will appear the same without the associated style sheet, but as long as the page still appears appropriately, it is sufficient. Many users with disabilities (such as those with color blindness) apply their own style sheets to Web pages; therefore, it's quite possible that the designer's style sheets will be overridden by the user's style sheets (Paciello '00).

Ideally, all Web sites would be accessible, but in reality, this is not the case. Most Web sites were not originally designed for accessibility, and there are expenses incurred in redesigning for it. Unfortunately, this means that if a Web site is not required by law to be accessible, it rarely is. For instance, most Web sites (75–98 percent) of for-profit and nonprofit organizations are inaccessible (Sullivan '00a; Lazar '03). Given the direct relationship between accessibility and profitability, one would expect that e-business sites would largely be accessible. However, one study finds that only 9–16 percent of e-business sites are considered accessible (depending on which set of guidelines, Section 508, or WAI, is used) (Loiacono '04). Why are so many Web sites inaccessible? It's possible that low levels of accessibility are due to persistent myths in the Web design community. One myth is that an accessible Web site must be all text and no graphics (Lazar '04). Other myths include the view that users with disabilities only represent a small number of potential customers and that they don't use computers. Finally, some Webmasters don't like others dictating the design of their sites, although this is a misunderstanding. Accessibility doesn't change how a Web site appears to users without disabilities. Most of the accessibility features are equivalents, provided behind-the-scenes, to the users who need them. For users without disabilities, the experience is seamless, and they don't know the difference.

Similar to the privacy statements that many Web sites include, it's suggested that a site also includes a universal usability statement. The purpose of a universal usability statement is to let users clearly know the usability aspects of the site (Hochheiser '01). A universal usability statement might include information on which browsers have been tested, which plug-ins are needed, if style sheets are used, the expected download time at various connection speeds, and if the site is accessible for users with assistive technologies. These are important facts, which, without a clear statement, are not obvious or easy for a user to figure out. A downloadable universal usability statement template is available at http://www.universalusability.org/about/template.html. A sample universal usability statement is displayed in Figure 7.2.

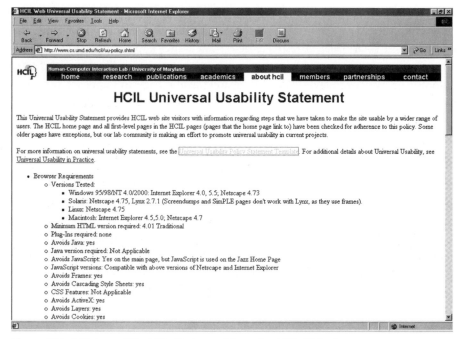

Figure 7.2 A Universal Usability Statement from the HCIL Web site.

Browser Diversity

The Web environment is quite different from past information systems. Although the Web development team can try to learn as much as possible about the target user population, once the Web pages are posted, anyone can view the Web pages (unless they are password protected) using a browser. The two most popular browsers are Internet Explorer and Netscape Navigator. There are a number of other browsers, such as Neoplanet, Opera, Mozilla, Firefox, and Lynx, that are used as well. This variety would not be a problem, except that different browsers can interpret HTML differently. The same Web page can appear differently in different browsers because of the way the browsers read HTML. This is a problem. And to make it worse, different browser versions (4.0, 5.0, 6.0, etc.) can respond to HTML differently. Moreover, the same version of the same browser on a different platform (Internet Explorer 4.0 on a PC versus Internet Explorer 4.0 on a Mac) can act differently.

How different can a Web page look when viewed in different browsers? A quick look at the Web site for Michael English serves as an introduction (see Figures 7.3 and 7.4). The newsbytes section displays properly in Internet Explorer, but not in

Figure 1.1 A nonstandard Web page design, which can confuse users (page 5).

Figure 6.2 The NASA Web site for children shows appropriate use of graphics and animation for children (page 141).

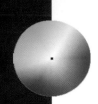

Southwest Airlines Home Gate
The Home of Southwest Airlines on the World Wide Web

Figure 5.7 The Southwest Airlines homepage as it appeared until 1999, using metaphor-based navigation (page 118).

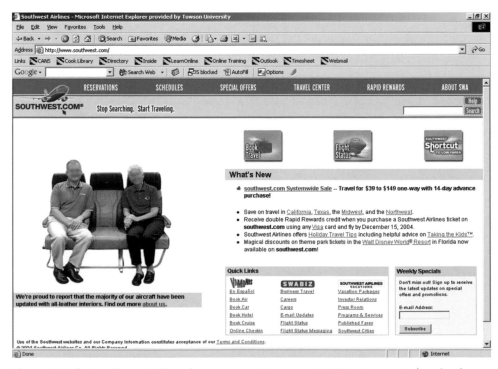

Figure 5.8 The Southwest Airlines homepage as it appears in 2005, using topical navigation (page 118).

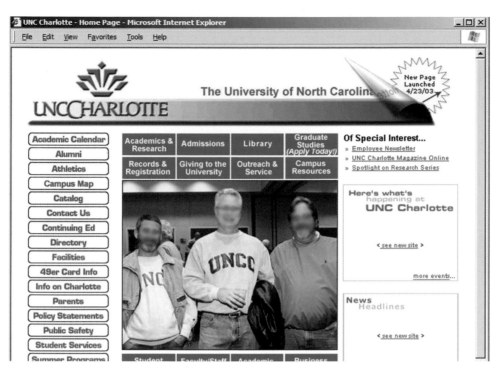

Figure 5.10 The old version of the UNCC homepage (page 121).

Figure 5.11 The new version of the UNCC homepage, where link choices are better organized and better located (page 121).

Do this

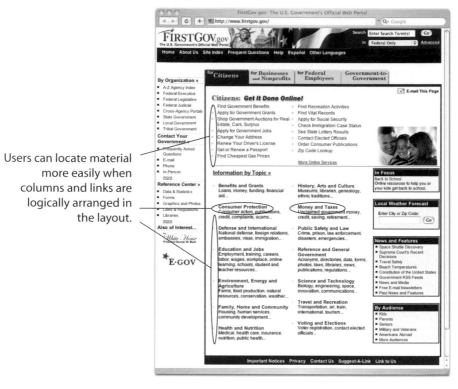

Users can locate material more easily when columns and links are logically arranged in the layout.

Don't do this

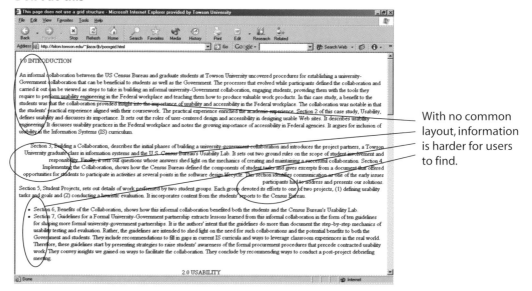

With no common layout, information is harder for users to find.

Figure 6.6 A comparison of a page layout using grids and columns, and one not using any type of standard layout (page 146).

Figure 6.7 Various text colors on a white background (page 148).

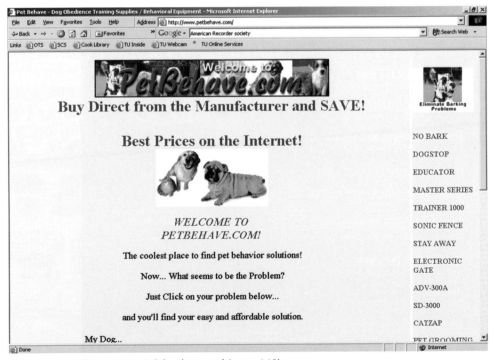

Figure 6.8 Red text on a pink background (page 148).

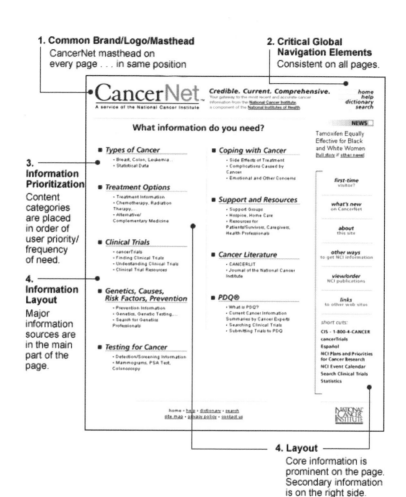

1. Common Brand/Logo/Masthead
CancerNet masthead on
every page . . . in same position

**2. Critical Global
Navigation Elements**
Consistent on all pages.

**3.
Information
Prioritization**
Content
categories
are placed
in order of
user priority/
frequency
of need.

**4.
Information
Layout**
Major
information
sources are
in the main
part of the
page.

4. Layout
Core information is
prominent on the page.
Secondary information
is on the right side.

Figure C.3 Separate critical core information from secondary
information (page 352).

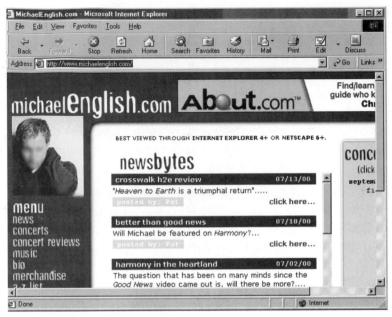

Figure 7.3 The Michael English Web site, displayed correctly in Internet Explorer.

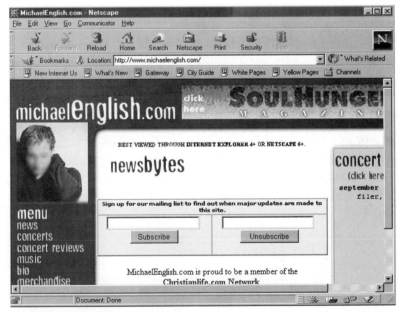

Figure 7.4 The Michael English Web site, displayed incorrectly in Netscape Navigator (a section is missing).

Netscape Navigator. In Netscape Navigator, the newsbytes section does not appear at all.

The site notes that it's best viewed in Internet Explorer 4+ or Netscape 6+. It's interesting to note that, at the time these screenshots were taken, Netscape 6+ had already been unveiled to the press, but a full working version was not yet available for downloading at the Netscape Web site. Since many universities and IT departments do not install the first release of any software, but wait for a later version in which the bugs have been fixed, certainly a large majority of users were not using Netscape Navigator 6 at that time.

Despite what some developers think, even Netscape 4.x still has an installed base of users. Although most browsers are available for a free download, users do not frequently upgrade their browsers. Most users do not install their own browsers; browsers are usually installed by the IT department or a friend or colleague who enjoys using technology (Nielsen '00). Users are therefore unlikely to be comfortable or familiar with how to install a browser. In fact, one estimate is that it takes two years for an overwhelming majority of users to upgrade one browser version. Therefore, once a browser is installed and working properly on a user's machine, the user is unlikely to change it. Furthermore, in many organizations (such as companies and universities), for security reasons, users are not allowed to install their own software; they must use the software provided in the computer lab or installed on the department network. Therefore, it's unacceptable to require that users have the latest browser since they might not know how to upgrade or change their browser, they might not be comfortable doing it, or they might not be allowed to install software personally.

It seems that there is a need for standardization on the Web. There should be one set of standards, and everyone should follow them, right? Well, a set of standards does exist. The World Wide Web Consortium has defined a set of standards for the languages and protocols used on the Web. For instance, there is a standard for HTML, which is now at HTML version 4.01. For more information on World Wide Web Consortium (also known as W3C) standards, go to http://www.w3.org. The W3C also offers a validator service available at http://validator.w3.org where you can submit your Web page URL and it checks it for compliance with HTML standards.

If you follow W3C HTML standards, however, it does not mean that your Web page will appear correctly in all, or even any, of the browsers. The major browser companies design their browsers to be different. The browser companies try to win market share by adding new features that will work in their browser only. These companies want to differentiate their product from their competitors', not produce a standard browser. And unfortunately, it appears that the differences in browsers are becoming more significant. Therefore, when designing Web pages, it's important to consider how they will look in all browsers. It may be difficult to make Web pages appear exactly the same in all browsers, but a reasonable goal is to make sure that they appear properly in all browsers.

Browser Usage Data

Since there is no definitive list of Web users, it's impossible to do a census or a strict random sampling of users to determine what browser (and versions) they are using. A number of organizations have tried to estimate current browser usage, however, all of the estimates suffer from some bias. For instance, in 2000, BrowserWatch, found 59 percent of users using some version of Internet Explorer, 26 percent using some version of Netscape Navigator, and the rest using 10 other browsers. During mid-2004, estimates from http://www.w3schools.com/browsers/browsers_stats.asp found that nearly 78 percent of users were using some form of Internet Explorer, and that nearly 15 percent were using Mozilla. Another 4 percent were using either Netscape or Opera. Another great resource is CNET's browser reference, available at http://www.browser.com, which has various browser resources. Older versions, as well as newer versions, can be downloaded, in many cases, for free. At http://www.anybrowser.com/, it's possible to test a Web page to see how it appears in different browsers. To test how a Web site appears in Lynx, a viewer is available at http://www.delorie.com/web/lynxview.html.

Common Browser Incompatibility Problems

There are a number of common browser incompatibility problems that occur frequently and require the attention of the Web development team. The next sections discuss some general and specific browser incompatibility problems. It's hoped that these common pitfalls can be avoided. In general, Internet Explorer tends to be more lenient than Netscape Navigator when interpreting HTML tags. However, Netscape version 6.0 and above allows for more flexibility.

Missing End Tags. Many HTML tags are container tags, which means that there is an opening tag and a closing tag. The closing tag usually starts with a slash, and the text between the container tags displays differently, as dictated by the container tags. If an end tag (such as `</table>`) is missing from a Web page, Internet Explorer assumes that the end tag was supposed to be there, whereas Netscape Navigator will not display the table at all. This is a problem, especially when a Web page uses tables for navigation. In Netscape Navigator, if a table is used as a container for the navigation and content, and if a `</table>` tag is missing, the entire Web page will not appear.

Consider the following HTML code:

```html
<html>
    <head></head>
    <body>
        A table will appear only in Internet Explorer <p>
        <table border="2">
        <tr><td>Name</td><td>Phone Number</td></tr>
        <tr><td>Fred </td><td>434-555-2354</td></tr>
        <tr><td>Ginger</td><td>654-555-1146</td></tr>
        <tr><td>Larry</td><td>636-555-3234</td></tr>
        <tr><td>Moe</td><td>565-555-3561</td></tr>
        <tr><td>Curly</td><td>756-555-7453</td></tr>
        <tr><td>Schemp</td><td>786-555-7654</td></tr>
    </body>
</html>
```

The preceding HTML code is meant to display a table with a list of names and corresponding phone numbers. However, the `</table>` tag is missing. The table appears correctly in Internet Explorer, yet does not appear at all in Netscape Navigator (see Figures 7.5 and 7.6).

An example of this problem is apparent on the past Web page for the Surry County Health and Nutrition Center. The homepage appears normally in Internet Explorer, but does not appear properly in Netscape Navigator (see Figures 7.7 and 7.8). This occurs because the text indicating for a user to enter the site is included in a table, but the end `</table>` tag is missing.

This problem of browser incompatibility is easily fixed by making sure that all end tags are included. This is not a browser problem as much as a problem with sloppy HTML. Missing end tags can also cause problems when using cascading style sheets (CSS), so it's a good policy always to include the appropriate end tags.

Incorrect Nesting of Tags. HTML tags must be nested appropriately. If a Web designer incorrectly nests tags on a Web page, Internet Explorer allows for more

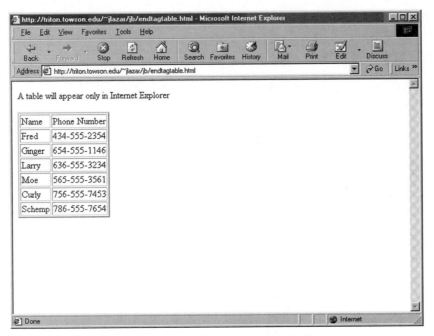

Figure 7.5 The table appears appropriately in Internet Explorer.

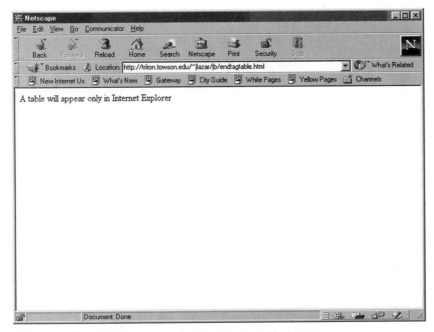

Figure 7.6 The table does not appear in Netscape Navigator.

Figure 7.7 The line to enter does not appear in Netscape Navigator; therefore, the user has no way to enter the site.

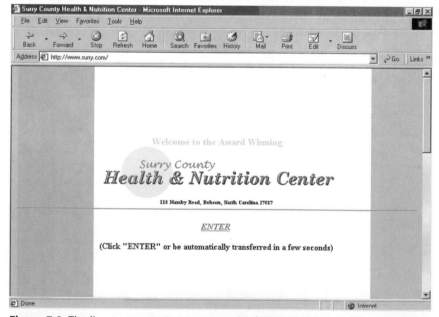

Figure 7.8 The line to enter appears appropriately in Internet Explorer.

flexibility, but Netscape Navigator is less forgiving and requires that HTML formatting tags are correctly nested.

In general, this is the correct way to nest HTML tags:

```
<tag 1><tag 2>Hello out there!</tag2></tag1>
<tag2><tag3>Hello again!</tag3></tag2>
```

The following is an example of incorrect nesting:

```
<tag 1><tag 2>Hello out there!</tag1><tag3>Hello
again!</tag2></tag3>
```

Consider the following inappropriately nested HTML code:

```
<html>
    <head>
    </head>
    <body>This text should appear plain. <b>This text
    should appear bold. <i>This text should appear bold
    and italic. </b>This text should appear italic only.
    </i>
    </body>
</html>
```

Notice how the HTML tags are nested incorrectly. After the first sentence, the <b> tag makes the second sentence appear bold. However, at the end of the second sentence, if a new style tag (such as <i>) is used, an end tag </b> should be used first, before the new style tag. Tags should be nested correctly, as in the following example:

```
<html>
    <head>
    </head>
    <body>This text should appear plain. <b>This text
    should appear bold. </b><i><b>This text should appear
    bold and italic. </b></i><i>This text should appear
    italic only. </i>
    </body>
</html>
```

Inappropriate nesting of HTML code can be a problem in different browsers, as Figures 7.9 and 7.10 demonstrate.

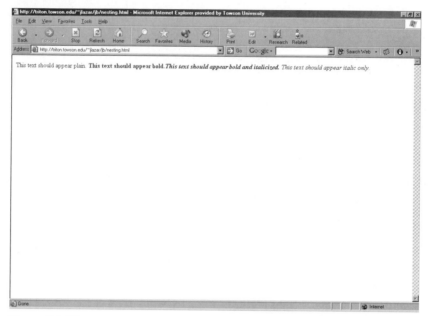

Figure 7.9 When tags are incorrectly nested, text still appears correctly in Internet Explorer.

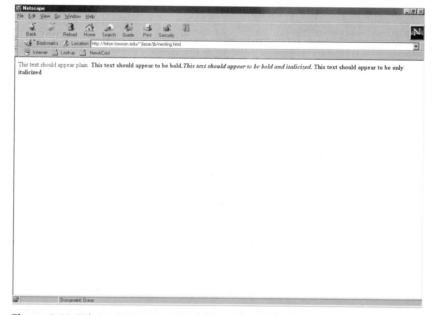

Figure 7.10 When tags are incorrectly nested, text does not appear correctly in Netscape Navigator.

In Internet Explorer, shown in Figure 7.9, the first three sentences display correctly, and the fourth sentence displays in italic text. In Netscape Navigator, shown in Figure 7.10, the first three sentences display correctly, and the fourth sentence displays in bold (but not italic) text.

Compatibility of Advanced Programming Features. Web pages can be designed with more interactivity and more control over design by using JavaScript (JS), cascading style sheets (CSS), and dynamic HTML (DHTML). JavaScript is a scripting language that adds interactivity to a Web page by allowing the page to respond to user actions, to detect conditions in the browser, and to respond accordingly. Cascading style sheets allow for more control over the presentation of content by providing absolute positioning control and allowing easier site maintenance. Dynamic HTML allows for a customized user experience by responding to user actions, using a combination of JS, CSS, and the Document Object Model. Unfortunately, browser compatibility is an issue with these technologies.

Internet Explorer and Netscape Navigator support these technologies differently. Therefore, it's necessary to check the documentation for browser support for specific JS, CSS, and DHTML features, and then to test the pages in a number of different browsers and browser versions. As long as the major browsers support the specific feature needed, the feature is safe to use. The user may disable CSS or JS, or the user might apply their own style sheets, so it's a good idea to check what a page would look like if CSS and JS features are unavailable. Since browsers allow users to turn off these features, it's relatively easy to check for compatibility. The page should still work and be usable with CSS and JS turned off. The Web page doesn't have to look or act the same, but the bare minimum functionality should still be in place.

Unique Browser Features. There are some features that are not a part of the W3C HTML standards and are supported by one browser only. For instance, the <multicol> tag displays text in columns of equal width, and is supported by Netscape Navigator, but not by Internet Explorer. The <marquee> tag creates scrolling text, and works in Internet Explorer, but not in Netscape Navigator. The <iframe> tag creates a floating frame within a document, and is supported only by Internet Explorer. There are some HTML features that are supported by the W3 HTML standards, but are not supported by the major browsers. In most cases, if an HTML tag is not a part of the W3 Consortium standards, and is not supported by the major browsers, it should not be used when designing a Web page, since doing so would be asking for trouble. The exception might be when designing for a corporate intranet, and if the Web development team knows exactly what browser will be used because it's an enforced corporate policy.

Solutions for Multiple-Browser Design

It's important to consider that in most cases, users will be using a number of different browsers, as well as different versions of the browsers. A large number of people will not be using the latest browser version. Generally, the best policy is to design Web pages that will appear properly, regardless of the browser, and will provide maximum flexibility to the user. By learning about the targeted user population's computing equipment in the requirements gathering, you may find that, say, 95 percent of the users are using a version 5.0 browser or higher. Even if a large majority of targeted users are using Internet Explorer 6.0, it's not a good idea to design a Web page that will appear properly only in Internet Explorer 6.0. Although it's far from ideal, if you must use HTML tags that are specific to one browser, then it's suggested that you do one of the following:

1. Make it very clear that for a maximum user experience, the user must use a specific browser. A strong statement such as "This Web page will display properly in Internet Explorer 5.5 or higher only " should be included. A link to download the specific browser should be included. This solution should be used in extreme circumstances only, if at all. Not only could this hurt the user experience, but also the Web site will appear to have been designed by an amateur.

2. You can ask people to select from two or three different Web sites. One Web site could be maximized for Netscape Navigator, and one could be maximized for Internet Explorer. It's also possible to ask users to select from a site that uses Flash and one that does not. Some sites offer users the choice of a Web site that is maximized for text browsers or slow Internet connections.

3. You can write JavaScript code that will automatically deliver the appropriate Web page to the user. If the content requires that you use browser-specific tags, then you can set up two different versions of the page and create a script that will automatically recognize the user's browser and then retrieve the Web page that is appropriate. This is a common technique to ensure maximum usability when browser-specific features need to be used.

The following JavaScript example will perform the task described in the third choice above.

```
<script>
   if (navigator.appName=="Netscape")
   {
      top.location.href='nnhome.html'
   }
   else
   {
      top.location.href='iehome.html'
   }
</script>
```

What Exactly Is This Code Doing?

- It checks to see what browser is viewing the page (note that you can use `"Microsoft Internet Explorer"` instead of `"Netscape"`.)

- If the browser is Netscape Navigator, the JavaScript will show the user the file nnhome.html, which is the Web page appropriate for those using Netscape Navigator.

- If the browser is not Netscape Navigator (potentially meaning that it is Internet Explorer), the JavaScript will show the user the file iehome.html, which is the Web page appropriate for those using Internet Explorer.

Of course, the filenames can be changed to anything that you want. The same technique can be used to test for browser version and platform. And `else if` in Javascript can be used to test for multiple browser brands.

Chapter Wrap-Up

When creating or redesigning a Web site, it's important to make sure that it can be used by as many users as possible.

- Web pages need to be designed to address technology diversity (screen resolutions, browser brands, and versions), as well as user diversity (older users, users with disabilities, etc.).

- Browser incompatibilities can negatively affect the experience of the user when viewing a Web site. Therefore, it's necessary to plan in advance to consider browser incompatibilities in the design process.

- Web developers should always include end tags, should correctly nest their HTML tags, and should never use HTML tags that are supported by one browser only and are not part of the W3C HTML standards.

- Flexibility should be built into Web pages so that diverse users can use them.

Following these guidelines can increase the number of potential users to your site, and make a statement that the organization sponsoring the Web site is respectful of user diversity.

Design Exercise

Imagine that you are designing a Web site for a senior retirement village in Florida. The users are primarily 50 years or older. What would important design features be? What would you specifically want to avoid in design? Midway through development, the client notifies you that they must follow government rules for accessibility (from Section 508). How would you change the site? Would you make any changes to the graphic design? Would you make changes to the back-end code? How would the two versions of the site (the early version designed for older users, and the new version, designed for older users and users with disabilities) differ?

Discussion Questions

1. Why do Web pages look different in different browsers?

2. What are the two major sets of guidelines for making a Web site accessible?

3. Name three different assistive technologies.

4. What categories of Web sites do government policies related to Web accessibility usually cover?

5. What are three design features that make a Web site easier for older users to use?

6. Why are clear frame names important?

7. What does a universal usability statement cover?

8. Why is it unreasonable to expect users to upgrade to a new browser version?

9. If a Web page cannot be designed to work properly in multiple browsers, what is a good method to ensure that users with different browsers can view appropriate Web pages?

Suggested Reading

Alliance for Technology Access. (2000). *Computer and Web Resources for People with Disabilities*. Berkeley, CA: Hunter House Publishers.

Birdi, K., & Zapf, D. (1997). "Age Differences in Reactions to Errors in Computer-Based Work." *Behaviour and Information Technology*, 16(6), 309–319.

Clarke, J. (2001). "Key Factors in Developing a Positive User Experience for Children on the Web: A Case Study." Proceedings of the Human Factors and the Web 2001. Available at: http://www.optavia.com/hfweb/index.htm.

Ellis, R. D., & Kurniawan, S. (2000). "Increasing the Usability of Online Information for Older Users: A Case Study in Participatory Design." *International Journal of Human-Computer Interaction*, 12(2), 263–276.

Fox, S. (2004). Pew Internet and American Life Project. "Older Americans and the Internet." Available at: http://www.pewinternet.org/pdfs/ PIP_Seniors_Online_2004.pdf.

Ghaoiu, C., Mann, M., & Ng, E. (2001). "Designing a Humane Multimedia Interface for the Visually Impaired." *European Journal of Engineering Education*, 26(2), 139–149.

Hanna, L., Risden, K., & Alexander, K. (1997). "Guidelines for Usability Testing with Children." *Interactions*, 4(5), 9–14.

Hirsch, T., Forlizzi, J., Hyder, E., Goetz, J., Stroback, J., & Kurtz, C. (2000). "The ELDer Project: Social, Emotional, and Environmental Factors in the Design of Eldercare Technologies." Proceedings of the ACM Conference on Universal Usability, 72–79.

Hochheiser, H., & Shneiderman, B. (2001). "Universal Usability Statements: Marking the Trail for All Users." *Interactions*, 16–18.

Hysell, D. (1998). "Meeting the Needs (and Preferences) of a Diverse World Wide Web Audience." Proceedings of the ACM 16th Annual International Conference on Computer Documentation, 164–172.

Inkpen, K. (2001). "Drag-and-Drop versus Point-and-Click Mouse Interaction Styles for Children." *ACM Transactions on Computer-Human Interaction*, 8(1), 1–33.

Lazar, J., Beere, P., Greenidge, K., & Nagappa, Y. (2003). "Web Accessibility in the Mid-Atlantic United States: A Study of 50 Web Sites." *Universal Access in the Information Society*, 2(4), 331–341.

Lazar, J., Dudley-Sponaugle, A., & Greenidge, K. (2004). "Improving Web Accessibility: A Study of Webmaster Perceptions." *Computers in Human Behavior*, 20(2), 269–288.

Lazar, J., & Preece, J. (2001). "Using Electronic Surveys to Evaluate Networked Resources: From Idea to Implementation." In J. Bertot (Ed.), *Evaluating Networked Information Services: Techniques, Policy, and Issues* (pp. 137–154). Medford, NJ: Information Today.

Loiacono, E., & McCoy, S. (2004). "Web Site Accessibility: An Online Sector Analysis." *Information Technology and People*, 17(1), 87–101.

Mead, S., Spaulding, V., Sit, R., Meyer, B., & Walker, N. (1997). "Effects of Age and Training on World Wide Web Navigation Strategies." Proceedings of the Human Factors and Ergonomics Society Annual Meeting, 152–156.

National Institute on Aging. (2002). "Making Your Web Site Senior-Friendly." Available at: http://www.nlm.nih.gov/pubs/checklist.pdf.

Niederst, J. (1999). *Web Design in a Nutshell*. Sebastopol, CA: O'Reilly and Associates.

Nielsen, J. (2000). *Designing Web Usability: The Practice of Simplicity*. Indianapolis: New Riders Publishing.

Nielsen, J. (2002). "Kids' Corner: Website Usability for Children." Available at: http://www.useit.com/alertbox/20020414.html.

Paciello, M. (2000). *Web Accessibility for People with Disabilities*. Lawrence, KS: CMP Books.

Shneiderman, B. (2000). "Universal Usability: Pushing Human-Computer Interaction Research to Empower Every Citizen." *Communications of the ACM*, 43(5), 84–91.

Slatin, J., & Rush, S. (2003). *Maximum Accessibility*. New York: Addison-Wesley.

Sullivan, T., & Matson, R. (2000a). "Barriers to Use: Usability and Content Accessibility on the Web's Most Popular Sites." Proceedings of the ACM Conference on Universal Usability, 139–144.

Sullivan, T., Norris, C., Peet, M., & Soloway, E. (2000b). "When Kids Use the Web: A Naturalistic Comparison of Children's Navigation Behavior and Subjective Preferences on two WWW Sites." Proceedings of the 2000 Conference on Human Factors and the Web. Available at: http://www.pantos.org/ts/papers /wkutw/.

Worden, A., Walker, N., Bharat, K., & Hudson, S. (1997). "Making Computers Easier for Older Users to Use: Areas Cursors and Sticky Icons." Proceedings of the ACM Conference on Human Factors in Computing Systems (CHI), 266–271.

8

Physical Design

After reading this chapter, you will be able to:

- Write HTML code by hand using a text editor.
- Be familiar with the major Web development applications.
- Understand how to code table-based navigation.
- Understand how to code frame-based navigation.
- Gather content for Web pages.

Introduction

This chapter discusses physical Web site design—the process of turning conceptual design requirements into a physical Web site through developing the code. The conceptual requirements should clearly state the number of Web pages, content, graphics, and navigation schemes. There are several different approaches to turning conceptual requirements into coded Web pages. Web developers might decide to write the code by hand or use a number of software applications for assistance. The idea behind these applications is that they allow developers to work in a WYSIWYG (what-you-see-is-what-you-get) environment, where they can manipulate the layout on the screen, and the software application creates the code. These applications, such as FrontPage and Dreamweaver, also provide a number of usability-related features.

HTML is the core of the Web programming experience. While a number of plug-in technologies (e.g., Java applets and Acrobat files) and different languages and programming tools (e.g., Javascript and cascading style sheets) can be used within a Web page, the core language required is HTML. The World Wide Web Consortium (W3C) sets the standards for HTML (http://www.w3.org). The most current version, HTML 4.01, has been the standard since December, 1999 (see http://www.w3.org/MarkUp/Activity for more information about HTML, including XML-related work for the future). Version 4.01 is, by far, the version that current browsers support (although various browsers, with their own quirks, support it differently). Past versions of HTML were 2.0 (adopted in 1994), 3.2 (adopted in 1996), and 4.0 (adopted in 1997).

Most programming guides note which HTML tags are deprecated. A deprecated tag is an HTML tag that was a part of the standard, but that the W3C has decided to remove, in favor of other approaches. This is most common for HTML tags related to style (such as the `<font>` tag), where the newer standards suggest that cascading style sheets are used. While CSSs are theoretically an excellent idea, at this point, various browsers still implement style sheets differently; therefore, in some situations, it can be problematic to use them. This is one of the inherent challenges in Web design, where neither outcome is perfect. If you use deprecated tags, it may work with the older browsers. If you use style sheets in place of the deprecated tags, you must worry about the compatibility issues for style sheets, and some older browsers that don't support them. One way to address this is to write the code that will serve up a different style sheet based on the user's browser. This code can be written in JavaScript. Code that serves up a specific Web page is available in Chapter 7.

While HTML code forms the foundation for Web pages, several methods exist for turning conceptual requirements into coded pages. Developers can actually hand code using a plain text editor, such as Pico or Notepad. Word processors can serve as plain text editors, and some word processors now allow files to be saved automatically in HTML format. Web developers commonly use Web development applications, such as Microsoft Frontpage and Macromedia Dreamweaver. The following sections detail these various coding methods.

Coding by Hand Using a Text Editor

The most basic way to create a Web site is to code it by hand. This method is especially appropriate for small Web sites. In these situations, it is always a good idea to have a code reference book. Since ideally the layout throughout the site should be similar, it is often a good idea to use a template. The Web developer can create an HTML file that includes all of the layout (color, style, etc.) and navigation information, without the content. That file can then be copied numerous times, and the content can simply be inserted into each Web page. The Web developer does not have to type the same code over and over. In some cases, style sheets can be appropriate, and they can help with later maintenance, since a change in one file (the style sheet .css file) can immediately affect the style on all the pages on the site. If style sheets are used, the style sheet should be created first, so that all the Web pages are developed with the style sheet in mind.

When coding by hand, no special software tools are needed. The only requirement is to use a text editor. The text editor can be as simple as Notepad (on MS-Windows) or Pico (see Figures 8.1 and 8.2). The Web developer simply saves the text file with the .html extension. When hand coding, there are no features in the text editor to check the code for correct spelling and usage. In such cases, the code validator provided by the W3C can be useful in identifying problematic areas of the written code. The code validator is available at http://validator.w3.org and is free (see Figure 8.3).

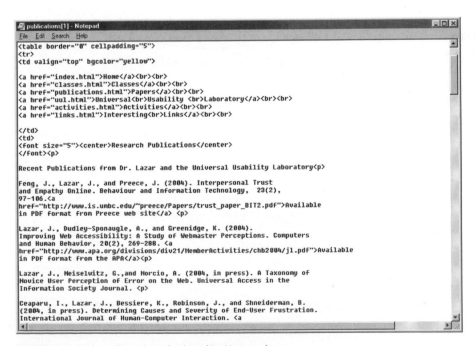

Figure 8.1 Web coding done by hand in Notepad.

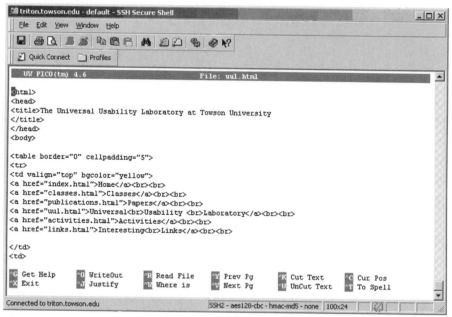

Figure 8.2 Web coding done by hand using Pico, a text editor.

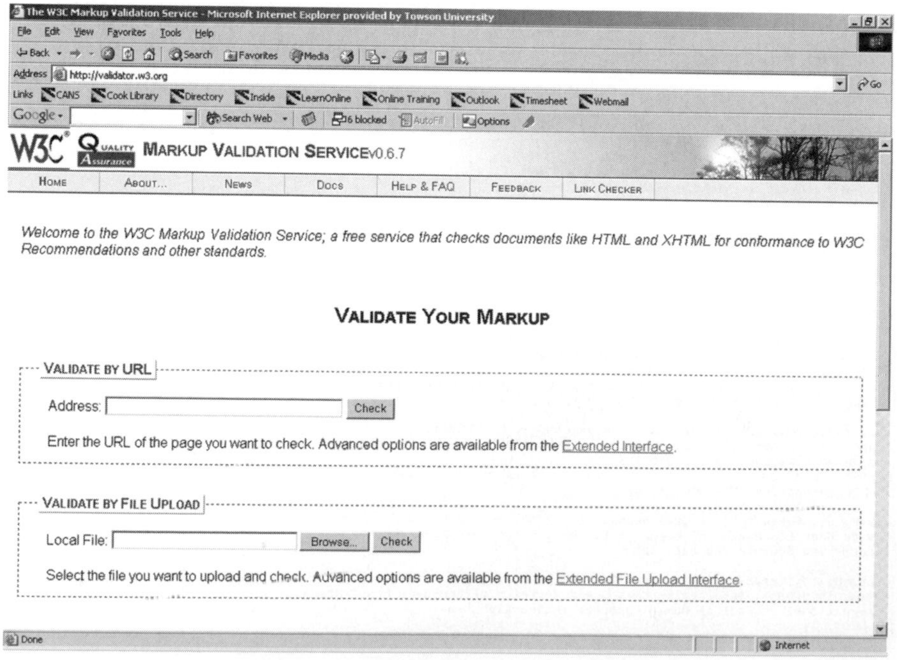

Figure 8.3 The World Wide Web Consortium code validation engine.

Web Development Applications

Many software applications have been created specifically to assist in the process of Web development. These applications can provide the Web developer with advanced HTML functionality, and in many cases, can create JavaScript and cascading style sheets. A number of helpful features, such as checking for linkrot (linked URLs that are no longer valid), and estimating the download time using different connection speeds, can help the Web developer with usability issues. Leading Web design applications include Microsoft FrontPage and Macromedia Dreamweaver. These applications work by letting Web developers create Web pages in a WYSIWYG environment, in which they describe how the Web page should appear without specifying the HTML code. The Web design application creates the HTML (and in some cases, JavaScript) code "on the fly." Web developers can then fine-tune the HTML code. A brief description of two of the major Web development applications, Dreamweaver and FrontPage, follows.

Macromedia Dreamweaver

Macromedia Dreamweaver provides advanced Web design features that can save Web developers time. Dreamweaver provides basic Web functionality, including text color and size, links, and bulleted lists. Dreamweaver also allows Web developers to create Web pages that incorporate tables, frames, forms, and JavaScript mouseovers, without writing any code by hand. Dreamweaver has a number of nice features, including the ability to create cascading style sheets and clickable image maps. Another helpful feature is that it will not modify HTML code originally created in another application when it is imported. A screenshot of Dreamweaver MX 2004 is shown in Figure 8.4.

Dreamweaver has a few nice features related to usability. For instance, as stated in Chapter 7, browser compatibility is a major problem in Web design. Dreamweaver includes an option for testing how a Web page will appear in the various versions of various browsers. When you name the browser and version that you want to target your site to, Dreamweaver will test your pages for compatibility with the browsers (see Figure 8.5). Dreamweaver will also check your Web page for compatibility with accessibility guidelines. While not as powerful as the standalone automated accessibility testing tools discussed in Chapter 9, these Dreamweaver features can go a long way to ensuring that there are no major accessibility flaws in your Web site. A screenshot of this feature is shown in Figure 8.6, at the bottom of the screen. To access this Dreamweaver feature, click File → Check Page → Check Accessibility.

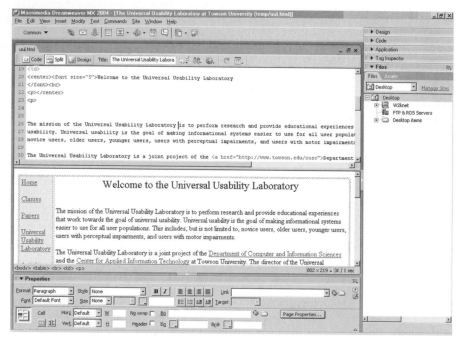

Figure 8.4 A screenshot of the Dreamweaver application.

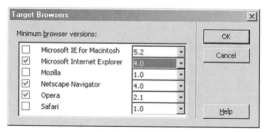

Figure 8.5 Dreamweaver dialog box that allows you to test for browser compatibility.

Microsoft FrontPage

Microsoft FrontPage is a part of the Microsoft Office package. The interface layout is similar to those of the other Office Suite applications, such as MS-Word. Microsoft FrontPage has many of the same features as Dreamweaver, such as the ability to control text presentation and create tables, frames, forms, and

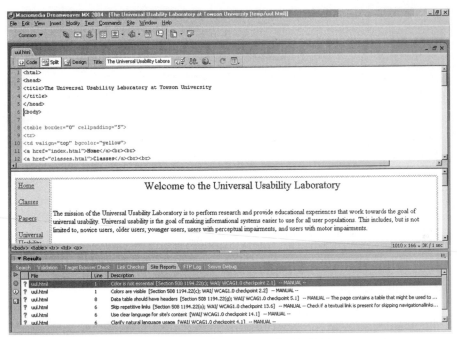

Figure 8.6 Dreamweaver feature that allows you to check a Web page against accessibility guidelines.

mouseovers. But FrontPage also has added features that allow the Web developer to provide more powerful functionality without writing any extra code. These features are called FrontPage extensions, and they work only if the Web server (on which the Web site will be hosted) is using the FrontPage server extensions. (Contact the ISP or Webmaster to determine if the server is running FrontPage extensions.) The FrontPage extensions provide a number of features without requiring the Web developer to create or install CGI scripts. For instance, FrontPage extensions allow the Web developer to insert search engines, time stamps, and form validation without writing any additional code. User responses to forms can be automatically saved in a Web page or text file, again, without the Web developer having to write any additional code. A screenshot of FrontPage (version 2002) is shown in Figure 8.7. One of the nice usability-related features of FrontPage is that, in the lower right-hand corner, it provides the estimated download time for a page, given various connection speeds. FrontPage also offers tools similar to Dreamweaver, for testing Web pages for accessibility.

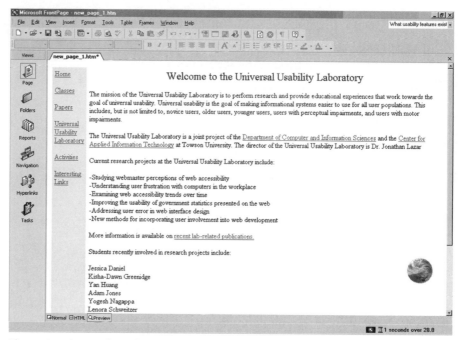

Figure 8.7 Screenshot of Microsoft FrontPage.

How to Code Navigation

Navigation on the top or left side of Web pages is frequently designed using tables or frames. The next few pages discusses how to code these different approaches.

Table-Based Navigation

HTML provides support for tables, primarily for presenting rows and columns of data. However, tables are frequently used to control the layout of a Web page, providing an ideal manner for presenting navigation. The table serves as a container of sorts for the two main elements on the Web page: the navigation and the actual content. At a minimum, this means that the table has two cells. The cell on the left is for navigation, and the cell on the right is for the content (see Figure 8.8). Please note that if you use tables for page navigation, you should use clear titles and identifiers to provide navigation hints for users with disabilities who might be browsing the page nonvisually or nonlinearly. The following HTML code is an example of how to create table-based navigation. The page that results from this code is shown in Figure 8.8.

```
<html>
   <head>
      <title>An example of table-based navigation</title>
   </head>
   <body>
      <table cellspacing="3">
         <tr>
         <td bgcolor="yellow">
            Navigation<br>
            Choice 1<br>
            Choice 2<br>
            Choice 3<br>
            Choice 4<br>
         </td> <td valign="top">
            Place all of your content here. In this
            second cell of the table, you can place all
            content, and the navigation will remain in
            the first table cell on the left. More
            content. We want more content.
         </td>
         </tr>
      </table>
   </body>
</html>
```

What Exactly Is This Code Doing?

- The `<table>` tags create the table.

- Choice 1, Choice 2, Choice 3, and Choice 4 are items that represent links to the different sections of the Web site. They can be replaced with something like `<a href="history.html">History</a>`, which would take users to the Web page on history when they click that link.

- The `<td>` tags specify the table cells.

- The first `<td>` tag creates the table cell for the navigation, and the `bgcolor="yellow"` specifies that the table cell should have a yellow background, which creates the appearance of a separate navigation strip on the left side of the screen.

- The second `<td>` tag creates the table cell for the content. The `valign="top"` serves to keep the content at the top of the table cell. The default is at the center, so without `valign="top"`, the content would appear in the center of the screen.

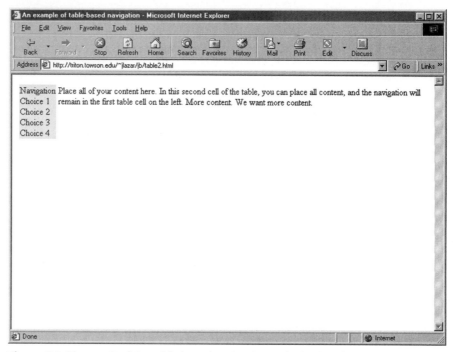

Figure 8.8 The result of the table-based navigation code displayed in this chapter.

Another way to provide table-based navigation is to place the navigation at the top of the screen, instead of at the left side. This can be done by creating two table rows. The first row provides the navigation, and the second row provides the content.

```
<html>
   <head>
      <title>An example of table-based navigation on the
         top</title>
   </head>
   <body>
      <table cellspacing="0">
         <tr bgcolor="yellow">
            <td>Choice 1</td>
            <td>Choice 2</td>
            <td>Choice 3</td>
            <td>Choice 4</td>
         </tr>
         <tr>
```

```
          <td colspan="4">
          Place all of your content here. In this
          second row of the table, you can place all
          content, and the navigation will remain in
          the first table row on the top. More
          content. We want more content. Content!
          </td>
      </tr>
    </table>
  </body>
</html>
```

How is this example different from having the navigation on the left side of the screen?

In this example, we are creating two rows of data, not two data cells. The first row is specified yellow, marking it as our navigation bar. We split the first row into four separate cells, so that we have adequate space for each of our navigation choices. This is done by specifying four <td> tags within a table row. Since there are four table cells in the top table row, we will have four table cells in the second table row, unless we specify otherwise. By specifying <td colspan="4">, we indicate that our second table row should only consist of one table cell for our content (in other words, the table cell should span all four columns). Figure 8.9 shows table-based navigation with navigation at the top of the screen.

There are a number of other possibilities for providing navigation on a Web page with tables. For instance, navigation bars on the left and the top can be provided simultaneously. However, all uses of tables for navigation are based on these two simple examples of using tables as containers for navigation and content.

Frame-Based Navigation

Frames can be used to implement navigation in Web pages. A frame occurs when the browser window is divided into a number of virtual windows, allowing more than one HTML document at a time to be displayed in the window. When setting up a framed document, there are a few different HTML documents involved. It is the combination of documents that makes up the framed browser window. Each document can be scrolled individually. For example, see the screenshot of the Association for Information Systems Special Interest Group on IS Education (AIS SIGED), as shown in Figure 8.10.

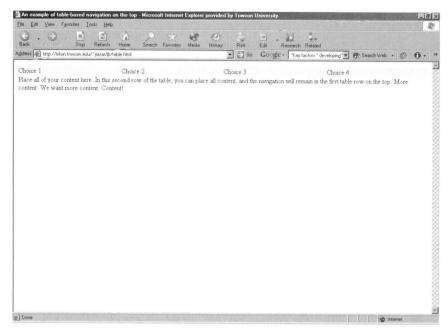

Figure 8.9 Table-based navigation, with navigation at the top.

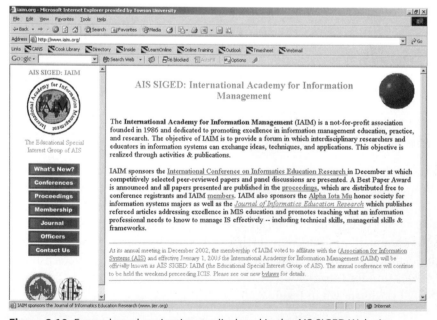

Figure 8.10 Frame-based navigation, as displayed in the AIS SIGED Web site.

A framed document requires at minimum, three HTML documents. The frame-set document specifies what size the frames will be and what the source documents will be. The frameset document is the file that the user actually accesses with the URL. For instance, if a frameset document specifies that the browser window will consist of two frames, one frame that takes up 25 percent of the screen on the left, and the other frame that takes up 75 percent of the screen on the right, then there are actually three HTML documents involved: the frameset document, which creates the frame layout, the HTML document that goes into the left frame, and the HTML document that goes into the right frame. Usually, navigation goes into the left frame and content goes into the right frame.

Here is an example of the code required to create a frameset document:

```
<html>
  <head>
    <frameset cols="25%,75%">
    <frame src="navigation.html" name="navigation">
    <frame src="content.html" name="content">
    </frameset>
  </head>
</html>
```

This code sets up a framed document with two frames in the document, one frame on the left side of the screen (25 percent) and one frame on the right side (75 percent). The documents that should go into each frame are stated (navigation.html, content.html), and names are given to each frame. Names given to the frames can be anything, but it is strongly suggested that the names chosen are related to what type of material will be in those frames (e.g., content, navigation, search, or contact) rather than the layout (e.g., top, left, bottom, or middle). For users with disabilities, the names of the frames, if chosen well, can help facilitate navigation throughout the Web site. These names will also become important when we look at the code for our source documents. An example of frame-based navigation appears in Figure 8.11.

Next, we need to create two other HTML documents, one for the navigation and one for the content. For the content, we create a plain HTML document with our content. However, for the navigation, we need to pay careful attention to be sure that we create our navigation correctly. If we simply place a list of links in the HTML document, then when the user clicks a link, it will change the Web page in the navigation frame and the navigation will no longer be persistent for the user. We don't want this to happen because it ruins the purpose of the navigation. Instead, we want the navigation to function in the following manner: When

Figure 8.11 An example of frame-based navigation.

the user clicks on the navigation in the left frame, the HTML document in the right frame changes, but the navigation stays in place. This can be done by placing the following code in the navigation document:

```
<html>
    <head>
    </head>
    <body>
        <a href="http://triton.towson.edu/~jlazar"
            target="content"> Navigation choice 1</a><br>
        <a href="http://triton.towson.edu/~jlazar/classes
            .html" target="content"> Navigation choice 2
            </a><br>
    </body>
</html>
```

Note the use of the `target` attribute. When the user clicks on the link or navigation choice 1, the default is that the document changes in the frame that the user clicked in, which is the navigation frame. But the code listed above includes a target, which specifies that when the user clicks the link, it should place the new document, not in the current frame, but instead in a different frame, the frame named `content`. The main content frame was named `content` in the frameset document. By targeting our frames correctly, we can use frames to keep our navigation consistent throughout the Web site. It's important to note that frames can cause some confusion for users. Many users do not understand the concept of frames, and therefore, may have problems printing and bookmarking framed documents. For instance, when users navigate through a frame-based site, the URL in the browser address bar does not change. Therefore, the URL cannot easily be bookmarked (users can bookmark one specific document frame, but not the entire frame layout, by right-clicking the mouse button on the frame), nor can it provide any location information. Frames are another tool in the toolbox of the Web development team, however, some might feel that frames should not be used.

Navigation can also be provided without any frames or tables. It's possible to place links to all important sections of the Web site at the top of a Web page in plain text. This is a simple, yet effective way to provide navigation, as long as the navigation stays present throughout the site.

Gathering Content for Web Pages

It's the responsibility of the client organization to provide content for the Web site. Although the Web development team is responsible for a number of tasks, it's generally not the responsibility of the Web development team to create content. The Web development team might, however, be provided with content on paper, which will need to be developed into an electronic format. The Web development team might also be provided with access to those who can verbally describe the content. If word processing files (or other data files) exist, it is ideal if they are provided to the Web development team. If data files exist, the Web development team can simply cut and paste the content into the HTML files. If the Web site is being redesigned, much of the content is already contained in the original HTML files, so it can simply be copied and pasted into the new HTML files. There are a number of tools available to convert documents from one format to another. For instance, if older versions of PDF files exist, they can be converted into HTML documents using tools such as the one available at http://www.adobe.com/products/acrobat/access_simple_form.html.

One note of caution: Unfortunately, in some situations, the Web development team is forced to delay progress because the client organization does not deliver the content on time. This is frustrating for all concerned.

Functionality Testing: Does the Code Work?

The pages must be tested for functionality and browser compatibility. This is a separate process from usability testing (which is described in Chapter 9). Once the Web pages are coded, it's important to test them to determine if they are functionally correct. The Web pages should be accessed through a browser. At that time, the Web developer can ascertain that the text and layout appear appropriately. When a problem occurs, many times the error is as simple as forgetting to include an end tag. For instance, if `</a>` is not included at the end of a link, all of the text after the link will appear underlined, as a link. Debugging a Web page is relatively simple, because many problems are visually obvious. In addition, Web development applications will generally detect any inappropriate code. Advanced Web programming, such as JavaScript, Java applets, or CGI scripts should also be tested to ensure that they work properly. All links should be tested to make sure that they take the user to the appropriate page. The W3C provides a validator service, available at http://validator.w3.org/, which checks a Web page for compliance with HTML standards.

When Web pages are developed, it's also important to test them to be sure that they appear appropriately in the major browsers. The results of the requirements gathering should strongly influence the testing. If the target user population is relatively homogeneous in browser usage, then this should be a focus of the browser compatibility testing. If 90 percent of the target user population uses Internet Explorer 5.5 or higher (such as an organizational intranet), then this provides an important benchmark. However, the Web pages should look appropriate (not necessarily the same) in recent versions of Internet Explorer and Netscape Navigator, as well as Lynx. Many of the Web development applications provide the capability to check automatically for compatibility with different browsers and versions. Web developers not using an application to design a Web site can download old browser versions at http://www.browser.com. It's also possible to test a Web page to see how it appears in different browsers at http://www.anybrowser.com/.

In this chapter, we discussed the major issues involved in the process of physical Web design.

- Web developers may write code by hand, or use a Web development application.
- Tables and frames are frequently used for page layout.
- Tools that can help with converting various file formats, or with seeing how the current version of the Web site will appear in different browsers, are also available on the Web.

Design Exercise

Take the sketches that you completed for the Design Exercise in Chapter 6. These were two different Web pages, presenting information on skin care protection from the sun. One page was geared toward 10–12-year-olds and the other page was geared toward adults. Code each of these pages by hand or by using a Web development application. Add the features you described in the Chapter 6 Design Exercise. See how the pages look once they are coded and offer a short list of suggestions for improvement.

Discussion Questions

1. What are some advantages and disadvantages of using a Web development application?
2. Why might developers use tables, and how might tables be superior to frames?
3. When a team is creating a frame layout with three frames, how many HTML files are required?
4. Why is it important to choose clear names for the frames?
5. Why is it important to test for browser compatibility?

Suggested Reading

Holzschlag, M. (2005). *Spring into HTML and CSS*. Addison-Wesley: Boston, MA.

Niederat, S. (1999). *Web Design in a Nutshell*. O'Reilly: Sebastopol, CA.

Sebesta, Robert W. (2006). *Programming the World Wide Web*, 3e. Addison-Wesley: Boston, MA.

Yuen, P. K. and Lau, V. (2003). *Practical Web Technologies*. Addison-Wesley: Boston, MA.

Usability Testing

After reading this chapter, you will be able to:

- Perform an expert-based review, such as a heuristics or guidelines review, and determine when one is appropriate.
- Decide what type of location is best for a user-based test.
- Choose representative users for a user-based test.
- Write up a task list for a user-based test.
- Write up satisfaction questions to ask users at the end of a usability test.
- Understand the various metrics that can be used to measure user performance.
- Identify automated usability testing tools.
- Identify the interface flaws discovered during usability testing and rank their importance.

Introduction

One of the hallmarks of user-centered design is usability testing. Usability testing is different from functionality testing, code walkthroughs, or any other type of testing that focuses on whether or not a technology actually works. Usability testing, sometimes called usability engineering, is not concerned about whether the technology (hardware, software, Web site) is functionally correct. Rather, it focuses on whether a specific technology is easy to use. There are three types of usability testing: user-based testing, expert-based testing, and automated testing. The goal of usability testing is to discover flaws in the interface related to ease of use. Even if good design guidelines are followed, it's impossible to guess in advance how users will interact with an interface and what aspects will be problematic. The only way to find out what truly works and what is frustrating is for users to test a system by means of usability testing. Expert-based and automated testing also provide suggestions for improving the usability of an interface.

Usability testing has been widely used in developing large-scale software applications, and has been popular for years with large-scale applications because it generally saves money and results in more satisfied users. So far, usability testing has not been a standard part of Web development, but this situation is starting to change. Today, usability testing of Web sites is especially important. With traditional software applications, a license or copy of the application is purchased and the investment is then already made, and often there are not many choices available of a certain type of software application. Compare this with Web sites offering similar items; if users find one site hard to use, they can simply switch to another because switching costs are low or nonexistent. The usability of a Web site is of paramount importance. As discussed in previous chapters, a Web site's ease of use can influence how users perceive the sponsoring organization. Usability testing is the best way to ensure that the developmental planning and research results in Web sites that are easy to use. And if flaws related to ease of use are discovered, they can be fixed, making sure that the final Web site meets the needs of users.

Ideally, usability testing would be done with hundreds of users in an advanced usability laboratory. In the real world, usability testing attempts to find and fix as many problems as possible, as quickly and cheaply as possible. The testing does not have to be done in an extensive laboratory setting. Most Web development projects don't have the budget to rent a usability lab, nor do they have the time to test 100 users or even the access to 100 users. Any usability testing is better than no usability testing. If the project budget/timeline/access allows testing with five users only, then this is better than no testing. While testing at least 5–10 users is preferable, the more users who participate in the usability testing the better, because the numbers of users relates to how many usability problems are identified.

It's useful to see the patterns that occur among users during usability testing. For example, if one user mistakenly looks on the history page of a Web site for information about current events, it's probably an aberration. But if eight out of ten users mistakenly look on the history page for information about current events, it probably indicates a problem that will occur with additional users. That is, more users testing an interface would be better, but some users are better than none.

Usability testing is usually performed once a working interface (or an interface prototype) has been created, but before the final working system (and an interface) is delivered to users and implemented. In addition, periodic usability tests might be useful if systems (or users) change over time, to ensure that the information system remains easy to use. For a Web site, this usually means that the coding for most of the site has already been done. In some cases, it can be useful to test sample page templates (known as mockups or wire frames), before content is added to the pages. Some developers suggest first testing with paper prototypes of what an interface might look like before any coding is done. Paper prototyping is discussed in Chapter 4 and is also used in Case Study A: kodak.com. Regardless of what type of usability testing is conducted, it should take place when there is still enough time for the results to make an impact on the final design. A usability test, where none of the suggested changes in the interface can actually be made, is in reality a worthless test.

How much usability testing should be done? You should do as much as time allows. Certainly, a combination of all three approaches (user-based tests, expert-based tests, and automated tests) is superior, but in reality, most Web development projects don't allow the time for this. In fact, many Web sites are implemented without any usability testing at all. Therefore, the best type of usability testing is the one that can actually be implemented in time to impact the final site design.

Expert-Based Reviews

Expert reviews are one type of usability test. Some developers consider it a usability test only if actual users are involved, and they consider an expert-based test an expert review or a usability inspection. However, both users and experts may have useful suggestions to improve the usability of a Web site. An expert-based review is when an expert in interface design examines a series of Web pages, using a variety of structured approaches. The main difference between an expert-based test and a user-based test is that usability experts are experts in interface design, but not necessarily in the tasks that users will perform. The opposite is true of users, who are experts in the tasks, but are not as knowledge-able about interface design. Expert-based tests tend to focus on the interface itself, whereas user-based tests tend to focus on using the interface to perform the tasks. Usability experts usually comment on problems that violate usability guidelines, such as problems with color consistency or terminology. Often, experts find the larger usability problems and users pinpoint smaller problems related to task concerns, which are not as obvious to the experts.

Some researchers advocate testing with users only, their point being that expert reviewers are not experts in the task domain that is represented in the interface, and being unrepresentative of the user population, cannot offer useful feedback. In reality, what frequently happens is that both experts and users are testers, depending on factors such as schedule pressures, costs, and the availability of users. For instance, one usability firm indicates that most of their clients first ask for a heuristic evaluation (see more on this technique later in the chapter) with a usability expert to root out any major usability problems. After the expert heuristic evaluation, the clients usually want user-based usability testing to be performed in a lab setting with 5–10 users.

If there are any usability experts on the Web development team, they should not be used for expert reviews. Only outside usability experts should be used. The idea behind an expert review is to get a different viewpoint, from someone who is an expert in usability and interface design. Therefore, an expert reviewer must be someone who is not involved in the actual Web development project. If a member of the Web development team is a usability expert, that person should not offer a separate viewpoint as part of the expert review. Furthermore, if a member of the Web development team notices a problem related to usability at this stage of development, the issue should have been pointed out earlier.

Expert reviews share some characteristics with user testing in that they can take place in any type of setting, such as a workplace, a usability lab, or over the Web. The reviewers themselves can come from consulting firms, usability labs, or universities. These expert reviewers, much like the users, normally expect to be paid to review a Web site. However, the expert reviewers are not representative users. Because of this difference, the techniques those expert reviewers use are different from user-based usability testing. There are various types of expert reviews; the three most commonly used are heuristic evaluations, guidelines review, and consistency inspection.

Heuristic Review

In a heuristic evaluation, an expert compares a Web site to a short list of design heuristics that usually consists of 5–10 design rules. The expert reviewer checks the Web site to see if it violates any of these general design rules. Heuristic evaluation is quite common since it is quick and does not require a large number of experts. At the same time, the experts must be familiar with the heuristics used in order to ensure that they can perform an effective review. Again, what the expert finds tends to be general flaws in the interface, not interface flaws specific to the task. There are a number of sets of heuristics. For instance, the heuristics for creating a credible Web site by Fogg (in Chapter 6) is one form of heuristic review. A shorter set of heuristics, based on the guidelines for creating an accessible Web site (from Chapter 7) are discussed in this chapter. Probably the best known set of usability heuristics is Shneiderman's 8 Golden Rules of Interface Design, which applies to all types of computer interfaces, not just Web design. Additional sets of Web design heuristics include: Hilberg and Lazar's heuristics for Web-based applications and Abras, Ozok, and Preece's heuristics for online communities (see the following Hands-On Examples). Other sets include Barnum's heuristics for Web design (Barnum '01) and Nielsen's Top 10 Mistakes in Web Design available at http://www.useit.com/alertbox/9605a.html.

Heuristics are frequently shorter versions of longer sets of design guidelines. For instance, the Web Accessibility Initiative has a set of 10 heuristics, which is a shortened version of the Web Content Accessibility Guidelines, Priority Level 1

Shneiderman's 8 Golden Rules of Interface Design

Hands-On Example

1. Strive for consistency
2. Cater to universal usability
3. Offer informative feedback
4. Design dialogs to yield closure
5. Prevent errors
6. Permit easy reversal of actions
7. Support internal locus of control
8. Reduce short-term memory load

(Shneiderman '05)

Hands-On Example

Short List of Heuristics to Design Accessible Web Sites

A shortened version of the full guidelines from http://www.w3.org/wai.

- **Images and animations.** Use the `alt` attribute to describe the function of each visual.
- **Image maps.** Use the client-side map and text for hotspots.
- **Multimedia.** Provide captioning and transcripts of audio and descriptions of video.
- **Hypertext links.** Use text that makes sense when read out of context. For example, avoid "click here."

- **Page organization.** Use headings, lists, and consistent structure. Use CSS for layout and style where possible.
- **Graphs and charts.** Summarize or use the `longdesc` attribute.
- **Scripts, applets, and plugins.** Provide alternative content in case active features are inaccessible or unsupported.
- **Frames.** Use the `NOFRAMES` element and meaningful titles.
- **Tables.** Make line-by-line reading sensible. Summarize.
- **Check your work.** Validate. Use tools, checklist, and guidelines at http://www.w3.org/TR/WCAG

(see Chapter 7 for more information on accessibility). Sometimes, heuristics are more useful than long design guidelines because the brevity of the heuristics makes them more likely to be used. Long design guidelines can be useful, but only if they are actually used. This parallels some of the research on minimalist documentation (Carroll '90). Less documentation can actually be more useful, since a large set of documentation is unlikely to be used. The bottom line is that heuristics are useful because they are actually used.

Guidelines Review

A guidelines review is similar to a heuristic evaluation, except that the expert reviews a Web site against a much larger list of design guidelines (potentially 15–200 guidelines). There is no clear border (say, 10 rules) between heuristics and guidelines. Some developers use the terms interchangeably. Regardless of which term is used, it's clear that guidelines are longer and more detailed than heuristics. Some organizations and computer companies have their own set of design guidelines. For instance, there are guidelines provided by Apple for the OS X operating system (Apple '04) and by Microsoft for the Windows operating

Abras, Ozok, and Preece's Usability Heuristics for Health Online Communities

Consistency and Accessibility

Consistency
- Consistent navigation
- Familiar language
- Necessary navigation buttons provided on each page

Accessibility
- Able to find the site using any search engine
- Archived discussions easily accessible
- Site and board are useful

Navigation
- Easy navigation
- Layout of the site and board intuitive
- Original search page easily accessible
- Members' ability to obtain information easily

Organization
- Familiar icons
- Layout of discussion board organized by topic or string depending on need
- Directions on how to use the site and board are provided

User Control
- Feeling in charge of the system
- Fast pace of interaction
- Consistent design of the site and the board

Searchability
- Site and board are accessible at all times
- Search sequence easy to remember

There are also separate heuristics for sociability in health online communities, as well as separate heuristic sets for academic online communities.

(Abras '05)

Hilberg and Lazar's Heuristics for Web-Based Applications

- Avoid non-traditional use of widgets
- Keep the user informed
- Provide application specific navigation
- Simplify data entry
- Avoid excessively long pages and scrolling
- Avoid long download times
- Provide online help and documentation
- Test the application with multiple browsers and versions

(Hilberg '03)

system (Microsoft '04). Other design guidelines exist for specific types of applications. Design guidelines for specific organizations or interfaces can contain hundreds of design rules, so this type of review takes a long time and is not as commonly performed as a heuristic review. One example of design guidelines includes the full Web Content Accessibility Guidelines from the Web Accessibility Initiative at http://www.w3.org/TR/WCAG10/, part of which is listed in Chapter 7. As stated previously, the accessibility heuristics in this chapter are a shorter version of the full guidelines set.

Another extensive set of Web design guidelines comes from IBM, and is available at http://www-306.ibm.com/ibm/easy/eou_ext.nsf/EasyPrint/572. These guidelines deal with the Web design process, and include a separate set of guidelines for e-business sites. The Research-Based Web Design and Usability Guidelines, an excellent set of design guidelines from the U.S. Department of Health and Human Services, is available at http://www.usability.gov/guides/index.html. Due to the length of design guidelines, they cannot be fully included in this book; however, they are all available as free downloads, so the URLs are provided. One shorter set of design guidelines for e-commerce, from Fang and Salvendy, appears in the Hands-On Example on the next page. In addition, design guidelines are heavily used in developing automated usability testing applications (see later sections in this chapter).

Consistency Inspection

In a consistency inspection, an expert reviews all of the Web pages on the site to ensure that the layout, terminology, and color are the same. For instance, if most pages of a site have navigation on the left, and the corporate logo at the top left-hand corner of the page, then the user will expect to see this arrangement on every page. Font faces and sizes should also be consistent. Interface consistency is important, because when a series of interfaces are inconsistent, it can lower user performance and satisfaction, and increase the error rate. Users can become disconcerted or disoriented when similar pages do not appear consistently. For instance, if most pages appear similar, but two pages differ from the common layout (different color schemes, no navigation on left or corporate logo), users may mistakenly perceive that they have left the Web site. Templates or wireframes of Web sites are encouraged in early stages of design because they increase the likelihood that all pages will follow a consistent format. Also, if an organization uses interface design guidelines, it's likely that the consistency is spelled out in detail, which will also ensure interface consistency.

Customer-Centered Rules for Designing E-Commerce Web Sites

Homepage

- Web page should be clean and not cluttered with text and graphics
- The width of a page should be less than the width of the browser window to avoid horizontal scrolling

Navigation

- Text on the links or buttons should be self-explained and descriptive
- When linking to another product-related Web site, link to the exact product page instead of the homepage of that site

Categorization

- Categorize products in a way that is meaningful to regular customers
- The depth of the categories should be no more than three levels

Product Information

- Present accurate, consistent, and detailed descriptions of products
- Provide accurate and full pictures of products
- Present the size of products in a measurable and comparable way

- Present the inventory information of a product in the beginning
- Present products in a table with enough information to make a purchasing decision such as prices and features for easy comparison
- Present related charges up front and in an accurate way
- Same products should be presented in the same page, same position
- Products shouldn't be removed from the page because of out-of-stock

Shopping Cart

- In the shopping cart page, provide a link that directs the customer back to the page he or she left for continuing the shopping

Checkout and Registration

- Only ask for necessary and meaningful information such as name and address, no marketing questions
- Allow customers to browse the site without logging in

Customer Service

- Provide a 1-800 number for customers to call
- Clearly state the return policy in a prominent place

Table 3: Fang and Salvendy, "Customer-Centered Rules for Design of E-Commerce Web Sites," *Communications of the ACM*, Vol. 46:12ve, pp. 332–336, December 2003 © 2003 ACM, Inc. Reprinted by permission.

User-Based Testing

User-based testing is the most common type of usability testing. In usability testing, representative users (people who are part of the target user population) attempt to perform representative tasks. The testing can take place in many different types of locations (a fixed usability lab, an office workplace, over the Internet). Testing can be conducted with five users or with 300 users. The usability testing can have quantitative goals, or be informal, where users record what they did not like about the interface. Any type of usability testing is valuable, and while more usability testing is better than less, some usability testing is better than none. If both expert-based testing and user-based testing take place, the expert-based tests should come before the user-based tests. For all types of user-based testing, the following steps guide each stage from the initial selection of users to the final processing of testing results.

1. Select Representative Users

Users who truly represent the target user population must be recruited to take part in the testing. It is essential to have a representative set of users. Having users who are unrepresentative of the user population is like asking teenagers what they think of the AARP (American Association of Retired Persons), or asking senior citizens about the newest set of Pokémon cards. College students should not be chosen to perform usability testing on a management information system to be used by senior executives. Does the choice of users really make a difference? Would you want airline pilots to test an interface to be used by doctors and nurses in a hospital? Airline pilots would not have the knowledge in the task domain to effectively use the hospital computer system. Most likely, airline pilots would not have previously worked in a hospital, nor would they be working in a hospital in the future. They would not have experience using hospital computer systems, nor are they expected to use such systems in the future. The feedback from airline pilots about what they think of a hospital system interface would be as worthless as doctors' perceptions of an interface for piloting a jet.

One of the first issues to address in user-based usability testing is how to recruit the users. This step can be harder when designing new Web sites than when redesigning an existing site. Hopefully, the client organization can provide a list of potential testers who accurately represent the target user population. Potential users should be contacted to find out if they accurately represent the target population of users and if they are willing to take part in usability testing. As with jury duty, users are usually compensated for taking part in usability testing. This compensation can be in the form of money, food, or a simple thank you. Compensation is related to how interested the users are in the Web site, how important they think the Web site will be, and the monetary value of their time. Those who are very interested in using the potential site might be willing to perform usability testing for free. Those who are not as enthusiastic about the site might be willing to participate for $10–$30 an hour. To get medical doctors to test a Web site might cost a few hundred dollars an hour per doctor. While a greater number of users taking part in a test would obviously be superior, a minimum of five users is a good idea. Remember that it's important to have users who are representative of the target user population.

2. Select the Setting

Usability testing can take place almost anywhere. The location is influenced by the access that the Web development team has to equipment and to the users themselves. Many large companies and governmental organizations (such as IBM and the U.S. Census Bureau) have in-house usability laboratories and teams of experienced usability professionals. Consulting firms can provide expertise in usability, and can be hired to do usability testing. If you need to rent usability equipment, some companies will let you rent portable usability equipment or an entire usability laboratory by the hour.

A Formal Usability Laboratory. Formal usability testing can take place in a usability laboratory in which there is special equipment, made especially for usability testing. Usually, there is a chair and desk with a computer. The user sits at the desk, with a camera mounted either on the wall or on top of the computer. The camera records the actions and/or facial expressions of the user. The actions on the screen of the computer are also recorded to see what the user is doing. These two views, one of the user and one of the screen, are recorded side-by-side or picture-in-picture, usually in digital format. The user wears a microphone to assist in recording comments. The observer (a usability professional) may sometimes sit next to the user.

However, it is preferred to have a small room adjacent to the usability laboratory with a one-way mirror that separates the user from the observer. A drawing of this typical layout is shown in Figure 9.1. The observer watches the user through the one-way mirror, but the user cannot see the observer. The one-way mirror makes the user more comfortable and reduces nervousness about being observed. The idea is that when users perceive that they are being watched, they act differently. Although users must know that they are being recorded (by law), at the same time, once users begin their tasks, they tend to forget that they are being watched. Small and inconspicuous cameras can help to ensure that users do not feel self-conscious. An example of this layout is shown in Figure 9.2. The user on the left is separated from the observer on the right by a one-way mirror.

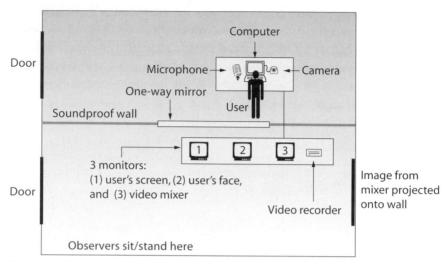

Figure 9.1 A drawing of a typical formal usability laboratory.

Figure 9.2 A user (on the left), is participating in user-based testing in a formal usability laboratory. The observer (on the right) is watching the user through a one-way mirror and a video camera. Photo courtesy of Userworks, Inc.

Workplace Testing. Another possible location for usability testing is the workplace. It's possible for a Web development team member to visit the user's workplace (or home) and observe the individual's interaction with the Web site. The advantage of this approach is that the user is in his or her natural environment, and most likely feels comfortable interacting with the computer. In addition, it might be easier to get access to users in their workplace environment, since they do not need to take large amounts of time from their day to travel to a usability laboratory. Portable usability equipment can be taken to a workplace or home, set up to record the user's actions, and still remain inconspicuous. The usability equipment, similar to a fixed usability lab, can record the interaction on the screen, the user's facial expression, and the user's voice, using portable recorders and cameras. However, this equipment is expensive and sometimes not feasible for testing small numbers of users.

Portable usability equipment is sold under such names as "lab-in-a-bag" and "lab-in-a-box." The equipment generally breaks down into two parts. One part stands next to the user's computer—a microphone and a small video camera. It's mobile and attached via wires to the moderator's equipment, which should be located away from the user so that he or she does not feel that they are being watched. Figure 9.3 shows a user, with the only visible equipment being a small camera and a microphone. Figure 9.4 shows an observer monitoring a user with portable usability equipment. Next to the observer is the portable box, which provides the observer dual-monitor views of what is on the user's screen, what the user's face looks like, and comments from the user.

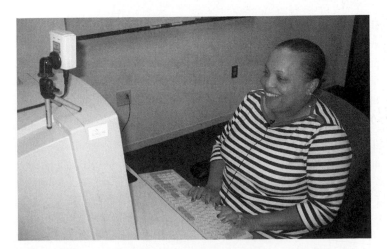

Figure 9.3 The user is seated at a workplace computer. The camera, on top of the monitor, and the microphone, attached to the user's shirt, are the only signs that the user is being recorded.

Figure 9.4 The observer is in a separate room, watching the incoming video of the user. The observer is also recording data on a laptop computer. Photo courtesy of Userworks, Inc.

Another possibility is for an evaluator simply to sit next to a user in their workplace or home, and ask them questions about their interactions with a Web site as they are using it. This scenario is not as structured as with the portable usability lab, but it's still a valuable approach for learning about how users interact with a site. Just recording these comments with pencil and paper can be useful.

Remote Usability Testing. Another type of usability testing is remote usability testing, sometimes called Web-based usability testing, where the user and the evaluator are not physically located at the same location, but are connected via the Web. The user performs usability testing by accessing the Web site via the Web. The evaluator might communicate with the user in real-time or the evaluator might talk with the user at a later time.

Web-based usability testing has several advantages. Generally, it allows more users to take part in the usability testing because they don't need to be available to come to the usability lab. Also observers don't have to be present to watch users in their workplace setting. Via the Web, users can perform usability testing on a site any time, day or night. Factors that are outside the Web development team's control (such as download speed) are not present in the usability lab, but they are apparent when the users performing usability testing are distributed across the country. Remote usability testing seems like a natural method in which to test a Web site.

The main disadvantage of Web-based usability testing is that the observer cannot record every user action, or be able to listen to what the user has to say. But there are a number of techniques that can be used to collect this data through Web-based usability testing. Videoconferencing can be used to allow the observer (evaluator) to watch what the user is doing. The user can talk by phone to the observer as part of the think-aloud protocol (there is more information about this later in the chapter) or the evaluator can remotely view the user's screen using software such as PCAnywhere. The user's system can provide some type of data logging that allows post-hoc review of statistical data. If there are many users performing remote usability testing, a chat room or bulletin board can be set up for them to share their comments and discuss their suggestions. After users have completed the tasks, they can be presented with a Web-based questionnaire asking their opinions on the Web site. Realistically, there are many ways to have remote users perform usability testing. Be creative!

3. Decide What Tasks Users Should Perform

In usability testing, users are asked to perform a set of tasks, and the Web development team (or usability evaluator) learns about the usability problems of the system through this process. The tasks and instructions for performing the tasks should be determined in advance. When users participate in the usability test, traditionally they are given a list of tasks to perform, on a sheet of paper. The tasks should represent common tasks that the users will be expected to perform. In requirements gathering, the users might have stated what they would like to accomplish with the site, or the clients might have indicated what tasks they expect users to perform.

In the case of informational Web sites, these tasks are usually related to information gathering. Users should be sent on a "scavenger hunt" to find information on the site. For an e-commerce site, users can be asked to find a product and purchase it. For an online community, tasks might be related to logging onto the site, and searching for postings, or actually posting a message. The wording of the tasks should be clear and unambiguous. Users should be asked to find a specific piece of information or perform a specific task. They should not be asked to do something like "look for information on our graduate program," because that is too vague, and it doesn't model how users will actually need to interact with the interface. Users should be asked to find things that they do not already know, because if the tasks ask for information that users already know, they will tend to report what they know and not actually use the interface to find the information.

In most usability testing scenarios, users are asked to attempt the tasks without any outside assistance. This matches the user's natural environment, where the user would attempt tasks without assistance from anyone else. Since the test tasks should be representative of common user tasks, the computer equipment should also be representative of the common user computing equipment. A sample task list is available in the Hands-On Example below. Usability testing took place on the new Web site for the Center for Applied Information Technology at Towson University. There were two different, well-defined user populations: current graduate students and prospective graduate students. Because the tasks of the two populations are different, there were two separate task lists, one for each population. The task list in the Hands-On Example below is for prospective graduate students.

4. Decide What Type of Data to Collect

There are a number of different types of data that can be collected as a part of the user-based test. This data includes quantitative measures, direct user feedback through thinking aloud, coaching methods, and satisfaction surveys. Various combinations of these data should be collected. In addition, although it

---

Hands-On Example

Sample Task List for Prospective Graduate Students

1. What is the first day of classes for the Fall 2005 semester?
2. What are the names of the six graduate-level certificates that CAIT offers?
3. Who is the director of the graduate program at CAIT?
4. Who is the director of the entire center?
5. What is the mailing address for the center?
6. Can a student at the center enroll online?
7. How many credits are required for a certificate?
8. How many credits are required for a master's degree?
9. What are the tuition fees per course for the Fall 2005 semester?
10. Where would students park for the center? Are permits required?
11. Are graduate assistantships offered?
12. What are the general requirements for admission? Are GRE scores required?
13. Does Towson University offer on-campus housing for graduate students?
14. Find the contact information (e-mail address and phone number) for the following members of the center's faculty and staff: Dr. Jonathan Lazar, Dr. James Clements, Dr. Ali Behforooz.

is rarely used in usability testing (it is more frequently used in experimental research), human physiological measures, such as blood pressure, heart rate, and muscle movement, can measure the usability of an interface.

Quantitative Measures. Quantitative measures of performance using the interface can be taken. This data can measure how many tasks were successfully completed (task performance), how long it took the user to complete a specific task (time performance), and the number of errors and time spent recovering from the errors. This data can be manually recorded by the observer, or, like response time, can be logged by the computer. The quantitative measures of task and time performance are the most common quantitative measurements of usability and have been named standard metrics for usability by the U.S. government (National Institute of Standards and Technology '99). In interfaces where task performance, or low error rates are especially important, benchmarks can be set for performance (e.g., 80 percent of users must be able to complete all of the tasks correctly within five minutes). For interfaces where errors can be disastrous (e.g., online banking), threshold rates for error can be decided upon (e.g., no more than one error per person in the banking tasks). The usability goals might even be different for different user groups. Through a series of usability tests, various iterations of the interface can be designed, until the quantitative goal (e.g., 80 percent of users completing the tasks in five minutes) is reached. One example of quantitative goals is listed in the table on the following page. In the usability testing of an intranet site at the U.S. Census Bureau, user groups and corresponding usability goals were defined, as illustrated in the table (Lazar '04).

Thinking Aloud Protocol. Another way to collect data on interface usage is more qualitative. Users are encouraged to verbalize their thoughts as they attempt to complete their tasks. Users may point out parts of the system that are satisfying, parts of the system that are confusing, or they may express their thoughts on how to improve the interface. These comments should be recorded on video or audio (with the user's prior permission, of course), or should be recorded by an individual (the observer or moderator) whose purpose is to take notes of the session. Another possibility is to have two users working together, a process that helps to increase the amount of discussion about the system. The technique of having two users test the system simultaneously is called co-discovery learning or constructive interaction. Users might also be asked to review a videotape of their actions at a later time, and provide retrospective comments. The thinking aloud protocol can be helpful in understanding interfaces where users have low task performance, but it isn't clear why the task performance is low.

Sample Quantitative Usability Goals for the Testing of a U.S. Census Bureau Intranet Site

User group	Importance (1 = not important, 3 = very important)	Task performance	Time performance	User satisfaction (1 = not important, 3 = very important)
Administrative application designers and developers	2	75 percent	< 60 seconds	2
Hardware, software, Web site, and intranet designers	3	100 percent	< 45 seconds	3
Hardware, software, Web site, and intranet developers	3	100 percent	< 45 seconds	3
Hardware, software, Web site, and intranet testers	3	100 percent	< 45 seconds	3
Persons responsible for any electronic product design	2	75 percent	< 60 seconds	2
IBM FactFinder Contractors	3	100 percent	< 45 seconds	3
Census Bureau Usability Lab personnel	3	100 percent	< 60 seconds	3

Coaching Method. In most usability testing methods, the user attempts to perform tasks without outside help. In the coaching method, the user is assisted by the evaluator, who provides advice about how to use the system, and asks many questions of the user. The user may also ask questions about the system, such as "What does that icon represent?" Use of the coaching method is controversial. On one hand, it can help the user get through a series of interfaces he or she is having problems with. On the other hand, skeptics say that the coaching method does not accurately represent how a user would interact with a system in a workplace or home setting. The goal of a user-based test is to watch the user interact with an interface in as natural a setting as possible. The coaching method may not reach that goal.

Satisfaction Surveys. Users can be required to answer questions while they are attempting the tasks. For instance, if a user is given a list of tasks, after each task there can be a question such as "Were there any parts of that task that you found confusing?" Users can also be requested to fill out a questionnaire at the end of the usability session. Questions to ask at the end of the session might include:

"What did you like most about the Web site?"

"What did you like least about the Web site?"

"What changes to the Web site would you suggest?"

It is especially important to ask the users questions about parts of the interface that might have been controversial during the Web development process. If there were any components of the Web site that were not requested by users, or any parts that the clients were specifically concerned about, it might be useful to solicit the users' opinions on these aspects of the interface. For instance, "What did you think about the color scheme?" In addition, there are validated questionnaires, such as the Questionnaire for User Interaction Satisfaction (QUIS) that can be used to ascertain the user's overall satisfaction with the system (see the following Hands-On Example). Other surveys to evaluate how the site has been used, as discussed in Chapter 11, are typically used after a site has been launched and has attracted users.

Along with user feedback, the observers also watch the users, and make notes on task performance. Sometimes, the users may perform actions without realizing it, or a number of users might make the same mistake, or choose the same incor-

Hands-On Example

Sample Section of the Questionnaire for User Interaction Satisfaction

The Questionnaire for User Interaction Satisfaction is a standard, validated questionnaire, used frequently at the end of a usability testing session. It is split into 12 different sections, covering topics such as screen layout, appropriate use of terminology, and multimedia. Each section can be used independently. More information about the QUIS is available at http://www.lap.umd.edu/quis. One section of the QUIS follows:

Overall System Reactions

Please circle the numbers which most appropriately reflect your impressions about using this computer system. NA = Not Applicable.

3.1	Terrible	Wonderful
	1 2 3 4 5 6 7 8 9 NA	
3.2	Frustrating	Satisfying
	1 2 3 4 5 6 7 8 9 NA	
3.3	Dull	Stimulating
	1 2 3 4 5 6 7 8 9 NA	
3.4	Difficult	Easy
	1 2 3 4 5 6 7 8 9 NA	
3.5	Inadequate power	Adequate power
	1 2 3 4 5 6 7 8 9 NA	
3.6	Rigid	Flexible
	1 2 3 4 5 6 7 8 9 NA	

rect paths to a goal. For instance, if a majority of users attempt to find a specific piece of content by using the site navigation, when in fact, that content isn't listed in the site navigation, observers should note this, and suggest that the content be listed in the site navigation.

5. Before the Test Session

Before the usability testing session begins, any questions that the user has should be answered. In addition, the user should be asked to fill out an informed consent form. Such a form should provide information about what will take place in the usability test, and inform the user that his or her participation is voluntary, confidential, and that they are free to end the session at any time. If the user is

Hands-On Example

Sample Informed Consent Form

Purpose of the Project:

The researchers (names here) are conducting a usability study to learn more about how to improve the interface of a new Web site. The users are not being tested. Rather, the goal is for users to utilize their expertise and help test the Web site.

Procedure:

Users will be asked to fill out this form. Then they will be given the URL of a new Web site, and a list of tasks to perform. After completing a series of tasks, the users will be asked to fill out a survey, giving their perceptions of the new Web site. The user's voice and actions will be recorded via video. The video will not be shown outside of the usability lab, and at no point will the user's name be attached to the video.

Confidentiality:

Participation in this usability study is voluntary. All information will remain strictly confidential. The descriptions and findings may be used to help improve the interface of the Web site. However, at no time will the user's name or any other identification be used. The user is at liberty to withdraw consent to the experiment and discontinue participation at any time without prejudice. If you have any questions after today, please contact (name) at (phone).

I have read and understood the information on this form and had all of my questions answered.

_____   _____
Participant's Signature   Date

_____   _____
Usability Consultant   Date

being videotaped or recorded, the user must be aware of this and agree to it. In addition, users should be reminded that the interface is being tested—users aren't. Users are simply the individuals testing the interface. A sample informed consent form appears in the preceding Hands-On Example.

6. During the Test Session

During the test session, the users should be minimally interrupted. Since the goal of the usability test is to replicate actual user conditions, in most cases, the user is in their workplace or home, and would not be interrupted by an outside person. If the observer needs to interrupt the user, it should be infrequently.

7. Debriefing After the Session

After the user has indicated that they have completed the session, they should immediately be asked to fill out any questionnaires. This way, the information is still fresh in the user's mind. After the user has filled out the questionnaire, debriefing should take place. This debriefing should consist of asking the user for any final thoughts about their experience, and thanking the user for participating. If it was agreed that the user would be paid for participation, payment should be made at this time. After the usability test is completed and the user has left, the observers should make notes on all aspects of the usability session, before these details are forgotten. This protocol should be used, regardless of whether the usability testing is in a formal usability laboratory, a workplace setting, or via the Web. The only difference is that, over the Web, more time may elapse between sending the user instructions and actually performing the usability testing.

Automated Usability Testing

Because of the time and expense of running traditional user-based usability tests, and because comparing Web pages to long guideline lists can be overwhelming, a number of software companies have been working on developing software tools that can assist with improving the usability of a Web site. The idea behind an automated usability testing tool is for the computer to analyze a Web page (or a series of Web pages) against a set of usability guidelines, and point out the design flaws. These guidelines tend to be well-known Web usability guidelines such as the Web Content Accessibility Guidelines, Section 508 guidelines for the

Web, or Guidelines for Developing Web Sites for Older Users (all of these guideline sets are in Chapter 7). Automated usability testing does not replace usability testing, but rather, is akin to an expert review. Automated usability testing software can help those who do not have the time or budget to do more traditional user or expert-based testing, but who still understand that usability is important. As previously stated, the best type of usability testing is user-based testing, but any type of usability testing is better than no usability testing. Different automated usability testing tools focus on different aspects of usability. For instance, most of the current software tools focus on accessibility, rather than general usability. This might be because usability guidelines related to accessibility are well-defined and tend to be code related, whereas general Web usability guidelines tend to be more general and subjective.

Automated usability testing tools come in a number of different formats. They are available on the Web, as a part of a Web development application (see Chapter 8), or as a stand-alone application. A limited version of WEBXACT (http://www.webxact.com/) is available for free on the Web (see Figure 9.5). WEBXACT will test a Web page for accessibility against either the Web Content

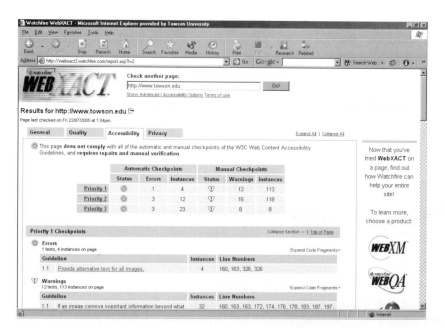

Figure 9.5 WEBXACT, a Web-based tool for automating the accessibility review of a Web page.

Accessibility Guidelines or Section 508, and will provide a report of the accessibility problems. WEBXACT, previously known as Bobby, has also added features that test for broader usability issues.

Other applications can be downloaded from the Web for free. WebSAT (available at: http://zing.ncsl.nist.gov/WebTools/), was developed by the United States National Institutes for Standards and Technology, and tests Web pages against general usability guidelines. A-Prompt (http://aprompt.snow.utoronto.ca/) developed at the University of Toronto, checks a site against the Web Content Accessibility Guidelines. Dottie (http://www.som.fit.edu/abecker/Accessibility/main.html), a tool developed at the Florida Institute of Technology, checks a site against the usability guidelines for older adults.

Stand-alone software packages are also available for purchase. These are more powerful tools that spider through and examine an entire Web site. In addition, these tools usually provide automated fixing of the problems discovered, or at least provide wizards to guide the developer through fixing the problems. These tools include InFocus (http://www.ssbtechnologies.com/) and RAMP (http://www.deque.com/), which focus on testing sites against the Section 508 rules for the Web (see Figures 9.6 and 9.7). These tools work on the same basic

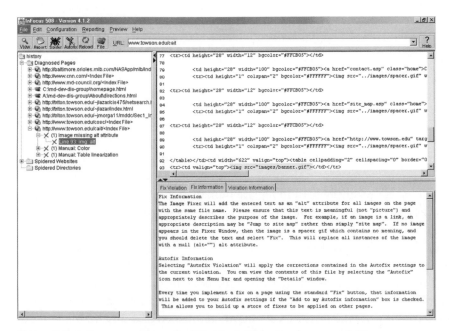

Figure 9.6 InFocus, a software tool that tests Web sites for accessibility.

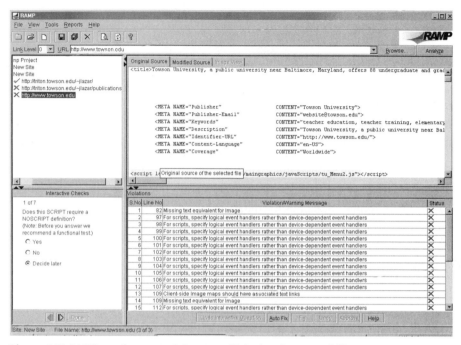

Figure 9.7 RAMP, a software tool that tests Web sites for accessibility.

concept of multiple windows displaying the code (with problem areas high-lighted), providing information on why an accessibility guideline was violated and information how to fix it, and showing an overall view of pages on the site that have been examined, along with other pages recently examined and fixed.

Automated usability testing tools can be useful to find and fix interface flaws quickly, especially those related to Web accessibility. However, the main weakness of automated usability testing tools is that they are only as good as the usability guidelines incorporated into the application, and how those guidelines are inter-preted. It is still relatively hard to replace human usability expertise with a com-puter. For instance, a usability guideline may state that all Web multimedia content must have alternative text for users with disabilities (using an `alt` tag). If the Web page has the following code: `<img src="president.jpg" alt="picture here">`, then technically, an automated usability testing tool would not flag this as a problem, since it includes an `alt` tag. However, the `alt` text, "picture here," is meaningless for someone who is counting on the `alt` text to understand what the picture is about. An automated usability testing tool can follow rules, but there are still gray areas where experts or real users are needed to test an application. Also, some automated usability testing applications have manual checks, which can be problematic because they are hard to interpret. For instance, if a page uses color or tables on a Web page, the application may flag it as a manual check, which notes that a Web page uses a feature that potentially could be an accessibility problem. However, human expertise is then required to determine if the color usage or table usage, actually violates Section 508 rules. These manual checks can be problematic because they can be hard to interpret and decide about.

Incorporating Testing Feedback

After the usability testing is completed, the Web development team should take some time to discuss the findings. Were there aspects of the Web site that users consistently found frustrating? Was there language that was unclear? Did the users have to go through too many menus to find the information they were looking for? Was the amount of screen scrolling overwhelming? Were the navigation schemes confusing? Did the Web pages take too long to download? Were there too many links or too many graphics? Was too much mouse movement required? These are common problems that have been found in the usability testing of major Web sites. It's important for the Web development team to determine the biggest usability problem, based on the usability tests.

The Web development team should decide the major lessons learned from usability testing. Then they should write them up in the form of actionable suggestions. The suggestions should be written so that they can be understood and used by the developers and designers. Suggestions for improvement, with specific examples, are far superior to general problem statements. Problems should not be noted only; suggestions for improvement, with examples of wording, new graphics, or improved layout, should be offered. If there are many design problems noted, all problems will not be able to be addressed in the allotted time period. The problems (and solutions) should be ranked in terms of importance. There should be at least three pieces of information for each usability problem noted: a suggestion for fixing the problem, the urgency of the problem (must fix, should fix, might fix, or some sort of likert scale), and the estimated time to fix the problem. For instance, changing the wording on one page of the site is not time-consuming, but changing the entire navigation layout on every page is very time-consuming.

Depending on whether the usability testing is done by the development team itself, or by those on the outside, the type of communication needed may differ. If the usability testing is done by the development team, most changes can be directly made, although major changes may need to be approved by the management of the client organization. If the usability testing is done by an outside group, its findings should be clearly communicated to the development team. Video and audio tapes, as well as quantitative data, can help to convince development team members, as well as managers, of the need for improvement. This can be a videotape of users having problems, written comments showing that users found the site confusing, or summary data showing that 75 percent of users did not find the information they were looking for. This data will help to convince the client that there are serious usability problems to be addressed. If major design changes are made based on findings from the usability testing, it may be necessary to make the design changes, and then do another round of usability tests to determine what problems exist with the new interface.

Usability testing is an important part of the Web development process. It ensures that there are no serious usability problems that will affect the ability of the users to interact with the Web site successfully.

- There is no one specific method or technique that is right for all situations.

- There is no specific "number" of users who can discover all usability problems.

- The usability testing approach needs to be tailored to each specific Web development project, the timeline, the resources and expertise available, and the budget.

- The more data that can be collected, using multiple methods, the better.

- With the rapid development times for Web development projects, it is unrealistic to test a Web site with 200 users and all types of usability testing.

- It is important to understand the need for usability testing, and to implement some type of testing with users and/or experts to uncover the major flaws.

Design Exercise

Imagine that you are involved in usability testing for a Web site being developed for an e-commerce company that sells violins, violas, cellos, and related musical items. Who would be representative users for testing the site? What would be the best ways to recruit the users? What would be appropriate tasks for users to perform (name at least five tasks)? Where should the user-based testing take place? What types of metrics would be most appropriate?

Discussion Questions

1. Why is usability testing important?
2. What are the strengths and weaknesses of user-based usability testing versus expert-based usability testing? What does each one address?
3. Why is it important to have representative users test the Web site?
4. What is an appropriate setting for a usability test?

5. What is the setup of a formal usability laboratory?

6. What is a heuristic review, who uses it, and how is it used?

7. Why are guidelines reviews not performed regularly for Web sites?

8. What are three methods of data collection in a user-based usability test?

9. How should users in a usability test be treated? What rights do users have?

10. What is a manual check on an automated usability test?

Suggested Reading

Abras, C., Ozok, A., & Preece, J. (2005). "Heuristics for Designing and Maintaining Online Health and Academic Support Communities." Paper under review.

Apple Computer. (2004). "Introduction to the Apple Human Interface Guidelines." Available at: http://developer.apple.com/documentation/UserExperience/Conceptual/OSXHIGuidelines/.

Barnum, C. (2001). *Usability Testing and Research*. Boston: Longman.

Carroll, J. (1990). *The Nurnberg Funnel: Designing Minimalist Instruction for Practical Computer Skill*. Cambridge, Massachusetts: MIT Press.

Cockton, G., Lavery, D., & Woolrych, A. (2003). "Inspection-Based Evaluations." In J. Jacko & A. Sears (Eds.), *The Handbook of Human-Computer Interaction* (pp. 1118–1138). Mahwah, NJ: Lawrence Erlbaum Associates.

Corry, M., Frick, T., & Hansen, L. (1997). "User-Centered Design and Usability Testing of a Web Site: An Illustrative Case Study." *Educational Technology Research and Development*, 45(4), 65–76.

Fang, X., & Salvendy, G. (2003). "Customer-Centered Rules for Design of E-Commerce Web Sites." *Communications of the ACM*, 46(12), 332–336.

Hammontree, M., Weiler, P., & Nayak, N. (1994). "Remote Usability Testing." *Interactions*, 1(3), 21–25.

Hartson, R., Castillo, J., Kelso, J., & Neale, W. (1996). "Remote Evaluation: The Network as an Extension of the Usability Laboratory." Proceedings of the CHI: Human Factors in Computing, 228–235.

Lazar, J., Murphy, E., & O'Connell, T. (2004). "Building University-Government Collaborations: A Model for Students to Experience Usability Engineering in the Federal Workplace." *Journal of Informatics Education and Research*, 6(3), 57-77.

Lazar, J., & Preece, J. (1999). "Designing and Implementing Web-Based Surveys." *Journal of Computer Information Systems*, 39(4), 63–67.

Levi, M., & Conrad, F. (1996). "A Heuristic Evaluation of a World Wide Web Prototype." *Interactions*, 3(4), 50–61.

Microsoft. (2004). "Official Guidelines for User Interface Developers and Designers." Available at: http://msdn.microsoft.com/library/default.asp?url=/library/en-us/dnwue/html/welcome.asp.

Millen, D. (1999). "Remote Usability Evaluation: User Participation in the Design of a Web-Based Email Service." *SIGGROUP Bulletin*, 20(1), 40–44.

National Institute of Standards and Technology. (1999). "Common Industry Format for Usability Test Reports." Available at: http://zing.ncsl.nist.gov/iusr/documents/cifv1.1b.htm.

Nielsen, J. (1994a). *Usability Engineering*. Boston: Academic Press.

Nielsen, J., & Mack, R. (Eds.). (1994b). *Usability Inspection Methods*. New York: John Wiley & Sons.

Ozok, A., & Salvendy, G. (2001). "How Consistent Is Your Web Design?" *Behaviour and Information Technology*, 20(6), 433–447.

Scholtz, J., Laskowski, S., & Downey, L. (1998). "Developing Usability Tools and Technique for Designing and Testing Web Sites." Proceedings of the Human Factors and the Web. Available at: http://www.research.att.com/conf/hfweb/.

Sears, A. (1997). "Heuristic Walkthroughs." *International Journal of Human-Computer Interaction*, 9(3), 213–234.

Shneiderman, B., & Plaisant, C. (2005). *Designing the User Interface: Strategies for Effective Human-Computer Interaction* (4th ed.). Boston: Addison-Wesley.

Tedeschi, B. (August 30, 1999). "Good Web Site Design Can Lead to Healthy Sales." *The New York Times*.

chapter 10

Implementation and Marketing

After reading this chapter, you will be able to:

- Choose an appropriate domain name.
- Ensure that the Web site is properly installed on the Web server.
- Register the Web site with search engines.
- Get other sites to provide a link to the new Web site.
- Suggest appropriate methods for marketing the URL.
- Write meta tags to help search engines find your Web site.

Introduction

This chapter describes the process of implementing and marketing a Web site. After a Web site has been coded and the usability testing has been performed, it's time to unveil the site to the world. Many people refer to this step as "going live." However, before the Web site can go live, a number of issues need to be decided, such as where the Web site will be housed and what the URL will be. Once the site goes live, it must be marketed to the target population of users. The client organization is obviously interested in garnering high user traffic, so it's important to let the target user population know that the Web site is there, waiting for them to visit.

Users generally find a Web site using one of four methods: guessing the URL, using a search engine, following a link, and being given the URL. The implementation of a Web site must support all four of these methods.

Housing the Web Site

Where do you house the Web site? This may seem like an odd question, since a Web site can be accessed from anywhere. However, a Web site is based at a Web server. Whenever a user requests a Web page, the request is sent to the Web server where the actual pages, the HTML files, are physically housed. The actual geographic location is relatively meaningless; however, there needs to be a "home" where these files reside. Usually, Web sites are built and tested on accounts or servers that are owned by the Web development team. When the Web site is ready to go live, the files are moved from the Web development team's server to the client's server. If the Web development team is a part of the client organization, the files should simply be moved from a development or testing server to a permanent server. If the Web development team is not going to be involved in the ongoing maintenance of the site, then the team should provide a backup copy of the site files, as well as documentation on the files and on the overall structure of the Web site to the client.

A client organization may decide to set up their own Web server with an Internet connection and run it out of their organization. This is generally the solution for large-scale Web sites (such as e-commerce sites), and this setup requires an intensive amount of work. However, small- to medium-sized Web sites are usually housed on the Web server at an Internet service provider. Internet service providers can provide access to the Internet, as well as e-mail accounts for a monthly fee. The fee is directly related to issues such as the connection speed (dial-up or broadband), the amount of server space provided, the number of services provided (e.g., Web site stats), and the customer service provided. Basically, the more that you pay for, the more that you get. Inexpensive residential customer plans might be bare bones, but more expensive ISP services for business might include advanced features such as the ability to run FrontPage extensions, the ability to run CGI scripts, database connectivity, and access to server logs.

Domain Name

The client organization needs to decide whether they want to reserve a domain name specifically for their Web site. If an organization called the Singing Grillers (people who like to sing while making dinner on the barbeque grill!) choose to purchase a domain name, the URL of the Web site might be something like http://www.singinggrillers.org. On the other hand, if the client organization chooses to use their ISP account for their Web pages without reserving a domain name, the URL would be http://www.ispname.com/~singinggrillers. The second URL is obviously harder to remember, and it doesn't look as professional when you advertise the site. In addition, while a user might be able to guess the first URL, the second URL is nearly impossible to guess. Furthermore, if the client organization ever wants to move their Web site to another ISP, the URL will change. If you change ISPs and have to change your URL, the entire marketing process must start again. It's like moving from one house to another. Everyone must be informed of the new address.

If the client organization reserves a domain name, that domain name will stay constant and the users will always know where to find the Web site. Web developers can find out what domain names are still available by checking out the Web site http://www.internic.net/ or one of the domain name registrars, such as http://www.register.com/. It's important to remember that a domain name should not be very long, or include words that are commonly misspelled. A domain name that is short and easy to spell will help users remember. For instance, www.barnesandnoble.com was shortened to www.bn.com, which is much easier to remember. More information on choosing appropriate domain names is available later in this chapter.

The Contract for Web Hosting

The Web development team can research and suggest appropriate choices for an Internet service provider, but if the team is not a part of the client organization, the actual contract for Web hosting needs to be made between the client organization and the ISP.

The Web development team might be hired to manage the Web site. But in many cases, the Web development team will end their involvement with the Web site once it has been implemented and working for a few weeks. The client organization will either manage the Web site, or hire someone else to manage it. Therefore, the contract for Web hosting should be negotiated by the client organization, not the Web development team. In fact, this arrangement should be clarified with the client organization, just to make sure that the client organization does not mistakenly assume that the Web development team will manage the Web site forever. The Web development team should also provide the client organization with any information that is required for maintaining the Web site.

Final Acceptance Tests on the Web Server

When the actual HTML files are moved to the permanent home of the site, one final test should be done. The Web pages should be examined by the Web development team to make sure that the files are all in the correct directories, that all file protections are set correctly, and that no links are broken. It is possible that when the files were installed, some of the files were not placed into the correct subdirectories. If this happened, when a user clicks on a link, it's possible that he or she will get an error message because it links to a file that is in the wrong subdirectory. If there are any advanced functionalities using CGI scripts, style sheets, or external JavaScript files, they should be tested to make sure they are in the correct location and working properly. At this point, the site is live. People can access it from anywhere on the Internet. The question is will anyone access your Web site? This brings us to our next task, marketing the Web site.

Marketing: Bringing Users to Your Web Site

"If a tree falls in the woods, and no one is there, does it make a sound?" This is a common saying. In the Web environment, this statement can be updated to, "If you create a Web site, and no one visits the site, does the site exist?" Having a site go live is frequently viewed as the last major challenge to implementing a Web site, but it is not. An important consideration is how to inform potential users about the existence of the site. Think of the Web site as a new product. Advertisements for cooking tools appear on the Food Network on cable television. Advertisements for clothing geared toward teenagers appear on MTV. When a new product is introduced, it must be marketed to the target audience. But Geritol® commercials will probably not appear on MTV, and commercials for the new CD from the Backstreet Boys will probably not be seen on the Golf Channel. This same marketing approach to a target population of users should be used when marketing a Web site.

How can you reach the targeted users? Users traditionally find and visit Web sites in one of four ways: by guessing the URL, by being given the URL, by following a link, and by visiting a search engine. In addition, users may go to a Web site that they have already bookmarked in their browser. In that situation, users have been to the site before, and the bookmarking feature is supported by the user's browser, and therefore, out of the hands of the Web development team. The following sections will detail each one of the methods that can be supported by the Web developers.

Guessing a URL

Frequently, users attempt to guess a URL. Given that users know the name of the organization, they try to determine the correct extension (e.g., .com, .org, .co.uk, etc.). Because this happens so frequently, URLs should be chosen in a way to help support user guessing. The domain name should be short, and it should either identify the name of the organization (e.g., http://www.llbean.com), or the acronym of the organization (e.g., http://www.aarp.org). The extension most likely to be guessed is the one that should be used. Dashes or unexpected letters should not be used. In addition, words that are commonly misspelled should not be included in a domain name. Consider the following possibilities for Omicron Delta Kappa, the leadership honor society. The actual Web site for Omicron Delta Kappa (which is generally known as ODK) is http://www.odk.org. This seems to be the best URL because it's easy to guess, ODK is a nonprofit organization, and the organization is frequently known by its acronym. Consider the following alternative URLs:

- **http://www.omicrondeltakappa.org**
  This has too many letters, and users can easily misspell the words.

- **http://www.omicron-delta-kappa.org**
  How would users know to use dashes?

- **http://www.odknet.org**
  Why would users guess to place "net" in the domain name?

- **http://www.odkWeb.org**
  Why would users guess to place "Web" in the domain name?

- **http://www.odk.net**
  Why would users guess to use "net" for a nonprofit organization?

If users are likely to guess names other than the official name of the organization, then those URLs should be reserved, and redirections should be set up so that users are taken to the appropriate Web site. For instance, a user who types in http://www.sesamestreet.org, or http://www.sesamestreet.com will automatically be directed to http://www.sesameworkshop.org. If users are likely to misspell a

URL in a certain way, those misspelled URLs should be used to reroute traffic to the appropriate location. For instance, for the Barnes and Noble Web site (a major bookseller), both the word Barnes and the word Noble can be spelled differently (e.g., barns and nobel). When a user types in http://www.barnsandnoblc.com/ or http://www.barnesandnobel.com/, they are rerouted to the correct Web site. The user can also type in http://www.bn.com, a shortened version, which is also less likely to be misspelled. Finally, domain names should be as short as possible, as the most popular Web sites have short domain names. URLs should be easy to guess, easy to remember, and easy to spell. It's especially important to support URL guessing, because, despite what designers tend to think, users have problems forming appropriate search queries for search engines, and typically view only the first 10 Web sites found in the search query (Jansen '01). Therefore, guessing the URL is an important way that users find a Web site.

Being Given the URL

Users can be given the URL by traditional marketing techniques. These techniques can be large-scale (i.e., expensive) or small-scale (i.e., inexpensive). Most large organizations use traditional marketing techniques, such as television commercials, radio spots, and newspaper and magazine advertisements. The URL of the organization's Web site can be placed at the end of these media advertisements, or new advertisements can be created to grab the attention of potential users. For instance, William Shatner (Captain Kirk of Star Trek fame) did a number of commercials for priceline.com. Television commercials for Ebay have people singing praises about the Web site. Television commercials and newspaper advertisements are expensive, and only large organizations and e-commerce sites have large enough budgets to spend on this type of expensive mass media advertisement. A large e-commerce site may have millions of dollars to spend on advertising, whereas an informational site for a local school may not have a marketing budget at all.

Organizations with small marketing budgets (mostly informational Web sites) can use small-scale marketing approaches. Many marketing techniques are inexpensive, or can be included with other promotional materials. For instance, Pennsylvania was the first state to include the URL of their Web site on their license plates. Although most organizations cannot place their URL on a license plate, any organization can place their URL on a license plate frame. URLs can also be placed on various types of giveaways, such as T-shirts, tote bags, refrigerator magnets, buttons, lanyard key chains, mouse pads, pens, coffee mugs, Frisbees, and leather portfolios. These inexpensive marketing tools should be distributed in places where many potential users of the Web site are expected. For instance, the University of Maryland Human-Computer Interaction Lab places their URL on a tote bag, which is distributed to those who attend their annual open house (see Figure 10.1).

Other marketing methods can be used at minimal cost. An important way of marketing a Web site is to include the URL on all related organizational materials, such as letterhead, business cards, newsletters, and promotional fliers. These materials are already budgeted for, so usually no added cost is involved. Many organizations have guidelines for materials (such as press releases, newsletters, and fliers) that are sent outside of the organization. For instance, a policy might specify that the organizational logo must be included in the upper right-hand corner, in red, and the organizational motto ("We're number 5—and improving!") must be present. These guidelines can simply be modified to require that the organizational URL is included on all publications released for distribution outside of the organization. These are inexpensive ways to market the URL of the Web site, and the existence of the site itself. One additional way of marketing a Web site is to add the URL to all outgoing e-mails from the client organi-

Figure 10.1 Advertising a Web site on a tote bag.

zation. Most e-mail programs allow a user to specify a signature file that appears at the bottom of all outgoing e-mail messages. Many users include a signature file that replicates a business card, with the postal address, phone, fax, and e-mail address. The URL for the client organization's Web site should also be included in all outgoing e-mail messages. Although this is not something that is within the control of the Web development team, they certainly can encourage the client organization to use this opportunity to let users know about the organization's Web site.

Linking to a URL

Marketing a Web site is not limited to advertisements or giveaways. If you want users to go to a Web site, you can reach them online. The most popular way is to get links to your Web site, placed on another Web site. First, determine what Web sites your targeted user populations are likely to visit. This type of information might have been collected during the requirements gathering. Ask those related sites to provide a link to your Web site. You can offer to reciprocate by providing a link to their Web site. Obviously, this is not a solution for e-commerce sites, which would not want to bring customers to their competitors. But this is a very appropriate approach for informational Web sites. If the client organization is a local or regional chapter of a national organization, or is affiliated in any way with a national professional organization, these partnerships should be used to direct traffic to the Web site by providing reciprocal links.

If a Web site already exists and is being redesigned, you can find out who already links to the site. Many search engines (such as Google) allow users to search for Web pages that link to a certain URL. As an example, one could use the search engine to find out which Web pages provide a link to the Web site for the Archdiocese of Baltimore http://www.archbalt.org (see Figure 10.2).

Another way to find linking opportunities is to look at online communities that the target user population might visit. There are many online communities where users with similar interests and hobbies gather to communicate and share resources. These online communities consist of communication tools, such as listservers, newsgroups, and chat rooms, as well as shared resources, such as Web pages and searchable databases. Online communities provide a gold mine of marketing opportunities because they offer a concentrated, dedicated group of users with a shared interest. Many e-commerce companies are getting involved in building online communities for this very reason (Preece '00). When you have an

Figure 10.2 Google can be used to find out which outside Web pages provide links to a site.

online community, you have people with an intense interest in a certain topic area, and if you can find an online community related to the topic of interest of your Web site, it's likely that you can draw those users to your Web site. Information about the new (or redesigned) Web sites can be posted on list-servers, newsgroups, and mentioned in chat rooms. A link to the new Web site can be added to the online community's Web pages.

Common sense is a good guide in finding appropriate communities. For instance, it would not be wise to post a message about a new Web site for college students majoring in chemistry to the newsgroup alt.fan.seinfeld (an online community for fans of the sitcom "Seinfeld"). Information about online communities can be found at http://lists.topica.com/ or http://groups.yahoo.com or http://groups.google.com/.

If your Web site is targeted toward a specific geographic area (such as school or a neighborhood club), it's possible to find online communities that will also be targeted toward that geographic area. For instance, many newspaper Web sites (such as the *Baltimore Sun* and *The Washington Post*) and city-based online communities (such as the Blacksburg Electronic Village and Seattle Community Network) have a section for local organizations, providing links to organizations in that geographic area.

Using a Search Engine

A majority of Web users use a search engine when they are looking for Web pages that relate to a specific topic. Users generally use a search engine when they know the topic of interest, but do not know where to find Web pages on that topic. Because users go to a search engine looking for Web sites, search engines are important places for marketing a Web site. Closely related to search engines are topical catalogs (such as Yahoo!), which actually list sites by topic of interest. Instead of typing in a series of search keywords (as in a search engine), with a topical catalog, you choose from a very large series of menus, and drill down to the specific topic of interest, where links to related Web sites are presented. There are a number of ways to make sure that a Web site is included in the search engine or subject catalog:

1. Go to the search engine and register the Web page yourself. Some of the search engines (such as Google and Yahoo!) allow users to add information about a Web site to the search engine or subject catalog (see Figures 10.3 and 10.4).

2. A number of services will submit your Web site URL to multiple search engines. This saves time and allows access to search engines that otherwise might not be known. You submit the URL of the Web site, and the service submits the Web site to 50–400 search engines. Some Web sites, such as http://www.addme.com (see Figure 10.5), are free and some, such as http://www.submit-it.com and http://www.worldsubmit.com, charge a fee for this service.

3. Many search engines (including Google) add Web sites to their databases by using spiders or robots to find sites on the Web. Spiders automatically search through sites on the Web, adding sites (and pages) to the search engine database. You can increase the likelihood that a search engine will find your Web site by adding some extra code in the HTML document. Meta tags can be used to assist the search engines. Using <meta> tags, you can specify a brief description of the Web page, as well as appropriate keywords. <meta> tags should be placed between

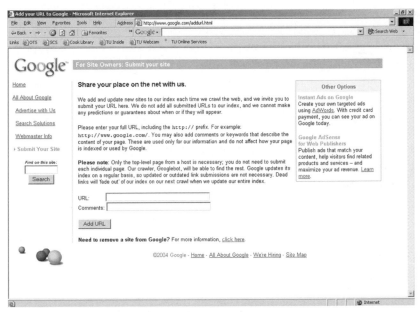

Figure 10.3 You can manually add information about your Web site to Google.

Figure 10.4 You can manually add information about your Web site to Yahoo!
Reproduced with permission of Yahoo! Inc. © 2004 by Yahoo! Inc. YAHOO! and the
YAHOO! logo are trademarks of Yahoo! Inc.

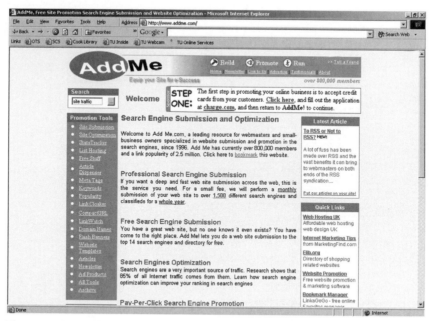

Figure 10.5 Sites such as Addme.com will submit your Web site to multiple search engines.

the <head> tags in an HTML document. The following code provides an example of how to do this:

```
<meta name="description" content="Dr. Jonathan
Lazar's Classes and Research and Guitar Chords and
Tofu Recipes"> <meta name="keywords" content="Lazar,
User Error, Tofu, Guitar, Interface Design, Towson">
```

Not all search engines will use these meta tags, but on the other hand, they will not hurt your download speed, so there is no downside to including them. Better to include them than not include them.

4. You can pay to have your Web site highlighted in a search engine such as Google. This may be an option only for organizations with large budgets. More information on this option is available at http://www.google.com/ads/.

5. If your Web site is in a specialized topic area, try to determine if there are any Web sites that serve as search engines for that specific area of study. For instance, for those working in the field of human-computer

interaction, there is a search engine called the HCI Bibliography. This site not only includes journals and books related to HCI, but also provides links to Web sites on HCI related topics (see Figure 10.6).

Considerations for Site Redesign

Most of this chapter is not of great concern to those who are redesigning an existing Web site. Implementation is a relatively simple step for those who are redesigning a site. In designing a Web site for the first time, the Web development team and the client have to grapple with the issue of where to host the site and whether to purchase a domain name. For those who are redesigning a site however, these decisions have likely already been made. However, it's certainly possible that the client organization has decided, as a part of the site redesign, to change the ISP or purchase a new domain name.

In most cases, the new Web site will remain in the same location as the old Web site. Having the redesigned site in the same URL location as the old site is impor-

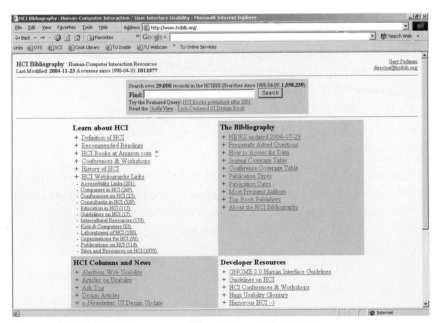

Figure 10.6 Specialized search engines, such as the HCI Bibliography, can be used to market a Web site.

tant, because this directly relates to the marketing of the Web site. If the Web site already exists, there are users who visit the site, who have links on their Web pages to the site, and who have the site bookmarked in their browser. Hopefully, through previous marketing, the Web site receives user traffic. In that case, you do not want to move the site to another URL location. The worst thing is for users to attempt to visit a site and find that it is no longer there.

When implementing a site redesign, it might be useful to place a small message on the Web site saying, "We hope you like our new Web site design. Here's why we did it. Contact us if you have any suggestions." It would be useful to do a small marketing campaign to the target population when a site redesign is completed. E-mail messages can be sent out over listservers or newsgroups to let users know that the Web site has changed, and to encourage them to revisit the site. The marketing should provide a good reason why users should revisit the site, such as: "Because we care about you, the user, we have made the Web site easier to use, and we now offer more content!"

If users have specific pages bookmarked, they should be able to find the same content at the same URLs. No user wants to see a "404-file not found" in their browser window. However, if the client organization feels strongly about changing the URL, then it is important to market this fact. A great deal of marketing (as described earlier in this chapter) should be done to let the users know that the Web site is moving. In addition, information about the new Web site and the new URL should appear when users request the old URL. When users request the old URL, <meta> tags can be placed on the old Web page to pull the user to the new Web page. These <meta> tags can be used in the following way:

```
<meta http-equiv= "refresh" content="5;
url=http://www.newurl.org">
```

where http://www.newurl.org is the new Web site that users should be directed to, and 5 is the number of seconds between the time the page is loaded and when the new Web page is requested. Although this is not a perfect solution, this is better than not directing the user to the new Web site.

The implementation stage of Web development is exciting.

- The Web site has been coded and has gone through both functionality and usability testing.

- HTML files are then transferred to the permanent host server, and the Web site "goes live."

- The whole world can now see the site that the development team has worked hard to create.

- Marketing of the Web site to the target user population must be done to let users know about the existence of the site. After all, the site can be a success only if users visit it.

Design Exercise

Imagine that you are in charge of marketing a Web site for a company that sells popcorn and taffy at a New Jersey beach. Although the beach is crowded during the summer only, the company sells its products all year long. The company hopes that a Web site will help with sales during the cold winter months. There are many happy customers within a few hours drive of the beach. What are some ways that you would market this site? How would you reach the customers who purchase items during the summer to inform them about the existence of the site? Name at least four ways that you would market the site to the target user population.

Discussion Questions

1. What is an online community, and why might it be useful for marketing?

2. What qualities make up a good domain name?

3. What does it mean for a Web site to "go live?"

4. What are two different methods of marketing a Web site through a search engine?

5. What are some methods of marketing a Web site that do not incur additional expenses?

6. Why is it important to determine which sites link to a Web site?

7. Why shouldn't dashes be used as a part of a URL?

Suggested Reading

Burdman, J. (1999). *Collaborative Web Development*. Reading, MA: Addison-Wesley.

Burgee, L. (2001). "Internationalization of Web Sites: The Next Great Challenge in Interface Design." Proceedings of the Human-Computer Interaction International (HCII) Conference, 106–110.

Cockburn, A., & Jones, S. (1996). "Which Way Now? Analysing and Easing Inadequacies in WWW Navigation." *International Journal of Human-Computer Studies*, 45(1), 105–129.

Eggen, D. (July 23, 2000). "States' Plates Say It." *The Washington Post*.

Jansen, B., & Pooch, U. (2001). "A Review of Web Searching Studies and a Framework for Future Research." *Journal of the American Society for Information Science and Technology*, 52(3), 235–246.

Lazar, J. (2003). "The World Wide Web." In J. Jacko & A. Sears (Eds.), *The Handbook of Human-Computer Interaction*, (pp. 714–730). Mahwah, NJ: Lawrence Erlbaum Associates.

Niederst, J. (1999). *Web Design in a Nutshell*. Sebastopol, CA: O'Reilly and Associates.

Powell, T., Jones, D., & Cutts, D. (1998). *Web Site Engineering: Beyond Web Page Design*. Upper Saddle River, NJ: Prentice Hall.

Preece, J. (2000). *Online Communities: Designing Usability, Supporting Sociability*. New York: John Wiley & Sons.

Sweeney, S. (1999). *101 Ways to Promote Your Web Site*. Gulf Breeze, FL: Maximum Press.

chapter 11

Maintaining and Evaluating Web Sites

After reading this chapter, you will be able to:

- Maintain content on a Web site.
- Evaluate Web site usage using surveys.
- Reach nonusers of a Web site and figure out why they are not users!
- Use Web site logs to understand user behavior.
- Decide when it is appropriate to redesign a Web site.

Introduction

After a Web site is implemented, if the Web development life cycle was followed properly, the site will meet the needs of the targeted users at the time of the site's implementation. But over time, this situation may change. Content must be maintained continuously because users might want new content and features, targeted users might change, and competition might increase. Over time, the technology might change as well. Periodic evaluations must be performed to determine if the Web site meets the needs of users, if there are any problems, and if changes need to be made. Outside factors, such as newer browser versions, or changing HTML standards, might necessitate a Web site redesign. Many large-scale traditional informational systems have been running for 15–20 years. Although this longevity is admirable, it's impossible to predict what the Web will be like 10 years from a given date. The technical foundations for the Web have been in existence since around 1990, and at that time, it would have been impossible to predict what the Web looks like today. Therefore, it's especially important to evaluate a Web site continuously to determine if it meets the needs of the users.

Maintenance of Web Sites

It is of paramount importance to maintain the data and information on a Web site. If the information is stale and out of date, users will not continue to visit the site. There should be a clear process for determining what needs to be updated, who has the responsibility for updates, and how frequently updates should be made. During conceptual design, the developer should have noted which Web pages will need to be updated most frequently. For instance, a calendar or a Web page that describes current events should be updated frequently. However, all Web pages should be updated frequently enough so that the information presented on the Web page is current. In addition, Web pages should note the date on which they were last updated. The date alone provides reassurance to the user that the information is current. If any Web pages change location, meaning that the same content is now located at a different URL, the old URL should provide information on where the content is currently located for at least one year after the content has moved.

Another type of maintenance involves making sure that all of the links on the site still lead to active sites. Linked Web sites are outside of the client organization's control. These outside sites may change URLs, or may simply disappear. Users can become frustrated if they receive a lot of "404-File not found" error messages, and if a Web site has numerous dead links, it can lower the user's perception of the quality of the site. Links can be checked by hand, or there are a number of Web sites that can check for dead links.

Evaluation of Web Sites

Evaluation is an important aspect of maintenance activities in traditional information systems. Without evaluation, it's impossible to know whether users are still happy with the system, whether changes need to be made, or even if a new system needs to be developed. There should be periodic evaluations of the Web site to ensure that it meets the needs of the users, and that there are no functionality or usability problems. Although the Web site originally might have met the needs of the users, those needs might have changed since the original Web site launch. There are actually two different approaches to evaluating a site: user perceptions and satisfaction, and actual statistics on the usage of the site.

Knowledge of user perceptions is gained through techniques such as surveys, interviews, and focus groups. Knowledge of Web site usage statistics is gained through examining Web site logs, information scent, and other techniques. Both methods examine Web site usage, but from different points of view. User perceptions of usage address how satisfied they are, if they feel that the Web site helps them meet their task goals, and how likely they are to return to the site. Surveys, interviews, and focus groups provide this type of feedback. Even informal e-mails to the Webmaster might contain a user's opinion of the site or a notification of a problem, such as old content, incorrect links, or a technical error. User feedback should receive attention! It's likely that if there is a problem with the Web site, for every user who e-mails about the problem, there are more users who experienced the same problem but did not send an e-mail about it. A link (or a Web-based form) should be provided on the site so that users can easily make suggestions or provide feedback. The following Hands-On Example provides an example of when user complaints sent via e-mail actually helped drive the redesign of a Web site for iBuy Lucent.

Redesigning the iBuy Lucent E-Commerce Site

Usability was not originally a concern for the iBuy Lucent e-commerce Web site. However, after the initial site release, users (customers) submitted many unsolicited e-mail complaints about the Web site. The complaints related to order status screens, search engines, screen layouts, and overall site navigation. Due to the complaints, it was decided that a redesign of the site was necessary. Follow-up phone calls to some of the users who complained, helped developers to understand the problems. Based on this feedback, the e-commerce site was redesigned for improved usability. Color schemes changed, links were added, data that had been presented on multiple screens was combined onto one screen, and the layout of data presentation was changed. After a new iteration of the Web site, some of the users who had originally complained took part in usability testing of the redesigned site. Usability testing showed that attractiveness and ease of use ratings for the new site were higher, and user task performance stayed constant for some users and improved for others (Smith '00).

Hands-On Example

Web site usage statistics can also be helpful in evaluating the Web site. For instance, in examining the data, if users use the search engine much more frequently than the provided site navigation, it might mean that the navigation is confusing. The usage statistics can tell which pages are most popular and which are not. It's possible to identify Web sites that are driving traffic to your site. A high number of errors on one portion of the Web site (e.g., registration forms) highlights an area that needs help.

Using Surveys for Evaluation

A popular technique for evaluating Web sites is a survey. The advantages of using surveys are numerous. They are low-cost, easy to develop, and can collect data from a large number of people in a small amount of time (an in-depth discussion of surveys is available in Chapter 4). When responding to surveys, users can indicate whether the Web site meets their needs and what they like and do not like about the site. These surveys are easier to implement than the initial surveys that were used to collect requirements for the new site because there is now an established population of users.

Surveys for site evaluation can be sent via e-mail, placed on a Web site, or sent via paper (if a list of mailing addresses is available). Web-based surveys can simply be placed on the site, and users can be asked to fill them out when visiting the site. When users access the existing Web site, they can be asked to fill out a short list of questions, usually implemented using HTML forms. These questions can relate to user content needs, user computing environment, or any of the other important topics discussed in Chapter 3. Those responses can then be used to determine whether changes need to be made to the site.

If users must log in to access the site, or if the target user population is very well defined (see Chapter 2), then a random sample of users can be drawn to participate in evaluation activities. Those selected can be informed when they log in that they have been selected to take part in the evaluation (see the Hands-On Example on the next page). If users aren't required to log in, then a strict random sample of users isn't possible, but a diverse sample of users is sufficient. Demographic survey questions can collect the data needed to determine if the responses to the evaluation survey are diverse. Or a random sampling of usage (not users) can be performed, where, for instance, every fifth user receives a pop-up survey.

There are a number of surveys to assist in Web site evaluation that have already been developed and tested. They include the Website Motivational Analysis Checklist (WebMAC) and the Information Quality Survey. Information about

Hands-On Example

Evaluating the Cleveland Freenet and the Texas Educational Network

Anderson and Gansneder conducted an evaluation of the Cleveland Freenet using electronic surveys. The Cleveland Freenet provides communication tools, such as bulletin boards, electronic mail, and databases. Users are required to log in every time they want to access the Cleveland Freenet. To develop the sample in their study, Anderson and Gansneder examined a log file containing all of the logins in a two-week period. Then they selected a random sample of 600 users, using SPSS, a widely used program for statistical analysis. The 600 randomly selected users received e-mail information about the survey. The same sampling methodology was used by Anderson and Harris in a study of the Texas Educational Network (TENET).

In both the Cleveland Freenet and the TENET, users were required to log in to access the networked resources. Therefore, a database of user information already existed. The researchers selected a random sample of registered, active users. This same methodology can be applied to any well-defined population of users, where the users must log in to utilize resources. Random samples can be drawn from databases of registered users. The population can be further segmented before the sample is drawn, in order to include only users who logged in within the previous two weeks (as in the Cleveland study), users who accessed specific tools or resources, or any other distinction. After the sample is drawn, when the selected users log in, they can be notified of the existence and importance of the survey.

(Anderson '95; Anderson '97)

these surveys follows. However, it's sometimes preferable to write evaluation questions that specifically relate to the target user population and mission of the Web site.

WebMAC Survey. The WebMAC, developed by Ruth Small and Marilyn Arnone, is a set of surveys used to evaluate the motivational quality of Web sites. Motivational quality is the concept of determining which features motivate users to spend time on a site and return later. These motivational behaviors, according to the authors, are determined by two factors, both of which must be present: Users must value the content or experience, and users must have a positive expectation for success within the particular Web site. The WebMAC series includes several different surveys related to different types of Web sites, such as business and education, to assist in determining where sites need improvement. For more information about the WebMAC surveys, go to http://digital-literacy.syr.edu/resources/Webmac.htm.

Sample Questions from the WebMAC E-Business Survey:

Place the appropriate number about this Web site on the line preceding each item.

3 = strongly agree

2 = somewhat agree

1 = somewhat disagree

0 = strongly disagree

NA = not applicable

_____ **1.** The homepage of this Web site is eye-catching and visually interesting.

_____ **2.** The information on this Web site is accurate and unbiased (or the bias is properly identified).

_____ **3.** The visuals (e.g., videos, photographs) and audio included on this Web site enhance the presentation of service(s) and information offered.

_____ **4.** The interface design makes the site easy to navigate.

_____ **5.** There are incentives at this site that motivate me to explore it.

_____ **6.** This Web site provides links to other relevant Web sites.

_____ **7.** This Web site provides enough information about the services offered.

_____ **8.** This Web site has a help function that I can use at any time.

_____ **9.** The screen layout of this Web site is attractive.

_____ **10.** This Web site provides information that allows me to judge the company's credibility.

_____ **11.** There is a menu or site map that helps me understand how this Web site is organized.

_____ **12.** I can control how fast I move through this Web site at all times.

_____ **13.** The information at this Web site is interestingly written.

_____ **14.** The information at this Web site appears to be current and up to date.

_____ **15.** The purpose of this Web site is always clear to me.

Hands-On Example

Evaluation Using Customer Satisfaction Surveys at IBM

Evaluation of industry Web sites takes place frequently. For instance, as IBM updated and improved their ease-of-use Web site http://www.ibm.com/easy, they used customer satisfaction surveys. Over time, the target user population broadened, going from HCI practitioners only, to include educators, executives, programmers, and developers. A total of 72 people, representing the different target user populations, participated in the evaluation surveys. Users of the IBM ease-of-use Web site were asked questions related to navigation, task efficiency, consistency, and overall user satisfaction. It was noted that the different user populations included within the survey respondents actually felt very differently about the effectiveness and usability of the Web site. In addition, users were not satisfied with the fact that over a period of time, updates to the content had not been made.

(Dong '00)

Information Quality Survey. An information quality survey was developed by Zhang, Keeling, and Pavur. It focuses on user perceptions of the quality of a Web site based on the homepage. They argue that if the user does not perceive the homepage to be high quality, then the user will not go any further into the Web site. This survey focuses on evaluation of the presentation, navigation, and quality of a Web site. Sample questions follow. More information on how the survey was developed is available in (Zhang '00).

Presentation

1. The use of graphics is very appropriate for this site.

Strongly Disagree		Neutral			Strongly Agree	
1	2	3	4	5	6	7

2. The design elements are not annoying or distracting.

Strongly Disagree		Neutral			Strongly Agree	
1	2	3	4	5	6	7

3. The amount of information displayed is just right.

Strongly Disagree		Neutral			Strongly Agree	
1	2	3	4	5	6	7

4. The colors in this Web site are pleasant.

Strongly Disagree			Neutral			Strongly Agree
1	2	3	4	5	6	7

5. This site organized its information in a way that is easy for me to understand.

Strongly Disagree			Neutral			Strongly Agree
1	2	3	4	5	6	7

6. The site's attractiveness invites me to go further into this site.

Strongly Disagree			Neutral			Strongly Agree
1	2	3	4	5	6	7

Navigation

7. The graphical presentation appears to be helpful in navigating.

Strongly Disagree			Neutral			Strongly Agree
1	2	3	4	5	6	7

8. I like the way the hyperlinks are embedded in this site's design.

Strongly Disagree			Neutral			Strongly Agree
1	2	3	4	5	6	7

9. Someone without knowledge about this company could easily find information.

Strongly Disagree			Neutral			Strongly Agree
1	2	3	4	5	6	7

10. Information links are located where I would expect them to be.

Strongly Disagree			Neutral			Strongly Agree
1	2	3	4	5	6	7

11. This site would enable me to get precise information quickly.

Strongly   Strongly
Disagree   Neutral   Agree
1   2   3   4   5   6   7

12. This site has a navigationally efficient layout.

Strongly   Strongly
Disagree   Neutral   Agree
1   2   3   4   5   6   7

Quality

13. Information appears to be believable.

Strongly   Strongly
Disagree   Neutral   Agree
1   2   3   4   5   6   7

14. I understand the purpose of this site.

Strongly   Strongly
Disagree   Neutral   Agree
1   2   3   4   5   6   7

15. I would recommend this site to a colleague.

Strongly   Strongly
Disagree   Neutral   Agree
1   2   3   4   5   6   7

16. This site appears to make it easy to correspond with the company.

Strongly   Strongly
Disagree   Neutral   Agree
1   2   3   4   5   6   7

17. I clearly understand the services and products of this company by looking at this site.

Strongly   Strongly
Disagree   Neutral   Agree
1   2   3   4   5   6   7

18. Viewing this site gives me a good image of the company.

Strongly   Strongly
Disagree   Neutral   Agree
1   2   3   4   5   6   7

Reaching Nonusers: Interviews and Focus Groups

An interesting situation can occur where users simply are not using a Web site. In situations like this, placing a Web survey on the Web site would not yield useful data, because what you want to find out is why people *aren't* coming to the Web site. In situations like this, the best technique is to access a population of users that includes potential users of the site, as well as actual users. For instance, if a professional organization has a Web site that almost no one uses, it would be good to contact a random sample of members in the organization, including many who *aren't* using the site, to find out why Web site usage is low.

Even if people are using a Web site on a regular basis, it's still helpful to evaluate the site with people who aren't currently using it, to find out what resources or changes, would entice them to use the site. An example of this occurred when evaluating the Blacksburg Electronic Village (BEV) (http://www.bev.net), an online community based on the town of Blacksburg, Virginia. To evaluate the online community, researchers sent paper surveys to the citizens of Blacksburg. By doing this, the researchers were able to access the entire population of Blacksburg, which was known to consist of many users of BEV. By sending surveys to the citizens of Blacksburg, researchers not only accessed users of BEV, but also accessed potential users who were not using BEV (Patterson '97).

Other approaches to understand users' needs include interviews and focus groups (discussed in detail in Chapter 4). If users can be accessed physically, then both interviews and focus groups can help with gaining an understanding of how users perceive the Web sites, and how satisfied they are. These techniques have been used in evaluating state library Web sites such as SAILOR (Bertot '96), DelAWARE (Bertot '98), and Online at PA (McClure '97). By talking face-to-face with potential and actual users, it's possible to learn more about why users do or do not use a Web site. This type of information gathering method tends to be less structured and offers less control for the researcher, so to gather information using these techniques effectively, it's necessary to have an experienced focus group moderator.

Web Usage Data

When users access a Web site, a trail of data is collected by the server that hosts the site. The trail of data tracks all user movements and choices—which site the user came from, what pages the user accessed, when the pages were accessed, requests to the site search engine, which links were clicked, and what requests were made in error. This Web site log data is very useful in tracking the usage patterns of the user population as a whole. Examining Web site logs provides a different, but useful approach for Web site evaluation. Web site logs can be examined in multiple ways, all leading toward an understanding of usage patterns. Web site logs don't unveil user perceptions or feelings, or a sense of satisfaction or frustration toward the site. However, much useful feedback can be gained. For instance, the statistics from a Web site search engine can be examined to determine which terms are being searched. The data on what terms users want to find can be compared to the terminology actually used on the site, to determine the match (or mismatches) between the user terminology and the Web site terminology. As previously discussed, confusing terminology can be a major problem in site design and navigation. This is just one example of how log data can be useful in examining usage patterns of a Web site.

When a user requests a Web page, the request is sent to a Web server, which responds to the request. In doing so, the user's Web browser sends a number of pieces of data to the server. When responding to the user's request, the Web server records data about the request, such as the time of the request, the IP address of the user making the request, and the file requested. From the data provided by Web site logs, it's possible to get a rough estimate of important information, such as how many users visit a site, what pages are most popular, and what types of users view the site.

How the server records the data partially depends on the Web server software. The Web developer (or Webmaster) can also specify what is to be recorded. The data can be recorded in a number of separate log files, or it can be recorded together. There can be as many as four separate log files—the transfer log, the error log, the referrer log, and the agent log—or this same data can be concentrated in onc log file.

The transfer log records the file requested, the time of the request, and the IP address of the user making the request. This data determines who is accessing the Web site, and which pages are most popular. An example of this is shown in the Hands-On Example on the next page. The error log records requests that were not able to be successfully fulfilled because the user entered the incorrect file name, or tried to retrieve a file for which file permission was lacking. This data determines where users frequently make errors. (For example, another Web site might be providing a link to an incorrect URL on the client's Web site.) It can indicate problems that need to be corrected.

Hands-On Example

A Sample of Transfer Logs for saber.towson.edu

24.175.78.198 - - [01/Jul/2005:14:41:07 -0400] "GET /webink/theInsert.js HTTP/1.1" 304 -
10.21.11.21 - - [01/Jul/2005:14:41:07 -0400] "GET /Homepage_Ani_077.swf HTTP/1.1" 304 -
10.21.11.21 - - [01/Jul/2005:14:41:08 -0400] "GET /webink/theInsert.js HTTP/1.1" 304 -
66.151.181.12 - - [01/Jul/2005:14:41:08 -0400] "GET /news/student/msg00780.html HTTP/1.1" 200 3178
67.138.46.120 - - [01/Jul/2005:14:41:09 -0400] "GET /tu/aboutlinks/did.you.know.html HTTP/1.1" 200 8439
10.21.11.21 - - [01/Jul/2005:14:41:10 -0400] "GET /tu/facultylinks/email-lookup.html HTTP/1.1" 304 -
10.21.11.21 - - [01/Jul/2005:14:41:10 -0400] "GET /tu/pageheads/pagehead.js HTTP/1.1" 304 -
24.187.74.75 - - [01/Jul/2005:14:41:11 -0400] "GET /webink/theInsert.js HTTP/1.1" 304 -
66.249.71.67 - - [01/Jul/2005:14:41:11 -0400] "GET /~roberts/301/P301Syllabus.doc HTTP/1.0" 200 81408
217.212.224.143 - - [01/Jul/2005:14:41:12 -0400] "GET /%7Educan/blurb.html HTTP/1.0" 200 5090
151.196.6.237 - - [01/Jul/2005:14:41:12 -0400] "GET / HTTP/1.0" 302 251
132.194.10.4 - - [01/Jul/2005:14:41:13 -0400] "GET /csme/mctp/Technology/Education.html HTTP/
    1.0" 200 35740
198.77.43.91 - - [01/Jul/2005:14:41:14 -0400] "GET /Homepage_Ani_077.swf HTTP/1.1" 200 83722
66.249.64.58 - - [01/Jul/2005:14:41:15 -0400] "GET /~larkin/210DOCS/exam2F2003.pdf HTTP/1.0" 200 146916
138.78.12.78 - - [01/Jul/2005:14:41:17 -0400] "GET /tu/facultylinks/employment.html HTTP/1.1" 200 416
64.231.38.48 - - [01/Jul/2005:14:41:18 -0400] "GET /favicon.ico HTTP/1.1" 404 4629
150.140.130.223 - - [01/Jul/2005:14:41:21 -0400] "GET /~schmitt/pyro/chapter2.html HTTP/1.1" 200 18631
10.27.1.86 - - [01/Jul/2005:14:41:21 -0400] "GET / HTTP/1.1" 304 -
10.27.1.86 - - [01/Jul/2005:14:41:21 -0400] "GET /tu/maingraphics/javaScripts/tu_Menu2.js HTTP/1.1" 304 -
10.27.1.86 - - [01/Jul/2005:14:41:21 -0400] "GET /tu/maingraphics/javaScripts/fw_menu.js HTTP/1.1" 304 -
10.27.1.86 - - [01/Jul/2005:14:41:21 -0400] "GET /webink/Announcement.js HTTP/1.1" 304 -
198.77.43.91 - - [01/Jul/2005:14:41:22 -0400] "GET /webink/theInsert.js HTTP/1.1" 200 1814
10.27.1.86 - - [01/Jul/2005:14:41:22 -0400] "GET /Homepage_Ani_077.swf HTTP/1.1" 304 -
10.27.1.86 - - [01/Jul/2005:14:41:23 -0400] "GET /webink/theInsert.js HTTP/1.1" 304 -
66.166.187.106 - - [01/Jul/2005:14:41:26 -0400] "GET /tu/alumni/welcome.html HTTP/1.1" 302 236
68.251.51.157 - - [01/Jul/2005:14:41:28 -0400] "GET /csme/mctp/Courses/PhysicalScience/ClassLog.txt
    HTTP/1.0" 200 73365
212.56.99.88 - - [01/Jul/2005:14:41:28 -0400] "GET /~flynn/toys.html HTTP/1.1" 200 8013
69.251.90.189 - - [01/Jul/2005:14:41:28 -0400] "GET /marketing/career/careers1.htm HTTP/1.1" 302 310
69.143.197.110 - - [01/Jul/2005:14:41:28 -0400] "GET / HTTP/1.1" 302 263
70.17.202.129 - - [01/Jul/2005:14:41:31 -0400] "GET /tu/maingraphics/javaScripts/tu_Menu2.js HTTP/
    1.1" 200 19891
70.17.202.129 - - [01/Jul/2005:14:41:31 -0400] "GET / HTTP/1.1" 200 21826
70.17.202.129 - - [01/Jul/2005:14:41:31 -0400] "GET /tu/maingraphics/javaScripts/fw_menu.js HTTP/
    1.1" 200 22885
70.17.202.129 - - [01/Jul/2005:14:41:32 -0400] "GET /webink/Announcement.js HTTP/1.1" 200 92
204.10.38.66 - - [01/Jul/2005:14:41:32 -0400] "GET /heartfield/reviews/Jovanovi.html HTTP/1.1" 200 9539
204.10.38.66 - - [01/Jul/2005:14:41:32 -0400] "GET /heartfield/reviews/Jovanovi.html HTTP/1.1" 200 9539
204.10.38.66 - - [01/Jul/2005:14:41:32 -0400] "GET / HTTP/1.1" 200 21826
70.17.202.129 - - [01/Jul/2005:14:41:33 -0400] "GET /Homepage_Ani_077.swf HTTP/1.1" 200 83722

The referrer log records the URL of the Web page that the user was viewing when he or she sent a request for the Web page. This data is useful because it spotlights which Web sites are driving user traffic to the client's Web site.

The agent log records the name and version of the user agent (the browser) that is sending the request for the Web page. This data can determine what browser is being used.

All of this data is recorded in log files, which can be long and difficult to read, since they can contain data on hundreds or thousands of requests per day. By itself, a log file doesn't tell a story. However, when the data in log files is summarized and presented, trends are revealed. For instance, based on the URLs that were requested by users but not available (404-File Not Found errors), it can be discovered which pages no longer exist. This might point to the need to either ask the sites that are referring to an incorrect URL to change their link, or have an automatic redirect at the incorrect URL that directs the user to the correct URL. The referrer log can also indicate which sites are linking to your Web site correctly. The agent log can track browser usage so that the primary browsers of the user population can be determined.

Since summary data and trend analysis can be difficult to determine by just reading the data, a software analysis package is traditionally used. There are various types of software. Some types run on a local Web server and others run on remote servers (where data is sent). Desktop versions of applications (where the data is downloaded to the desktop to be analyzed) are also available. Some of the most popular software/service in this area includes ClickTracks (http://www.clicktracks.com/), NetTracker (http://www.sane.com/), and WebTrends (http://www.webtrends.com/Default.aspx). For a complete list of tools and services, visit http://dir.yahoo.com/Computers_and_Internet/Software/Internet/World_Wide_Web/Servers/Log_Analysis_Tools/. Information visualization tools, such as Spotfire, can be used to analyze the data in Web site logs. Researchers working in the area of information scent have gone even further, using the data from past usage to predict future user behavior within a site, or how changes to the site would impact usage (Chi '00).

It's important to note that counting a Web hit is not equivalent to counting a user. If a user accesses a Web page with five files—the HTML file and four graphics, this totals five hits, but it's actually one page viewed by one user. When that same user views other pages on the Web site, these page views are recorded in the Web site logs, but this is still only one user. So, it's possible that a Web site claiming to have one million hits might have only 10,000 users. It's sometimes hard to identify unique users because some ISPs do not provide users with a unique and permanent IP address, but rather, reassign users an IP address from a pool of IP addresses each time they log on.

Regardless of how the data in Web site logs is presented, the question is, what do the statistics mean? The data itself doesn't tell a story, and while the software analysis packages can help summarize the data, they also do not tell the story. Trends in the data help point to the important evaluation issues for the Web site, which can be interpreted differently. And interviews or surveys with users can confirm these various data interpretations. Some common measures include long-term trends of page views (page views being different from hits). If, over a period of time (say, six months), the number of page views holds steady or increases, this is a good thing (as it means that the user population is steady or growing). At the same time, if these long-term trends for page views decrease, this might mean that it is time to reassess whether the current site is meeting the needs of the users. Feedback from users (such as e-mail complaints) can help to determine the cause of this. If the number of page views are consistent over time, yet fall short of what was hoped for, this might point to the need for more marketing to bring people to the site. Looking at hourly traffic patterns to the site over a long period of time (e.g., traffic is highest in the morning) can also give you a sense of the daily habits of users. If many users view the homepage but go no further within the site, this may indicate that there are problems with the homepage, related to the layout, technical problems, or graphical presentation.

While the measures discussed refer to usage patterns, Web logs can also reveal information about users. For instance, the data from the Web logs can present information about user browsers. This can be helpful to determine more about the target user population. Based on the geographic locations of the users requesting pages (which can broadly be gained from the domain names), a geographical analysis can be presented. The type of domain (such as .edu) from which users access the Web pages can also reveal information about the demographics of the users. While this might not be obvious with, say, 50 users, when data on thousands of users is collected, some interesting trends can be revealed.

When collecting user perception data and usage data, an effort should be made to track data on how user-centered design activities played a role in the success of the Web site. Earlier in the book, we discussed that those working in the field must frequently justify the costs of their user involvement activities. When possible, the outcomes of these user involvement activities should be measured. They can help to justify user involvement activities in the future. This is known as tracking the return on investment (ROI) for the user involvement activities. Although this is useful data that can help to justify the expenses of user involvement in the future, this type of data is rarely tracked. If user involvement in Web

Web site maintenance and evaluation involve a number of different tasks. Content must be continuously updated.

- Old and outdated links need to be trimmed.

- Periodic evaluations should be performed to determine if the Web site still meets the needs of the users.

- Satisfaction surveys and Web site logs can be used to assist with periodic evaluations.

- The site logs help to uncover usage trends over time.

- If the evaluation determines that the Web site no longer meets the needs of the users, then it might be time to redesign the site.

- At that point, the Web development life cycle starts again.

Design Exercise

You have been asked to lead a user evaluation of the Web site for a high school. The Web site has been up for one year. The target user population includes students, staff, and parents. What methods would you use to evaluate the site? How could surveys be used? Which group would make a good focus group? How would you reach nonusers of the Web site? How could Web site logs be used?

Discussion Questions

1. How is updating content different from redesigning a Web site?

2. When is it appropriate to redesign a Web site?

3. What are some of the different evaluation surveys available, and how do they differ?

4. What are Web site logs, and how are they useful when evaluating a Web site?

5. What is the difference between a hit and a page view?

6. What are good ways to evaluate why people are *not* using a Web site?

7. Over a 6-month period, what type of insights can page view data give you?

8. Why are the error logs useful data? How should they influence the site design?

Suggested Reading

Anderson, S., & Gansneder, B. (1995). "Using Electronic Mail Surveys and Computer-Monitored Data for Studying Computer-Mediated Communication Systems." *Social Science Computer Review*, 13(1), 33–46.

Anderson, S., & Harris, J. (1997). "Factors Associated with Amount of Use and Benefits Obtained by Users of a Statewide Educational Telecomputing Network." *Educational Technology Research and Development*, 45(1), 19–50.

Bertot, J., & McClure, C. (1996). *SAILOR Network Assessment: Final Report Compendium*. Baltimore, MD: Division of Library Development and Services, Maryland State Department of Education.

Bertot, J., McClure, C., & Lazar, J. (1998). *The DelAWARE Evaluation Project: Site Visit Report*. Dover, Delaware: Delaware Division of Libraries.

Buchanan, R., & Lukaszewski, C. (1997). *Measuring the Impact of Your Web Site*. New York: John Wiley and Sons.

Chi, E., Pirolli, P., & Pitkow, J. (2000). "The Scent of a Site: A System for Analyzing and Predicting Information Scent, Usage, and Usability of a Web Site." Proceedings of the CHI 2000: Human Factors in Computing, 161–168.

Dong, J., & Martin, S. (2000). "Iterative Usage of Customer Satisfaction Surveys to Assess an Evolving Web Site." Proceedings of the Human Factors and the Web. Available at: http://www.tri.sbc.com/hfWeb/.

Hert, C. (2001). "User-Centered Evaluation and Its Connection to Design." In C. McClure & J. Bertot (Eds.), *Evaluating Networked Information Services: Techniques, Policy, and Issues* (pp. 155–173). Medford, NJ: Information Today.

Hochheiser, H., & Shneiderman, B. (2001). "Using Interactive Visualizations of WWW Log Data to Characterize Access Patterns and Inform Site Design." *Journal of the American Society for Information Science and Technology*, 52(4), 331–343.

Hoffer, J., George, J., & Valacich, J. (2002). *Modern Systems Analysis and Design* (3rd ed.). Reading, MA: Addison-Wesley.

Larsen, L., & Henry, D. (1998). "Nightmare on Webstreet." Proceedings of the ACM SUGUCCS Conference on User Services, 157–162.

Lazar, J., & Preece, J. (2001). "Using Electronic Surveys to Evaluate Networked Resources: from Idea to Implementation." In C. McClure & J. Bertot (Eds.), *Evaluating Networked Information Services: Techniques, Policy, and Issues*, (pp. 137–154). Medford, NJ: Information Today.

Lazar, J., Ratner, J., Jacko, J., & Sears, A. (2004). "User Involvement in the Web Development Process: Methods and Cost-Justification." Proceedings of the 10th International Conference on Industry, Engineering, and Management Systems, 223-232.

McClure, C., & Bertot, J. (1997). *Evaluation of the Online at PA Libraries Project: Public Access to the Internet Through Public Libraries.* Harrisburg, PA: Pennsylvania Department of Education, Office of Commonwealth Libraries.

Navarro, A., & Khan, T. (1998). *Effective Web Design.* San Francisco: Sybex.

Patterson, S. (1997). "Evaluating the Blacksburg Electronic Village." In A. Cohill, and Kavanaugh, K. (Ed.), *Community Networks: Lessons from Blacksburg, Virginia,* (pp. 55–71). Boston: Artech House.

Powell, T., Jones, D., & Cutts, D. (1998). *Web Site Engineering: Beyond Web Page Design.* Upper Saddle River, NJ: Prentice Hall.

Preece, J., Rogers, Y., & Sharp, H. (2002). *Interaction Design: Beyond Human-Computer Interaction.* New York: John Wiley & Sons.

Rubin, J. (2001). "Introduction to Log Analysis Techniques." In C. McClure & J. Bertot (Eds.), *Evaluating Networked Information Services: Techniques, Policy, and Issues,* (pp. 197–212). Medford, NJ: Information Today.

Small, R., & Arnone, M. (2000). "Evaluating the Effectiveness of Web Sites." In B. Clarke & S. Lehaney (Eds.), *Human-Centered Methods in Information Systems: Current Research and Practice,* (pp. 91–101). Hershey, PA: Idea Group Publishing.

Smith, J., Bubb-Lewis, C., & Suh, Y. (2000). "Taking Order Status to Task: Improving Usability on the IBuy Lucent Website." Proceedings of the 2000 Conference on Human Factors and the Web. Available at: http://www.tri.sbc.com/hfWeb.

Stewart, C., Grover, D., & Vernon, R. (1998). "Changing Almost Everything and Keeping Almost Everyone Happy." *CAUSE/EFFECT,* 21(3), 39–46.

Stout, R. (1997). *Web Site Stats.* Berkeley, California: Osborne McGraw Hill.

Zhang, X., Keeling, K., & Pavur, R. (2000). "Information Quality of Commercial Web Site Homepages: An Explorative Analysis." Proceedings of the International Conference on Information Systems, 164–175.

kodak.com

Jack Yu
University of Michigan

Since the completion of this user-centered design project, kodak.com has expanded its emphasis from being primarily an informational and product sales Web site to include a focus on being the Web's premier photo community, offering users a variety of interactive picture enhancement, printing, storage, sharing, and learning opportunities online. Subsequent redesigns of the kodak.com homepage have reflected the ways in which Kodak's business has grown and continues to grow and change. Despite the change in the current site mission, this case study is one of the most-detailed case studies in user-centered design for a web site, and it is rare for a company to provide so much information on their design process. Jack Yu was a User Interaction Designer at the Eastman Kodak Company when he lead the kodak.com redesign effort. At the time of this book's publication, Jack has been on leave while pursuing an MBA degree at the University of Michigan Business school.

Background

Kodak is the world's largest manufacturer and marketer of imaging products and has one of the world's most recognized and respected brand names.

We make photographic films and papers for a wide range of consumer, entertainment, professional, business, and health-related uses. We develop, manufacture, and market traditional and digital cameras, photographic plates and chemicals, processing and audiovisual equipment, as well as document man-

*agement products, applications software, printers, and other business equip-
ment. We also provide photographic processing and repair and maintenance
services.*

Kodak products are sold throughout the world.

(From the Eastman Kodak Share Program Prospectus—
http://www.kodak.com/go/invest)

kodak.com, the Web site of the Eastman Kodak Company, caters to a very diverse
audience. Besides serving a broad consumer market for photographic products,
Kodak develops, manufactures, and delivers products and services for a variety of
business, commercial, and work-related applications, and the content served on
kodak.com is appropriately varied.

From 1995 to 1997, the kodak.com *top level*—including the homepage and the
pages to which it linked directly—retained essentially the same standard page
layout, visual design motif, and information architecture. Figure A.1 shows the
design of the Kodak homepage during this time and Figure A.2 shows a top-level
page from this time. The two-year period was one of tremendous growth for
kodak.com; traffic to the site grew to roughly a quarter of a million page views
daily, and many new types of content were added to the site. At the beginning of
1997, it became evident that the top level of kodak.com needed to be redesigned
to accommodate this tremendous growth. From the outset, our goal was to drive
the redesign with an understanding of the needs and desires of kodak.com's
diverse user population and the business goals of the company.

Mission of the Web Site

In 1997, Kodak utilized its Web site primarily in a marketing and communications capacity. The most abundant content on kodak.com included marketing
and technical support information for Kodak products, educational materials
about photography, and corporate information.

The primary function of the kodak.com homepage was to act as a gateway to the
tens of thousands of pages on the site. We wanted the redesigned version to play
this role effectively, and meet the following internal requirements.

1. Have the flexibility to *change* in appearance, content, and emphasis
    depending on company or user needs and priorities. If Kodak's business
    audiences changed, or a new product was launched, or an important
    announcement was made, or if we found that a certain area of the site

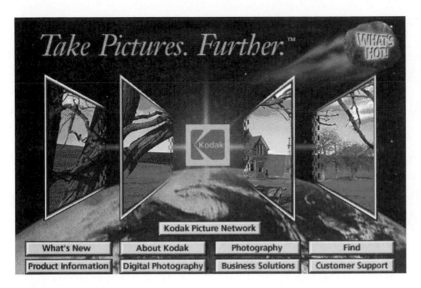

| What's New | Product Information | About Kodak | Digital Photography |
| Photography | Business Solutions | Find | Customer Support | What's Hot |
| Kodak Picture Network |

| Find | Customer Support |
Contact *webmaster@kodak.com* if this server presents any problems.

Preview Our New Home Page

Photo Credit for Pictures

Copyright and Privacy Practices

© Eastman Kodak Company, 1994-1997

Figure A.1 Kodak's homepage from 1995 to 1997.

just didn't work well, we wanted to be able to modify the homepage easily. The previous homepage did not allow for easy modification.

2. Present a compelling "teaser" for featured information on a regular basis.

3. Showcase outstanding photography. Kodak is the world leader in imaging; we wanted the homepage to convey this message through the display of dazzling imagery.

4. Convey the following attributes:

   a. Kodak is consumer-friendly.

   b. Kodak is an imaging technology leader.

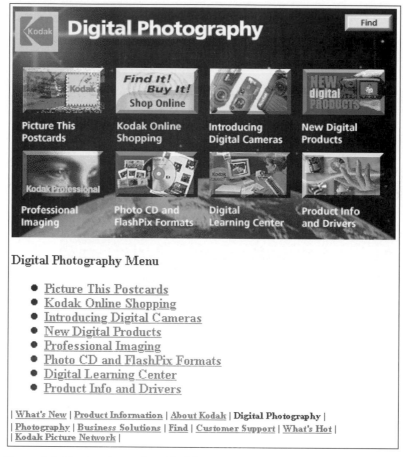

Figure A.2 Top-level page from Kodak 1995 to 1997.

c. Kodak has a worldwide presence.

d. Beyond the general consumer, Kodak also has a stake in professional, business, and government interests.

e. Kodak wants to build a community of people who repeatedly visit our Web site.

f. Kodak is selling products/services on the Web.

g. kodak.com has new and informative content that is continually updated.

h. kodak.com's content is diverse, i.e., interesting for a broad range of individuals.

Target User Population

There were a number of different user groups within the target user population for the Kodak Web site. We wanted the homepage design to cater to the following audiences, segmented by *information interest*.

1. **The consumer-imaging visitor:** one who is interested in imaging products and information for personal use. This represents a very broad segment of visitors, including the following:

   - a serious amateur photographer looking for advanced photography tips and technical information about films and cameras

   - a "point-and-shooter" looking for information about how to correct problem photographs and creative and innovative ways to share pictures

   - a "browser" seeking a new and compelling experience (such as Kodak Picture This postcards, Kodak Photonet online)

   - anyone looking to learn about new technologies or Kodak's progress and participation in them (such as digital photography)

2. **The "commercial-imaging" visitor:** one who is interested in imaging products, services, and solutions in the context of their work or profession. Efficient access to content, minimizing obstacles and "fluff," is key to the segment that includes business professionals, professional photographers, motion picture professionals, health professionals, government contractors, law enforcement personnel, printers, publishers, teachers, and others.

3. **The corporate visitor:** one who is interested in some aspect of Kodak as a company (as opposed to imaging information). This might include any of the following:

   - a reporter looking for corporate officer biographies or information about major corporate decisions and actions

   - a job seeker looking for employment opportunities

   - an investor interested in Kodak stock who wants to learn about the company's financial outlook and plans for future growth

   - a community leader looking for information about community events and sponsorships by Kodak

   - a person interested in environmental issues seeking information about Kodak's work processes and how they affect the environment

4. **The Kodak partner:** a person or company that has a relationship with or works with Kodak to provide solutions for others. Examples include

- a retailer or corporate reseller who sells Kodak products
- a software developer who creates solutions that use and/or interact with Kodak products and technology

5. **The surfer:** people who visit the Kodak site without any particular or specific information interest. They may be looking for fun and cool stuff or they may simply be curious about Kodak's Web presence.

We wanted the redesigned kodak.com top level to meet the needs of these different types of users; consequently, design development required input from various user groups.

Plan for Requirements Gathering

In order to establish user-centered requirements for the kodak.com redesign, we needed to gather as much data as possible regarding users' needs and current behaviors. A number of different techniques were employed to obtain this data. Since the site had existed for over two years, Web server logs and search logs were available and useful in indirectly monitoring users' interests. Other data gathering techniques, such as focus groups and usability tests, involved direct observation of test participants who represented the targeted user population.

Kodak business goals also heavily influenced the design requirements for the Web site redesign, and so interviews with the Web teams of many business units and corporate groups within Kodak were conducted. In cases where a business unit served a particularly hard to reach market segment—such as motion picture cinematographers or dentists—talking with business unit representatives was also an indirect way to determine user requirements because the representatives were experienced in working with users in their particular targeted market.

Web Server Logs

Analyzing Web server logs helped to determine what areas of kodak.com attracted the most traffic (hopefully corresponding to the areas of greatest user interest). Table A.1 shows the average number of daily visits for top-level pages; Table A.2 shows the average number of daily visits for second-level pages (those linked from top-level pages).

Table A.1 Average Daily Access for Top-Level Pages, February '96–January '97

Page	Average Daily Access	Percentage
Digital Imaging	2879	25.19
Photography	2353	20.59
Search	1980	17.32
Product Information	1033	9.04
What's New	1019	8.92
What's Hot	828	7.25
Customer Support	712	6.23
About Kodak	397	3.47
Business Solutions	228	1.99
Total access at this level	11429	100.00

Table A.2 Average Daily Accesses for Second-Level Pages, November '96–January '97

Page	Linked from	Average Daily Access
Kodak Picture This Postcards	Digital Imaging	13144
Digital Cameras	Digital Imaging	1337
Guide to Better Pictures	Photography	987
Feedback/Guestbook	Customer Support	954
Alphabetical Product Listing	Search, Product Information	903
Photo CD	Digital Imaging	651
Kodak Professional	Photography, Business Solutions	575
Product Types	Product Information	452
Digital Products Dealers	Customer Support	403
Professional Motion Imaging	Photography, Business Solutions	370
(Digital) Product Information	Digital Imaging	346
Software Drivers	Customer Support	344
Technical Information	Product Information, Customer Support	301
Table of Contents	Search	251
Press Releases	What's New, About Kodak	237
Zoomable Spatial Layout	Search	234
Digital Learning Center	Digital Imaging	228
Product Families	Product Information	224
Desktop Scanners	Digital Imaging	204
FlashPix	Digital Imaging	182

(continues next page)

Table A.2 (*continued*)

Page	Linked from	Average Daily Access
Kodak Online Services	Customer Support	164
Advanced Photo System	Photography	163
Corporate Information	About Kodak	159
Photography FAQ	Photography	142
Dye Sub Printers	Digital Imaging	136
FAQ	Customer Support	128
Call Kodak	Customer Support	128
Educational Solutions	Photography, Business Solutions	126
Capture, Manage, Store, Share	Product Information	122
Seminars/Events	Photography	121
Contact Kodak	About Kodak	111
Where to Buy	Customer Support	111
Business Units	About Kodak	94
Customer Chat	About Kodak	73
Business and Industry	Business Solutions	71
George Fisher, CEO	About Kodak	69
Graphical Overview	Search	68
Developer Relations	Product Information	62
Customer Equipment Services	Customer Support	62
Around the World	About Kodak	59
Photo CD Transfer Sites	Customer Support	55
Product Tradeshow Booth	Product Information	40
Service and Support	Business Solutions	35
Medical and Scientific	Business Solutions	32
Spatial Layout (Text)	Search	26
About this Server	About Kodak	25
Government Imaging Systems	Business Solutions	17
Image Magic	Photography	2

Search Logs

A search function was linked from the kodak.com homepage and from the footer of every page in the entire site. Data on the most popular searches made by users was available in the form of logs. Table A.3 lists the top 25 search requests in

Table A.3 Search Log Data for February–April 1997

Top 25 Search Topics	Number of Queries	Percent of All Queries
KODAK Picture This Postcards	17247	6.77
DC50, DC120, etc.	5589	2.19
Employment	4934	1.94
Sample pictures/Digital Images	4238	1.66
PHOTO CD	2548	1.00
Scanner	1629	0.64
Advantix film, Advanced Photo System (APS)	1586	0.62
FlashPix	1250	0.49
Film	1196	0.47
Xtol	1062	0.42
Printers	1062	0.42
Digital camera	992	0.39
Software	907	0.36
Prices	851	0.33
Diconix	819	0.32
Image Magic	709	0.28
Greetings	694	0.27
Digital imaging	644	0.25
Picture Disc	572	0.22
Super 8	571	0.22
Driver	551	0.22
Download	550	0.22
Camera	550	0.22
Photo enhancer	531	0.21
Infrared film	526	0.21
Above Total	51808	20.34
Total Queries	254933	

February–April 1997, along with the total occurrences of each query. This is interesting and useful data, because it showed that there needed to be easy access to the Kodak Picture This postcards feature and information on employment opportunities at Kodak. We knew that the Kodak Picture This postcards feature was the biggest traffic draw on kodak.com, but the fact that it was also the most popular search topic indicated that we needed to make it more easily accessible.

We did not realize that employment was as popular a topic as it was, representing the third most-searched topic on kodak.com. In the new design, both areas were linked directly from the homepage.

Interviews with Kodak Business Units

Eastman Kodak Company is a large corporation organized into business units that deliver products and services for specific markets. Examples of such business units include Kodak Professional, a unit that serves professional photographers and members of the printing and publishing industries, and Health Imaging, which markets medical imaging solutions to health care professionals, including radiologists, cardiologists, dentists, technicians, and hospital administrators. Each business unit has content developers and managers who handle the business unit's presence and content on kodak.com. Representatives from each business unit were interviewed to gain an understanding of

- the nature of their customers
- the customer needs to be met and the value to deliver via the Web
- the nature of their Web content
- other objectives they had for the Web

Focus Groups

Kodak enlisted the expertise of American Institutes for Research (http://www.air.org), a consulting firm specializing in behavioral and social science research, to plan and conduct these activities in different locations across the U.S. Focus groups were conducted with two different groups within the target user population of the Kodak Web site: "consumers" and "dealers." Consumers were defined as Web users who were interested in photography—purchasing at least four rolls of film annually but not employed as a professional photographer. Dealers were defined as retailers of digital photographic equipment, interested in using the Kodak Web site to find information about products.

Focus group sessions were held in three different U.S. cities: Lexington, Massachusetts; Dallas, Texas; and San Jose, California. Separate consumer and dealer focus groups were planned for each city, for six sessions. Because different moderators conducted the sessions, detailed moderator's scripts were necessary to ensure that the appropriate topics were covered (see Table A.4 for agenda of topics). See the following pages for an example of a detailed moderator's script.

Table A.4 Agenda of Topics for Consumer Focus Group

Introduction	5 minutes
Digital Imaging Associations	15 minutes
World Wide Web Usage	15 minutes
Kodak Web Site	10 minutes
Web Site Features	15 minutes
Discussion of New Product Concepts	20 minutes
Most Important Features	5 minutes
Conclusion	5 minutes
Total Time	90 minutes

Introduction for Consumer Focus Groups

Thank you for taking the time to meet with us today.

We should start by explaining the purpose of our research effort and the role you will play.

We are working with a film manufacturing company that is gathering information about the type of services that photographers might want to have on the World Wide Web. As part of that goal, the company is holding focus groups around the country with consumers who are photographers and who already use the Web. The client will use this information to design and modify their Web site.

The client who is sponsoring this session wishes to remain anonymous. I work for an independent research company, so please feel free to say whatever is on your mind concerning photography and the Internet. I will not be offended. The client wants to know what is working well, and what is not.

During our one and a half hour session, we are going to

- ask you to talk about your thoughts concerning digital photography
- ask you how you use the Internet

- ask you to comment on two concept services that might be available on the Internet

We are videotaping this session for future reference. Some members of the development team who are not here today would like to see the process.

As you can tell, this room is equipped with a one-way mirror. This makes it convenient for a few of our clients to watch, but not interfere with our discussion.

Keep in mind that there is no pressure to perform today. We want you to feel comfortable and enjoy yourself. If at any time you feel you want to withdraw from the study, you may do so. However, you will forfeit the honorarium.

This session will last about one and a half hours. We encourage you to enjoy the food and drinks while we conduct the discussion.

One more point. Before we get started, we would like you to read the statement that defines the terms of this session and requests confidentiality. If you are comfortable signing the form, please do so. When you have completed the form, please fill out the background questionnaire. Do you have any questions before we move on?

Selected discussion starters for consumer focus groups.

- What aspects of the Web do you like?
- What aspects of the Web do you dislike?
- What makes the Web attractive to use? What makes it cool?
- For what types of things do you use the Web?
- How many of you buy products and services through the Internet or Web?
- How do you pay for them?
- Would you be willing to pay less or more for products you buy on the Web in exchange for credit cards or financial accounts?

Let's return to the things you do on the Web.

- Do you use the web or Internet to communicate with friends? With family?
- If your pictures could somehow get onto the Web, how interested would you be in sending pictures to your friends? To your family?
- What would make using the Web fun for sending pictures to people?
- What would make using the Web difficult for sending pictures to people?
- Do you have any concerns about other people seeing your pictures on the Web?
- What kinds of things would you do with your digital images?
- Would you want to use digital manipulation on your images?
- Would you want to print out your images on other types of materials besides paper? Which materials?
- What would be the biggest problem with digital images?

We are going to start our discussion on the topic of how you send and receive information from Kodak. As we do so, let's keep the focus on your individual needs and feelings. We would like you to talk about how you currently receive information, and the types of information you need from Kodak. Let's start by talking about the types of information you currently receive from Kodak.

Selected discussion starters for dealer focus groups.

- What are some of the things you receive in the mail from Kodak? Does anybody receive new product announcements, product updates, product usage tips, or invoices?
- Do you receive phone calls from Kodak?
- Does anyone from Kodak send you faxes? What types of information do they send?
- How many of you receive electronic notes or e-mail from Kodak? What types of information does the e-mail contain?

Let's continue by talking about the types of information you currently send to Kodak.

- What are some of the things you send in the mail to Kodak? Do you send payments, problem reports, contracts, purchase decisions?
- When do you call Kodak? What types of information are you looking for when you call?
- Do you send faxes to Kodak? What types of information do you fax?
- How many of you send e-mail to Kodak? What types of information do you send in your e-mail?
- Who's having problems with communicating with Kodak?
- What would improve your communication with Kodak?

In today's discussion, we talked about mail, phone, fax, and e-mail. E-mail is sent via the Internet. However, we have not discussed a relatively new method of information delivery, the World Wide Web. The Web is the section of the Internet that contains Web sites or homepages for companies, groups, and individuals. I would now like to discuss the Internet and the Web further.

First, let's talk about the Internet.

- Does your dealership currently have Internet access?

- What would motivate you to get Internet access?
- What role could Kodak play in your decision to get Internet access?

Next let's talk about the World Wide Web. Kodak currently has a Web site and it contains some information about the company.

- What types of information do you think is found on Kodak's Web site?
- What information would you like to find on the site?

How many people have used the Kodak Web site?

- What types of things did you do on the Kodak Web site?

- What were your impressions of the Web site?
- How easy or difficult was it to find information on the Web site?
- How pleasing or unpleasing are the colors and graphics on Kodak's Web site?
- How would you improve the Web site?
- Concerning information delivery, how do you think the Web site would compare to mail, phone, fax, and e-mail?

Usability Testing

Usability testing was performed on kodak.com with the current homepage and top level in place, to determine usability issues to be addressed in the redesign. With Kodak's guidance, AIR designed the test protocol and recruited 12 individuals to participate. The test was conducted in Waltham, Massachusetts, and the testing sessions were videotaped for future review. Participants were screened to fit the attributes of the "consumer" focus group participant, described in the previous section. The purposes of the usability testing were to test the usability of the Web site in realistic situations for which a customer would visit the Web site and discuss the features and aspects of the Web site with the customers.

To represent the real browsing conditions of many kodak.com visitors, participants in the usability test used a 15-inch monitor and were connected to the Internet at 28.8 kbps. The usability test included several steps.

- Participants filled out an agreement form, agreeing to take part in the usability test.

- Participants received an introduction about the purpose and process of the test.

- Participants were asked to perform a number of information gathering tasks, such as "find a film that will work well in bright, sunny conditions."

- Participants participated in a post-test interview and provided overall feedback about the Web site.

The usability administrator sat with the participant during the usability test. Participants had some problems finding information about specific products, but they experienced even more difficulty when they looked for information without specific product names (such as advice for taking photographs). Users were given tasks to perform that would lead them to all of the links on the homepage. The search engine for the Web site was perceived as being hard to use. When doing searches, users commented that many of the Web pages were too cramped with text, and therefore, hard to read. The frequently asked questions page was perceived to be useful, but in some cases users weren't sure what "FAQ" meant, and therefore, advised that "Frequently Asked Questions" should be spelled out. In addition, users had trouble finding the location to e-mail questions and comments to Kodak.

During the interviews that took place after the usability test, participants commented that the kodak.com Web site seemed too cluttered. Users indicated that many of the resources that they wanted were available on the site, but they were hindered by the confusing terminology. Users also indicated that the search engine should be improved. Overall, users liked the resources offered at the kodak.com Web site and would be interested in revisiting the site if it was easier to use. All of this data was valuable in developing design requirements for the redesign.

The following are excerpts from the materials used in a usability test of kodak.com. The materials were developed and used by the American Institutes for Research (http://www.air.org) with guidance from Kodak.

Usability Test Materials

Introduction

Thank you for coming today. I work for the American Institutes for Research, a not-for-profit consulting group hired by outside companies to conduct research about the usability of products, software, and services. Currently, we've been asked by Kodak to evaluate their Web site.

I will guide you through the evaluation and interview you about your impression of the Kodak site. The session will be videotaped, and there may be an observer. Remember, we are not evaluating you in any way: We are interested in evaluating the content and information on the Web site. The information that you give us will be used to improve the site.

I will give you several tasks to complete using the Web site. The tasks will be printed on cards in front of you. I'll ask you to read each task aloud and then try to complete the task.

As you complete each task, I will ask you to think aloud and try to complete it. This will let me keep up with you.

Throughout the session, I will encourage you to express your opinions freely, to comment on what information is clear or unclear to you, and in particular, what you find confusing or difficult to understand.

Participant Tasks

Task 1—Top-Level Exploration (talk aloud warm-up)

Take a few minutes to explore this page. As you do, please comment on what you think each link means, and the sorts of things that you would expect to see if you were to click each link. Feel free to comment whenever you come across aspects and features of the Web site that you like, you don't like, you find confusing, or you find helpful.

Task 2—Product Information (search without knowing product name beforehand)

Try to find a film that will work well in bright, sunny conditions.

At first encounter with product information page: Please talk through what you think the different links on this page mean.

Return to the top page of the Web site, where you started.

_____ Backup _____ "Go" menu _____ Footer
Other: _____

Task 3—Product Information (search for a particular product name)

Try to find out a page of information on the Kodak Cameo Auto Focus Camera.

Return to the top page of the Web site, where you started.

_____ Backup _____ "Go" menu _____ Footer
Other: _____

Task 4—Digital Photography (digital learning center)

You have just heard about digital cameras and would like to learn more about what they can do. You wonder if the Kodak Web site contains any online tutorials about digital photography technology and how it is used. Try to find this information.

Return to the top page of the Web site, where you started.

_____ Backup _____ "Go" menu _____ Footer
Other: _____

Task 5—Customer Support (dealer locator)

Try to find a dealer who sells the DCS 420, a professional quality digital camera.

Return to the top page of the Web site, where you started.

_____ Backup _____ "Go" menu _____ Footer
Other: _____

Task 6—Digital Photography (sample digital image)

Pictures taken by digital cameras can be viewed on the Web. Try to find sample pictures taken by the DC40 camera so that you can see the quality of the picture.

Return to the top page of the Web site, where you started.

_____ Backup _____ "Go" menu _____ Footer
Other: _____

Task 7—Customer Support (frequently asked questions)

Try to find out whether walking through the X-ray machine at the airport will affect the film in your camera.

Return to the top page of the Web site, where you started.

_____ Backup _____ "Go" menu _____ Footer
Other: _____

Task 8—Customer Support (guest book)

Imagine that you have searched the Web site for an answer to a question about a Kodak product that you own, and you are unable to find an answer to your question. What would you do at this point?

If they did not answer that they would e-mail Kodak:

You have heard that there is a way on the Web site to e-mail questions to Kodak. Try to find it.

How long do you expect it will take before you get an answer?

What does the term "guest book" mean to you? Can you suggest a better name for this function?

Go back to the Customer Service page.

Is this what you expected under Customer Service?

Return to the top page of the Web site, where you started.

_____ Backup _____ "Go" menu _____ Footer
Other: _____

Task 9—Product Information (compare search possibilities)

Let's return to the Product Information page. Six of the links on the page can be used to search for information on products, and we are interested in determining how well each of the search strategies work. I am going to give you a couple of things to search for, and I will ask you to use a particular link on the page to do the search.

Try to find a page of information on the DC50 Digital Zoom Camera by clicking on the _____ link.

Now try it from the _____ link.

Which of the two search methods do you prefer?
_____

Is there a different way to find this information that you would prefer?

At the beginning of the session, I asked you to find an appropriate film to use in bright sun. Try to find this information from the _____ link.

Now try it from the _____ link.

Which of the two search methods do you prefer?
_____

Is there a different way to find this information that you would prefer?

In general, what do you think of having multiple ways of searching for products?

Return to the top page of the Web site, where you started.

_____ Backup _____ "Go" menu _____ Footer
Other: _____

Task 10—Product Information (search, compare navigation aids)

I'd like to direct your attention to a particular page. Click on the Find function. What do you think this page is used for? What is clear or unclear?

Now, I'd like you to look at this section over here (point to You can also search by:) What do you think is meant by each of these links?

Try out each of the links.

Would this be helpful to find what you need on the Web site? Which do you like best?

Post-Test Interview

- What were the three things that you liked best about this site?
- What were the three things that you liked least about this site?

- If you could change one thing about this site, what would it be?
- If you could add one thing about this site, what would it be?
- Would you go back to this site?
- Would you recommend this site to others?

Guest Book Messages from Visitors

Several hundred messages per day are submitted through the kodak.com guest book (a form by which kodak.com users can send questions, requests, comments, etc., to the company). Typically, the vast majority of these entries are requests for product support, requests for additional information, comments about the company and/or its products, etc., and less than two percent contain feedback about the Web site itself. However, these entries are the only regular means by which kodak.com users can provide direct feedback about the site. Therefore, we analyzed guest book comments from several months as part of our effort to understand user needs and desires.

We found that the majority of guest book feedback pertaining to the site itself was too generic to be useful (e.g., "Great site!"), and that most specific problems identified (e.g., broken links, misspellings, inaccuracies) were not helpful in identifying usability problems. However, some comments inspired our thinking about opportunities to improve kodak.com. For example, a few comments brought up the issue that the essentially static appearance of the existing homepage did not facilitate announcements of new product launches or the availability of popular applications (like the Kodak Picture This postcards feature); also, it gave no indication that new information was forthcoming or that the site was being kept up-to-date. This motivated the development team to make the new homepage more dynamic and flexible.

User Surveys

The results from a number of user surveys conducted on kodak.com yielded valuable information about user characteristics and preferences. We gained insights into the reasons users visit (e.g., business or personal reasons), the frequency with which users visit, connection speeds, monitor settings, browsing habits, demographics, etc. These insights were extremely valuable during the development of user requirements for the new site structure.

Requirements Collection and Site Design

Many different information-gathering techniques were used to collect data about users' needs and desires and Kodak's business objectives. The next steps were to develop design requirements based on the data and to begin the actual design process itself.

Business Unit Interviews

This exercise gave us a clearer understanding of some of the specific markets and audiences Kodak was trying to reach and some of the specific goals Kodak was trying to achieve through the Web. The following overall design requirements for the new kodak.com top level resulted from the interviews with business units.

- Present information in a user-centric way, without regard for corporate business unit boundaries.

- Provide information on applications of products as well as the products themselves.

- Provide a more intuitive and direct path to Kodak's various markets. ("Business Solutions" is not an adequate catchall.)

- Broaden the choices at each level so that the site is "shallower" (i.e., not requiring so many clicks to get to information).

- Provide areas for announcements, highlights, education, and enticement directly on the homepage.

- Provide branding and visual design guidelines that support the diversity of Kodak—its various businesses and markets and its worldwide presence.

Consumer Focus Groups

The consumer sessions focused on participants' expectations and understanding of digital imaging terminology and technology, impressions of the digital imaging marketplace, and expectations and preferences for Kodak's offerings on the

Web. Twenty-two consumers participated in the three consumer focus groups. Several interesting observations surfaced.

Many focus group participants were confused by terminology related to digital imaging and pictures. Some participants were not aware that Kodak made digital imaging products at all. In terms of general Web usability preferences, participants indicated that they disliked Web sites that took a long time to load, and that flashing pictures were annoying. Participants also sometimes found it hard to find the information that they were looking for. Regarding the Kodak Web site specifically, participants were excited at the possibility of sharing pictures with family and friends over the Web. Interestingly enough, none of the focus group participants had ever visited the Kodak Web site. However, the focus group participants indicated that they would be interested in visiting the site if it offered information on products and instructions about how to use those products, and also photography advice (about how to take good pictures, what type of film to use, etc.). Finally, participants were enthusiastic about the idea of Kodak delivering customer support for products directly through its Web site.

Dealer Focus Groups

The dealer sessions focused on the dealers' relationships to Kodak and how they could be improved because of Kodak's online presence. Dealers were asked to comment on their current communication with Kodak and indicate what Kodak could do over the Web to make that interaction more effective.

Twenty-seven digital equipment dealers took part in the dealer focus groups. The dealers who participated tended to focus on what resources Kodak made available on the Web. Some participants felt that the information sent out by Kodak through traditional means was geared toward larger consumer dealerships, not smaller organizations, or those who needed more technical information. Approximately half of the focus group participants had visited Kodak's Web site, and many of them felt that the site was geared toward consumers, but did not provide adequate information for the dealers. Such information could relate to new products, product availability, product specification sheets, and technical questions. The main advantage given for having this information available on the Web site was 24-hour-per-day availability. The participants commented that some information (such as dealer pricing information) should not be available to all (including customers). Overall, focus group participants did not like the design of the current kodak.com homepage. For instance, the difference between

"What's Hot" and "What's New" was not clear. The dealers reported that many of the categories were confusing; they requested easier paths for finding the information that they wanted.

Synthesizing Requirements

Based on our understanding of user needs and behavior, we defined a set of user requirements that guided the design of a new top-level site structure. Some of the requirements specifics follow.

Information Segments. Kodak.com visitors fall into a few broad segments based on information interest. We identified at least five major segments of information in which visitors could potentially be interested.

1. consumer photography and imaging
2. business and professional applications of imaging
3. Kodak as a company
4. working with Kodak to deliver products and/or services
5. nothing in particular

All of these information segments needed to be accommodated by the new top-level site structure, and eventually formed the basis for the information "chunks" we developed for the homepage.

Products versus Solutions. Some visitors come to kodak.com seeking information about a specific product; others come with a need or problem in mind but without knowing the product or service that best meets that need. Both needed to be accommodated by the new top-level site structure.

Technological Requirements. Based on surveys, guest book comments, feedback from focus groups, and existing literature on Web site usability, we made fast download times, pages viewable on monitors of varying resolutions, support for textual navigation, and other qualities requirements for our new top-level site structure. These requirements included the following.

- Total file size for the homepage, including graphics, should be kept to a minimum (ideally, around 45K).
- The main navigation and graphics should be viewable without scrolling on a low-resolution monitor. The width of the page should not exceed

472 pixels; no horizontal scrolling or window expansion should be necessary. The vertical constraint may be relaxed with proper design that gives clear visual indication of additional material and entices users to go there.

- No frames.
- No gratuitous, incessantly looping animations or blinking text.
- The page should be completely navigable with image loading turned off (for text browser users).

Conceptual Design

We had gathered a tremendous amount of knowledge—user needs and characteristics, content requirements, and marketing requirements. The next step was to use that knowledge and requirements to build the design of the homepage and top level of kodak.com.

As is usually the case with design, there was no systematic process we could follow to take us automatically from requirements to design. We had to rely on creative problem solving to generate a first prototype, which we could then improve upon using usability testing to drive design iterations. We assembled a multifunctional team consisting of visual designers, a project manager, a Web editor, a Web developer from one of Kodak's business units, a manager with a background in user experience, and usability experts to examine the requirements and brainstorm possible designs for a new top level for kodak.com.

Our primary focus was the design of the homepage. Once we settled on the design, we identified the need to create new top-level hub pages to pull together links to related pieces of content throughout kodak.com. For example, one hub page, "Digital Cameras and Technology," was developed to include links to Kodak's various digital products, including digital cameras, inkjet products, and CD products. We spent less time on the design of these hub pages relative to the time we spent on the homepage. We did not usability test the hub pages. The remainder of the links from the homepage pointed to existing "sitelets" (subsites) within kodak.com, which for the most part, we did not alter.

We had several multihour working sessions. Based on the user interface requirements we had defined, we knew that in order to make navigation more efficient, the new homepage would need to contain more links than the previous one. We also knew what content those links had to account for. Our challenge during the design process was to

- Establish the exact wording for the links, understanding that both the descriptiveness of the links themselves and their context among neighboring links on the homepage would impact usability.

- Divide the links into groups to help the user evaluate them more quickly and easily. In going from roughly ten to roughly thirty links, we knew we didn't want to simply add twenty more gray buttons to the current homepage.

- Design the look of the homepage, incorporating imagery into a primarily textual homepage to achieve a compelling look befitting the "World Leader in Imaging."

To achieve the first two tasks, we wrote the tentative names of the various sections of the site on sticky notes and spent many of our working sessions moving these notes around on large pieces of posterboard. We discussed the sections of the site, their relative importance to users and to the company, and how they could be grouped and organized. For inspiration, we conducted a benchmark comparison of 10 corporate Web sites, making note of

1. theme, if any
2. visual motif
3. organization of major sections of the site with descriptions
4. navigational model/tools
5. common page elements
6. number of choices from the homepage
7. how the following are handled on the homepage:
   — the path to product information
   — international content
   — online commerce, if any
   — special relationships (e.g., with dealers and/or developers)
   — feedback/guest book mechanism

Evaluating these sites helped us to identify design and interaction elements and effective words/labels.

Information Architecture

When we created groups, we discussed the wording of the links so that the juxtaposed links would not create confusion. After several sessions, we arrived at groupings that we thought were reasonable (see Table A.5).

Table A.5 Groupings for Links

Group 1	Group 6
Find	.Further
Site Map	Kodak Picture This Postcards
Product Catalog	Photo Chat
Customer Support	**Group 7**
Online Store	All About Photography
Group 2	Guide to Better Pictures
What's New at www.kodak.com	Digital Learning Center
Group 3	**Group 8**
About Kodak	Advanced Photo System
Press Center	Kodak Gold Films
Investors' Center	Digital Cameras and Technology
Career Center	**Group 9**
Group 4	Kodak Photonet Online
For Dealers and Developers	**Group 10**
Group 5	Periodic Feature
Professional Photography and Graphic Arts	**Group 11**
Motion Picture Imaging	Kodak around the World
Business and Office Applications	
Health and Medical Imaging	
Aerial, Space, and Scientific Imaging	
Government and Law Enforcement Imaging	
Imaging in Education	

Iterative Design with Usability Testing

We subjected our design to an *iterative design process*. That is, we conducted one usability test, fed the results of the test into the next iteration of the design, and tested again to refine the design further. The first usability test was paper-based.

Usability Testing, Round One

After developing a first draft of the links and groups we wanted for the new homepage, we subjected it to paper-and-pencil usability testing. This was called "round one" of usability testing. Twenty participants were recruited for the study, which consisted of three stages.

In the first stage, each participant was presented with a simple listing, on paper, of the links we intended to have on the homepage.

Links were presented in the major groupings (chunks) we had agreed upon, but no other visual design was employed. Each participant was given the same set of 30 tasks (presented randomly). Tasks were designed to cover a broad range of content on kodak.com, including information most frequently sought by users. For each task, the participant was asked to identify the homepage link most likely to lead to information that would support the completion of that task, and to give a rating of 1–3 of his/her level of confidence that the targeted information would be found using that link. This first stage was intended to examine how well our proposed homepage links were differentiated; that is, for a given set of representative tasks, whether the user knew which link to choose to find a particular piece of information.

Table A.6 shows the percentage of participants, for each task, who picked, as their first choice, the correct homepage link that would lead to the completion of the task. This was the most useful stage of the test, as it provided a preview of what it would be like for a user to use the new homepage.

In the second stage, we asked participants to go through the homepage links and describe what they would expect to find "behind" each link. This second stage was intended to examine the predictability of the links we intended to offer on the homepage. Table A.7 shows the percentage of participants making correct predictions for each link.

We found this stage of testing to be helpful because it identified unfamiliar or ambiguous terms, and terms for which the users' expectations differed from our intent. It also provided insight into possible misinterpretations of terms, and how pervasive these misinterpretations were likely to be. For example, we discovered that 80 percent of our test participants were unfamiliar with the term "Advanced Photo System," and did not realize that the term refers to an industry standard for general consumer photography. As another example, we constructed a link to "What's New at www.kodak.com" hoping that users would realize that it linked to recent updates to the Web site, not necessarily "what's new" with Kodak. However, we found that 75 percent of test participants did not make this distinction, and for the final design we dropped the words "at www.kodak.com" from the link.

In the third stage, again we went through the entire list of links on the homepage with each participant and explained the content we intended to offer under that

link. We asked the participant to give a rating on a seven-point scale of how well the link name we chose described the content we intended to offer "behind" it. In this stage, we attempted to discover how accurate the participants found the names we devised. We discovered that this stage of the study was not particularly useful, since participants tended to give us high accuracy ratings for almost every link. We discovered that because a link name is accurate does not necessarily mean that it is predictable, or well differentiated from surrounding links, or otherwise useful to the user.

As an illustration, a link marked "Information" may accurately describe what is found behind the link, but is not useful because it is not predictable or differentiable from other links. A specific example from our study is that we had a link marked "All About Photography" on our prototype homepage. Five of the thirty tasks could be completed using this link, but for four of the tasks, none of the twenty participants chose "All About Photography" as their first or second choice. Yet, when the participants were told the content that would be offered through "All About Photography" (tips for taking great pictures in various situations, suggestions on how to do more with pictures, information about photography clubs, seminars and events, information about Kodak photographic products, and more) all participants gave the name a high rating in terms of accuracy. The problem was that although the title "All About Photography" was accurate, it was not well differentiated from its surrounding links (many of which had to do with photography as well). In addition, because of the great diversity of information to which it pointed, it was difficult for users to predict what lay behind the link. We concluded that this methodology was not useful for measuring the usability of the proposed site structure, or for identifying changes that would increase usability.

When the results of the first set of usability tests came back, we were ready to perform our first iteration on improving the proposed homepage design. Based on the usability test recommendations, we cut down on the number of homepage links—subsuming some in others—and recasting the focus of some of the proposed hub pages. Of the homepage links that remained, we renamed the confusing ones.

Page Layout

Introduction

In addition to selecting the links that would appear on the homepage and top-level pages, we needed to determine how these links would be laid out and pre-

sented on each page. The page layout decisions affected not only usability, but also each page's ability to convey the aesthetic and emotional qualities we desired.

Focus on Text

In contrast to the previous homepage, which featured a large image map, we decided to make the new homepage primarily textual. There were multiple reasons for this. The first reason was speed. Existing research on Web usability points to greater speed and shorter download times as being of prime importance to users. Because text downloads faster than images, we chose to use textual links to enable users to navigate the site more quickly and without having to wait for images to download.

The second reason was flexibility. The previous homepage and top-level pages consisted of large image maps with up to eight links, accompanied by text link equivalents. Consequently, changes to these pages were very infrequent, and difficult to make. Usually, an existing item had to be removed in order to accommodate a new item. On rare occasions, new links were added without removing any of the existing ones, which was awkward in terms of visual design.

As an example, the introduction of the "Kodak Picture Network" (an online picture management/sharing service) in 1997 required a homepage link to learn about, join, and use the service. Of the existing homepage links at the time, eight were gray buttons at the bottom of the image map, and one—"What's Hot"—was a graphical link in the upper right hand corner. In order to provide a link to the "Kodak Picture Network," a ninth gray button was placed on top of the other eight—a solution that met the business requirements, but was not an elegant design solution. Because the new homepage was mostly textual, it could easily be modified to reflect the nature of the site. We could add, change, or remove links without much effort whenever necessary to accommodate new or changing content, address usability issues, and special announcements.

The Look of the New Pages

Designing the look of the new homepage proved to be a difficult task. We were dealing with several groups of links, and we wanted to present them in such a way that would not overwhelm the user. We also wanted to highlight photography and the great imagery that is expected of Kodak. We tried an exercise in which each member of the multifunctional working team sketched his or her

own concepts of what the new homepage should look like, and then laid the sketches out for all to see and from which to derive inspiration.

Ultimately, the duty of producing initial concept sketches of the new homepage fell to our lead visual designer, who produced very basic layouts for us to show participants in our second set of usability tests, where users were presented with actual screen layouts. The layouts were similar, involving two alternative arrangements of the same components, and usability test participants were evenly split between which layout they preferred.

The designer proceeded to create several composites of new homepage concepts, based on the layouts, with different color combinations and different uses of images. They were circulated among the kodak.com user experience group for comments. Many colleagues offered feedback, but they did not consistently favor one concept over another.

After we had refined the links and groups to address the issues raised in the first usability test, the visual designer again developed a composite design, incorporating the color scheme and visual elements from one of the composites that had received favorable comments (see Figure A.3). This prototype was used in the usability tests.

Physical Design

Developing Web Pages

The Web developers at kodak.com used and continue to use a variety of methods to implement Web pages. Most Web developers forgo so-called WYSIWYG ("What You See Is What You Get") authoring tools and instead manually edit HTML with or without the help of HTML editing tools (such as Allaire Homesite) because of the ability to control exactly what elements are used and better understand how the underlying code will interact with various Web browsers. Because browser compatibility is always an important issue, the Web developers who created the actual pages that comprised this particular redesigned site edited the HTML manually.

Web pages were constructed for use in the second usability test. This test was intended to require participants to actually use the page and follow links to existing sitelets on kodak.com. The site redesign did not include any changes in site functionality (e.g., development of new applications), nor did any of the redesigned pages contain scripts. Consequently, testing was limited to checking the

Figure A.3 Prototype of homepage used in phase 2 of usability testing.

new Web pages against different browser/platform combinations to ensure that the Web pages rendered as expected. There were no surprises uncovered during this stage of testing. The new homepage designed for usability testing is shown in Figure A.3.

Usability Testing

Introduction

Two rounds of usability testing were conducted during the iterative refinement of the homepage design. This section discusses the methods used in each test, and the impact each test had on the final design.

Computer-Based Usability Testing (Usability Testing, Round Two)

In our second stage of usability testing, which was computer-based, we sought to validate the changes we had made to the top-level site structure and test the homepage in actual usage situations. Thirty-three participants were recruited to complete ten information-seeking tasks, each using a working prototype of the new site structure. The homepage prototype was used in this stage of usability testing.

Top-level pages were prototyped as simple textual listings and groupings of links, without visual design elements. All links were functional and pointed to the appropriate content on kodak.com. As in the earlier usability testing, tasks were designed to cover a broad range of content on kodak.com, but this time with emphasis on information popularly sought by users as identified by corporate customer support staff. Each participant was given three minutes to complete each task successfully. Table A.8 shows the percentage of participants who were able to complete the tasks in the allotted time.

In addition to the task completion data, the usability test identified several specific potential improvements (based on feedback from test participants) to the homepage to increase its usability, such as labeling the major chunks of information, reducing the number of links, adding descriptors to more of the links, and removing the images along the left-hand side. These improvements were incorporated into the next and final iteration of the homepage design.

All that remained at this point was to finalize the visual design of the homepage. The visual designer worked with input from the rest of the team to develop the design that was presented to kodak.com users in the preview survey. After examining a few days' worth of survey respondents' comments, the designer made some final modifications to the design, which was used in the site launch, as shown in Figure A.4.

The other top-level pages were designed to follow the same groups of text links and visual design motif, as shown in Figure A.5.

Implementation and Marketing

Previewing the New Design with Users

Before the launch of the new Web page design, visitors to the kodak.com Web site were given a chance to preview the new design and offer their feedback. At the

Table A.8 Usability Test Results—Percentage of Participants
Completing the Task Successfully within Three Minutes

Task	Percent Completing	Number of Participants
General PhotoCD information	100	11
Job opportunities at Kodak	100	22
Making gift items from pictures	95	22
Business scanner	95	22
Avoiding glowing or red eyes in pictures	91	22
Using imaging in the classroom	91	11
Learn about the technology behind digital cameras	91	11
Online service to organize and share digital pictures	91	33
General scanner information	86	22
Inkjet papers	73	22
Digital camera connectivity problem	73	11
Discussion forums	64	11
Gift items that can be bought over the Web	64	11
Law enforcement imaging application	64	11
Where to buy a digital camera	64	11
E-mail Kodak	55	11
DC50 camera FAQ	55	11
Vacation photography tips	28	11
Getting photographic quality prints from DC120 camera	18	11
DC210 camera Windows compatibility question	18	11
Thermal printer comparison	18	11
Sample pictures	9	11

end of many Kodak Web pages, a link was provided where users who followed the link could view an HTML prototype of the new homepage. The links, while functional, pointed to "dead-end" pages that described the content to which each link would point. We did not link to the actual content in kodak.com because we didn't want users to navigate any deeper than the new homepage and be sidetracked or provide comments that were not about the homepage. Users then had a chance to fill out a short Web-based survey. The survey was linked from the footer of every page of the site.

The survey was not intended to be a representative sampling of all kodak.com users. Because we placed the link on every page and invited users to comment,

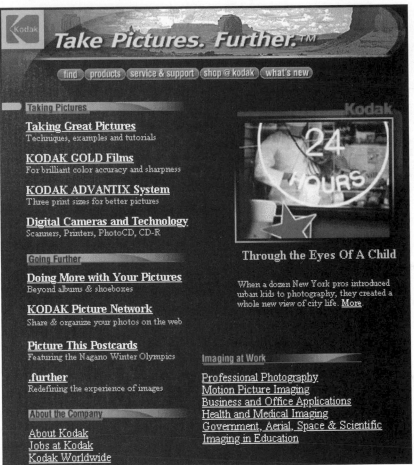

Also in the
Color Insert

Figure A.4 The final design used in the site launch.

we were not randomly sampling within a defined population and could not make any claims regarding the generalization of the results. Instead, we were simply trying to get as many opinions as we could about the new design. In this sense, the survey was quite successful, yielding opinions and comments from over 800 visitors. Respondents to the survey answered two questions: "How appealing is the overall design of the new Kodak homepage?" (see Table A.9) and "Overall, how does the new Kodak homepage compare with the current Kodak homepage?" (see Table A.10).

We carefully read each of the 710 open-ended comments offered by survey respondents, and separated them into three categories: positive (338 comments),

Figure A.5 An example of a top-level page in the site launch.

Table A.9 Results of Preview Survey: Overall Appeal

Response	Percent Respondents
Wow!!!	14.36
Very appealing	48.51
Appealing	25.87
Neither appealing nor unappealing	5.43
Unappealing	3.49
Very unappealing	0.65
Ugh!!!	1.68

Note: Number of respondents = 773

Table A.10 Results of Preview Survey: Comparison with Current Homepage

Response	Percent Respondents
Much better	48.29
Better	31.10
Somewhat better	9.97
Neither better nor worse	5.51
Somewhat worse	2.89
Worse	1.05
Much worse	1.18

Note: Number of respondents = 762

negative (162 comments), and neutral or both positive and negative (210 comments). A sampling of positive and negatives comments follows. The fact that the results were so positive gave us confidence that the design would be well received by users.

A Sampling of the Best

- I really like it! **I didn't know all this cool content was under the current homepage.**

- **This is one of the best homepage sites that I have visited.** I hope you'll let me know when it's ready for use.

- **Color scheme is excellent.** Shows great definition and makes sense in that it corresponds well with the Kodak image. Much improvement for the consumer who had to search for info in the previous version. Much more consumer friendly. Why not make picture network more accessible? Perhaps try framing at the top for quick reference to consumer pages, like picture network and postcard page. Overall, loads up nicely which isn't always the case today on the net.

- **It looks as though you've done your homework on what people are looking for on your site.** Very nice. Clean, visually appealing, not distracting.

- **The Colors seem to say "Kodak!"** Nice design and it makes it easy for users to find what they need.

- **Very well thought out!**—It appears that Kodak is a company that is very customer oriented and will be supporting our needs for years to come.

- **This page makes going around the Web site a great deal easier.** I was able to figure out more of where I needed to go. On the current page, I found it hard and unsure of the exact link I needed.

- **I look to Kodak for info on how to make better pictures and how to use your products to achieve this.** My impression is that the new homepage will make it easier to get the information I need.

- **It is neat, very "crisp," uncluttered.** It is object-oriented, which will be a tremendous assist in navigation. I really like the features presented on the page and will definitely bookmark so I can return to peruse when it is finished. I like the colors, which are traditional for Kodak products. It seems to be "quick" to respond, but the pages are not yet loaded in for testing out that component. (I hate waiting forever for a page to load.) It seems representative of the trademark Kodak quality.

- **Like Kodak products, it is excellent.**

- Having been a proponent of KODAK merchandise for the past forty years, I think **this Web site only fortifies my belief in Kodak's commitment to quality consumer products.** MAGNIFICENTLY DONE!

A Sampling of the Worst

- **It is a "muddled" list of things with little focus; neither aesthetic nor efficient.** I find it disturbing that a corporate giant like Kodak, whose business is largely "visuals," cannot put a decent, simple, clever, attractive homepage up on the Web. Of course, this is just my opinion.

- **Too busy.** Does not make a single, powerful statement. Confusing or at least not easy to grab at once.

- **While every element of the page is gorgeous, they are in violent competition for attention.** Brilliant color is visual chocolate—too much can make you sick.

- **Please leave the old homepage if you're not coming up with something better than that.** It is cluttered, hard to read, and the selection of colors does not account for Kodak's image at all. Why change something good just for the sake of changes?

- **I think you need to simplify the page even more. The viewer is hit with a very dense set of options made worse by the use of the black background.** Also, avoid scrolling. Many viewers may not realize more is below. Alternatively, decide that the information contained below is not important. It's better to lead people to another page than to try to put everything on the first page. Use cookies to find out what is most interesting for the viewer and give it to them again when they come back to the site. Usually a viewer will be coming back for similar information based on products they own or use. "Hot info" can be placed in a text area on the viewers screen in case they want to jump-start the process.

- **The new homepage might be somewhat "busy," I tend to prefer fewer links per page,** afraid that I'll overlook what I'm looking for, or miss links that might interest me because of the **visual overload from many links.**

Based on the results of the survey, we felt comfortable moving ahead with launching the redesigned top level as planned.

Marketing

Kodak issued press releases about the new site design. The teamwork and process that went into the design was featured in a local business publication. Because kodak.com was a Web site that had already existed, it was not necessary to address issues such as domain name registration, search engine registration, or marketing. Users already knew about kodak.com and how to access the site.

After the Launch

Surprisingly, we received very little feedback on the new site design. Because the design change from the old site to the new was so drastic, we expected to be inundated with user comments via the kodak.com guest book. In fact, we received no more guest book messages pertaining to site design after the launch of the redesign than before it—around one percent of the messages daily.

Because of the need to reassign resources to other work immediately following the launch, Kodak did not have the luxury of thoroughly studying the effects of the new Web site design. Instead, we relied on the knowledge that we had developed the site based on a rigorous user-centered design approach, using various techniques for requirements gathering and thorough usability testing. The endorsement of hundreds of kodak.com users who rated the new design favorably in the pre-launch survey confirmed that the new design was a success.

Ongoing Maintenance

The new design was based on text links organized into logical groups. No limit was set on how many links could appear in a group or how many groups could appear on a page. As such, it became much easier to add links, change links, or remove links without significantly affecting the overall look of the page. Change requests became much more frequent, although it is unclear whether this was the result of changes being easier to make, or that Kodak was doing more that required changes to be made, or both. Consequently, change requests needed to be addressed much more frequently than with the previous design—both for the homepage and for top-level pages.

The responsibility of handling change requests became the joint responsibility of three individuals—the site editor, the visual design director, and the user interaction design lead. They worked together to determine the best way to accommodate requests through adding, modifying, or removing links and changing groups, wording, and/or labels. The actual development of kodak.com content was, and continues to be, a responsibility distributed among Kodak's various business units and corporate groups.

asha.org—
Redesigning a Web Site for the American Speech-Language Hearing Association

Theresa O'Connell
Humans and Computers, Inc.

Defining the Mission and Target User Population

Redesigning a Web site is a challenge all by itself. But, like any other Web site, the American Speech-Language Hearing Association (ASHA) site added its own unique set of challenges.

Start with a wide variety of users—ranging from Web-savvy college professors to senior citizens just learning to surf. Divide these users into 16 distinct groups. Pull out a target user population of 103,000 professionals in two different fields, each with at least one graduate degree. Factor in up to 38,500 visits to the site on a busy day.

Add high pressure situations—parents trying to find help for a child with a suspected or newly identified disability, or someone who fears he's losing his hearing. Then expand all of this with a high priority responsibility to provide professional dues-paying members with all the latest and most important information on two wide fields of knowledge. Most importantly, throw in users' complaints that they can't find what they're looking for on the Web site.

You've just scratched the surface of the challenges of redesigning http://www.asha.org. Despite all the complexity, this is the story of a successful collaboration between a team of talented Web designers and a usability consulting firm. It's the story of a year long usability study that supported that team's goal to make ASHA's Web site its members' "most valuable and valued benefit."

The ASHA Web Site When the Usability Engineering Process Started

At the start of the usability engineering process, the American Speech-Language Hearing Association described itself as "the professional, scientific, and credentialing association for more than 103,000 audiologists, speech-language pathologists (SLPs), and speech, language, and hearing scientists." Its mission statement was "to ensure that all people with speech, language, and hearing disorders have access to quality services to help them communicate more effectively."

When ASHA started planning its Web site redesign, www.asha.org, had 3,000 to 4,000 pages on any given day. It provided information to ASHA members and others about audiology and speech-language pathology. The Web site was an integral part of ASHA. Every department contributed content. All ASHA employees were stakeholders in its success. Their most important users were the audiologists, speech-language pathologists, and speech, language, and hearing scientists who were ASHA members.

The site had three sections, each aimed at a different user group.

1. speech-language and hearing professionals
2. the public
3. students

The site's entry page led to a homepage for each of these three sections. The levels below organized most of the site's content in a deep information architecture.

Humans and Computers, Inc. (H&CI) is a small consulting firm, based in Upper Marlboro, MD, part of the Washington D.C. metropolitan area. It specializes in making technology compatible with people. Its main stock in trade is usability engineering.

Before the project started, ASHA invited H&CI to a meeting at the ASHA National Headquarters in Rockville, MD. The goal was a common understanding of the ASHA Web team's plans and how usability engineering could fit into them.

The ASHA Web team was unusual. They already knew a lot about usability and appreciated its value. They wanted to educate the Association about usability so that stakeholders would understand the reasons behind the team's design decisions. They had already identified the principal problem that would motivate most of their design decisions: Users had difficulty finding information on the site.

H&CI submitted a proposal that integrated usability engineering activities with the planned Web site redesign and development activities. Each step would draw on findings from previous user-centered design (UCD) steps and provide findings to feed into downstream activities (see Figure B.1).

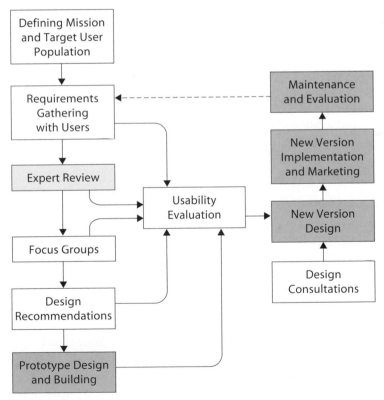

Figure B.1 The process used for ASHA. White boxes show activities where ASHA and H&CI collaborated. The light gray box shows the independent expert review by H&CI. Dark gray boxes show activities that ASHA performed independently of H&CI.

It's common practice that a usability engineering firm does not participate in all aspects of a Web site's redesign. Before H&CI joined the ASHA Web team, the redesign was already under way. The team was already addressing information architecture, site navigation, page design, universal usability design, and physical design. The H&CI role would include design consultations in all of these areas, and the expert review and user observation reports would also make design recommendations. But H&CI was not involved in executing design. Nor did it participate in implementation, marketing, or maintenance.

Usability Presentation

The ASHA Web team wanted the entire Association to be aware of the usability study and to participate in it from the start. The first step was to engage the people at ASHA National Headquarters. The ASHA Web team invited all the staff at the National Office in Rockville, Maryland, to a presentation.

H&CI called its presentation "Connecting the ASHA Community through Usability Engineering." This title became a theme of the later expert review. When members reintroduced it during a focus group, thinking it was their own new idea, we knew we had struck a chord.

The hour and a half long session drew a good crowd. The presentation shared goals and strategies. H&CI explained usability principles and key UCD processes and activities for the redesign. There was great interest in the ASHA Web site and excitement about the redesign. These people felt they had a stake in its success.

One good reason for a presentation to stakeholders is that it builds champions for the work ahead. This is what happened at ASHA. Before we knew it, we had stakeholder interviews scheduled from morning to closing time on three different days—and these were in addition to the interviews we'd already planned.

Requirements Gathering with Users

Requirements gathering activities didn't all occur at the same time or even at the same point in the project. We wanted to be flexible enough to take advantage of unexpected opportunities to refine our preliminary understanding of users' needs.

The first key activity was to build user profiles and categorize them into user groups. In order to do this, we had to understand users' needs, goals, and expectations for the new site. We had to be able to work with these goals within the context of ASHA's goals for the site. So, we needed to talk with users and we needed to talk with stakeholders. We invited all the National Headquarters employees and members to participate in requirements gathering.

Simple courtesy and managing expectations are vital to the success of any redesign effort. So, H&CI followed up every interview and focus group with personalized thank-you e-mails, encapsulating what we had learned from the user or stakeholder. We also told them that while all of their input was important and would help us do a better job, the ASHA Web team would only be able to implement some of it.

The first deliverable for requirements gathering was a description of users and their needs. The report also needed to recommend user groups to invite to focus groups and user observations. It had to set out tasks for users to perform during user observations.

Interviews at National Headquarters

ASHA considers its Web site so important that they have a group of executives, called the Web Strategy Team, to set its direction. Our first task was to interview these people. Everyone we contacted, from the Executive Director down the organization chart, invited us into their offices and shared frank opinions about the site.

We quickly realized that we had met our goal of engaging stakeholders. A three-day-long open house led to more meeting requests. There were 30 formal interviews plus informal chats. Some people brought colleagues or staff along for lively open dialogs. Finally, H&CI interviewed each member of the ASHA Web team. We planned a few questions, but for the most part, we encouraged the interviewees to drive the discussions.

The interviews backed up what we already knew: Many users found it very hard to find information on the site. Throughout ASHA, employees had developed paper resources to print and mail in response to requests for information published on the Web site. They did not expect the site to organize appropriately or quickly lead them to the content they needed to do their jobs.

This stakeholder feedback led to a big breakthrough. A reason for users' difficulties locating content began to come to light. The legacy Web site had been structured to reflect the organizational structure of ASHA. This structure assured that when a staff member contributed content, there would be no question about where to place that content on the site.

It wasn't surprising that members who weren't familiar with the details of ASHA's organizational structure might have problems finding information or functionality on the site. What was surprising was the fact that ASHA employees reported having the same problem. This was why they depended on their own paper resources instead of the site for quick answers. We had identified a major goal for the redesign: Revamp the site's information architecture to meet users' expectations, not ASHA's structure.

Ethnography in the Action Center

One of the interviews led to an invitation to observe call center personnel in the ASHA Action Center. Because our usability study plan was flexible, we could take advantage of this unexpected opportunity for a contextual inquiry of the site's most frequent users. These professionals were a rich source of information. Every day, they helped people who couldn't find what they sought on the ASHA site. They knew which site content was important to members, which content users couldn't find, and what kind of content the site needed to add.

Users' Feedback

The ASHA Web team began to send H&CI users' feedback about the site. Other ASHA staff offered to connect us to users. With ASHA introductions, we scheduled telephone and face-to-face interviews with members. Members told us they were dissatisfied because they could not find information on the ASHA site. They talked about their information needs and typical tasks on the site.

The telephone interviews emphasized the fact that the ASHA membership included people who were not very computer literate. We also learned that members working in school settings often had limited access to a computer, sometimes only moments between sessions with students. Often, they had to wait their turn on a shared computer. They needed simple and very fast access, but the site forced them to spend precious time exploring their way to information.

At the University of Maryland, so many SLP and audiology professors and students showed up for interviews that the only way to talk with everyone was in an impromptu focus group. They complained about problems finding information and having to remember their ASHA membership number to log in to the members-only part of the site.

Analysis of Web Logs

The ASHA Web team had a wealth of information about how people used the site. They monitored Web logs and shared their data and analyses with H&CI. The daily average number of users was 12,175. On a busy day, the site had up to 38,500 visitors, most of them return users. Sixty-seven percent started at the professional section homepage, making it the site's most visited page. Users spent an average of six to eight minutes in the professional section of the site. It appeared that a quarter of the site's visitors came to the ASHA site to monitor news in their fields.

The professional homepage linked to pages reserved especially for members. Access required registration and a login. Over a 20-day period, only 1,214 visitors had logged in to this most important part of the site. Visitors who did log in spent a long time—up to one minute and fourteen seconds on the login page. Users who stalled at the page that asked if they'd forgotten their password numbered 1,079. This confirmed what we had learned from the professors and students—logging in was a problem.

The second most visited page was the search results page. People knew what kind of information they were looking for and they wanted it fast. Their first strategy was the search engine.

Review of Other Professional Studies

Before the usability study, ASHA had commissioned studies on its members that helped to identify the kinds of information SLPs and audiologists sought on the site. This material contributed to a prioritized list of members' information needs.

Only 16,049 members had registered to use the members-only pages, the heart of the resources ASHA offered its members. We needed to show ASHA members the value these pages offered.

One of the primary concerns of SLPs in schools was a lack of time during the work day. Members in general had no more than four hours a week for work-related reading. An important trend began to emerge: ASHA members had a lot to do, and not much time to do it. They needed quick access to information and functionality.

Web Survey

ASHA developed a survey and posted it on the site. It asked users how often and why they visited the site. It sought users' opinions about what kind of information the site should have. It also collected information on workplaces and Web access.

The questions were clear, brief, and direct. "How many times did you access the ASHA Web site for your professional work in the last 30 days?" "What were you looking for?" The final question opened the door for users to share any comments they wished.

Respondents reflected the diversity of the site's users. Their frequency of use varied from once to 300 times over the last month. They had lots to say about the kinds of information they sought. They wanted up-to-date, easily accessible information; practical treatment tips and techniques; educational materials to give to patients; and information about running a practice.

They asked for better access to information about members and easier ways for members to connect to each other. They wanted the site to help them find jobs. They wanted to search the site by topic, an issue that ASHA was already addressing. Their requests foreshadowed what we heard in the focus groups.

The Web survey findings coincided with what we learned in other requirements gathering activities—users were dissatisfied because they couldn't find the information they sought. Improved navigation was at the top of their wish list. This emphasized the need for a new information architecture that reflected user needs, not ASHA's organization.

User Groups

As we continued to collect and analyze information, we came to the important point where we knew who the users were and what they wanted from the site. The requirements gathering report identified 16 groups of users who shared characteristics and needs and who performed the same tasks at the site. Although the report discussed the user population as it existed at this point in the study, we were able to identify trends that would help us meet the needs not only of present users, but also of future users.

1. **ASHA Action Center Staff.** It was surprising to the Web team that the first H&CI candidate for a focus group was the ASHA Action Center Staff. Although these highly computer literate professionals were the smallest user group, they were the site's most frequent users. They had the greatest need to access the breadth of information and functionality that the site offered.

Because of their close and constant interaction with users, Action Center users had first-hand knowledge of users' tasks and needs at the site. They could also pinpoint almost every aspect of the site that needed improved usability.

2. **ASHA Members in General.** There were many similarities among members. At the time of the usability study, 75 percent of them used Windows, but they were not highly computer literate. Although 1,000 of the site's pages were .pdf documents, many users didn't know what a .pdf file was or what the .pdf icon stood for. They didn't know they needed special software to read .pdf files.

The majority were women, many over 40 years old. To become a certified practitioner, a member needed to have a masters degree and pass a certification exam. Some members also had Ph.D.s. Members' principal tasks included seeking up-to-date information to use in their work and to give to their clients. They needed to register to take continuing education classes. They sought information about conventions and activities in their fields. Many had to maintain their contact information in ASHA's online directory.

Members' impressions of the site were poor. We knew that dissatisfied users sometimes transfer their poor impressions of a Web site to their impressions of the site's providers. Improving usability at www.asha.org was essential to ASHA's achieving its organizational goals.

3. **ASHA Members—SLPs in Schools.** Within the member population, we treated some subgroups as user groups in themselves. Comprising more than half of ASHA members, SLPs in schools were the largest of these user groups. Many worked at more than one school in a day. Their students were culturally and linguistically diverse. They rendered 83 percent of their services in a shared resource room.

SLPs came to the ASHA site to find new ideas and to search for colleagues outside of their school district. They sought information on specific speech and language disorders, and on how to work with parents. They looked for ways to collaborate with related service providers.

The site organization didn't reflect the way that SLPs in schools sought information. Because of this, some would not refer colleagues or students' parents to the site.

4. ASHA Members in Healthcare Settings. Almost 40 percent of ASHA members worked in healthcare settings. They primarily used the professional part of the site, but also sought information in the public section and referred patients there. To support them in their work, they wanted materials that were easily located, engaging, and readily understood.

5. ASHA Members—Faculty. One group of ASHA members had a markedly different profile from the others. These were the people who taught the next generation of ASHA members. University and college faculty users were much more computer literate than other members. They were adept at finding information on the Web. Faculty explored the site's professional pages. They were likely to rely on memory or to navigate from page to page to find information before trying the search engine.

A typical task was to find journal articles. They needed the ability to submit papers for ASHA conventions easily. They liked the site's look, but like other users, they complained that it was difficult to find the information they needed. They wanted sophisticated search functionality and easy login for the members-only pages.

6. Students. Most students were working on a Masters degree in speech-language pathology or audiology. They came to the ASHA site to prepare for their licensing exams, look for jobs, and access information on speech-language pathology and audiology.

7. eCustomers. Most eCustomers were ASHA members who purchased ASHA products to support their work.

8. ASHA Headquarters Staff (Exclusive of Action Center Staff). The site supported people of all job descriptions at the ASHA National Headquarters.

9. General Public. The general public had a wide range of needs and characteristics. They spanned every level of computer literacy. They included people with speech-language or audiology disabilities and caregivers to people with those disabilities. Some came to the site seeking information. Others sought an SLP or an audiologist.

Many of these users needed simple paths to information because of one important characteristic—they were under stress when they went to the site. For example, this group included parents who had just learned that their baby had a hearing disorder.

Other Professionals. Seven other user groups were identified, but we did not include them in focus groups or user observations.

10. advertisers and vendors

11. continuing education providers

12. educators in schools other than universities and colleges

13. international affiliates of ASHA

14. non-member SLPs and audiologists

15. the press

16. speech-language and hearing scientists

Outcomes

It's rare that a large association can include all of its user groups in Web site design. ASHA was no exception. H&CI had to prioritize and recommend the user groups that would provide the most valuable information for the usability study. ASHA decided that there would be two focus groups—one with Action Center employees, the other with SLPs in schools. Addressing the issues that these users experienced offered a great potential to improve the site experience of other users as well.

Usability Testing: Expert Review

The principal goal of the expert review was to uncover and prioritize the most important issues to address in the usability study. We wanted to know the site's strengths and where the site could be improved. Why bother to document the site's strengths? Because what works well in one place might be the solution for a problem somewhere else on the site.

H&CI needed to make a first set of design recommendations. We had to be on the lookout for any information that would require refining recommendations on areas to investigate in focus groups and user observations.

At every step in the expert review, H&CI had to keep in mind all we had learned about user requirements. We started by evaluating the site against user requirements within the framework of usability principles. Requirements gathering had shown us that two of the most important usability principles for this study were

- quick and easy access to information and functionality
- directing users' navigation efforts through design

We also assessed the site against guidelines such as ASHA's own Web writing guidelines. And even though ASHA wasn't legally obliged to conform to federal accessibility legislation, they wanted to be leaders in accessibility. So, we evaluated against federal accessibility standards.

These analyses led to recommendations to help the ASHA Web team make UCD decisions.

Expert Review Findings

The expert review report discussed 581 issues, prioritized according to their potential impact on user success and satisfaction. It cited strengths to build on and areas to improve. For each finding, it cited and explained usability principles and gave a usability engineering rationale. It identified areas to investigate during focus groups and user observations.

An electronic version of the report went to the ASHA Web team and to other stakeholders at ASHA. H&CI structured the report to help them process it quickly. Screen captures, drawings, and flow charts illustrated points. There were electronic links from discussions to screenshots and flow charts. Each finding was numbered for reference during discussions and traceability.

Seventeen topics identified by the ASHA and H&CI team each became a chapter in the report. Each stakeholder could go directly to topics of interest or concern. In each chapter, an electronic table of contents helped readers move directly to subtopics. Each chapter had an executive summary that set out major findings. The chapters were

1. Introduction and Background
2. The ASHA Community: Building and Connecting
3. Page Layout
4. Forms and Tables
5. Site Information Architecture

6. Site Navigation

7. Information Search and Retrieval

8. Language

9. Color

10. Graphics

11. eCommerce

12. Internationalization and Localization (Multicultural Affairs)

13. Universal Access: Special Needs Access

14. Access by Senior Citizens

15. Web-Based Technology

16. Pulling It All Together

17. Appendices (Explanations of Usability Principles; ASHA's Own Web-Writing Guidelines; Special Needs Access and Section 508; Technical Difficulty Reports)

It's not possible to summarize such a large report here, so we'll zero in on five chapters.

The ASHA Community: Building and Connecting

The site needed to make a better first impression. The entry page needed more information to show that the site offered great value (see Figure B.2). It needed to move users quickly to its content. Users' reactions to language on the site, especially in titles and labels, became a focus group topic.

A large portion of the site's users were more than 40 years old. A major problem they confronted was illegibility caused by small fonts. Plus, it was difficult for users with motor disabilities to click on small text links. To complicate things, most of these users were not expert enough to understand that they could change the font size on a Web page. This chapter stressed the need to accommodate users with low computer literacy.

Site Information Architecture

The existing information architecture did not lead members directly to members -only information and functionality. We already knew that the site's structure

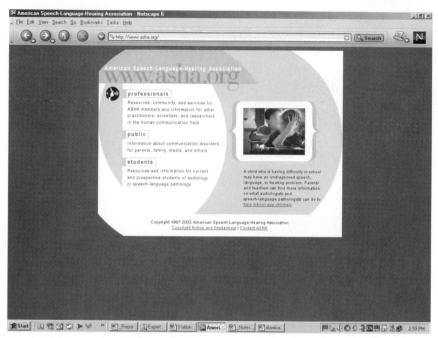

Figure B.2 Before the redesign, the site's entry page had room for more information to show users right from the start that the ASHA site held lots of value for them.

reflected ASHA's organization. In the focus groups and user observations, we needed to learn about users' mental models of where to find information and functionality.

Site Navigation

On most pages at the site's upper levels, there was empty real estate in the left and right columns—space to engage users with previews of the site's valuable content (see Figure B.3). The ASHA logo linked back to the professional homepage, the page where members could sign into their private part of the site. Following the convention of using the logo to link back to the site's homepage would fill users' expectations and give them a fast path back to their starting point.

It was important to do everything possible to make the search functionality simpler to use. The site needed to accommodate novice users with clear instructions on how to search. It needed to provide search functionality on its welcome page. The new search engine also needed advanced functionality to accommodate aca-

Figure B.3 Before the redesign, there was plenty of room in the site's left and right columns for links to invite users to visit other parts of the site.

demics who wanted to build complex Boolean searches. One problem was simply a matter of knowing the right search term. SLPs would know to look for information about swallowing under "dysphagia," but the public most likely wouldn't. ASHA was already building a thesaurus to address this issue.

Graphics

Graphics were, for the most part, one of the site's strengths. They almost always complemented or enhanced a page's content and functionality. As shown in Figure B.4, several of the site's pages included photos, which stressed the fact that ASHA was a people-oriented association. The site needed to build on this strength by using more photos of real people at ASHA National Headquarters and real members at work. We needed to check out this idea with users.

Brackets surrounded page titles (see Figure B.5), giving them a tentative aspect. This detracted from the site's ability to communicate its role as an authority in the fields of speech-language pathology and audiology. The brackets needed to

Figure B.4 Photos of real people at ASHA gave the site life.

Figure B.5 Before the redesign, brackets made page titles look unimportant.

go. And the titles needed to be presented as text, not graphics, so that people who used screen readers would know the title of the page they were on.

Special Needs

Users with visual disabilities use screen readers that "read" a Web page out loud in synthesized speech. To fulfill its goal of accessibility for users with special needs, the site had to accommodate screen readers better. Its alt tags needed to be more descriptive to give these users the same rich experiences as other site visi-

tors. Instead of only saying "continuing education," an alt tag also needed to tell users that the graphic showed a student in a classroom.

The American Psychology Association has published guidelines that have become de facto standards for describing people with disabilities. Sometimes the site conformed to these guidelines, but sometimes it didn't. For example, instead of saying "disabled children" the site needed to say "children with disabilities." It needed to conform to these guidelines all the time.

Outcomes

The Web team decided they would accept most of the recommendations and make changes over time. The highest priorities were going to go to the information architecture and site navigation. This, in turn, would mean major changes to page layout.

Requirements Gathering with Users: Focus Groups

We came to focus group planning with a list of goals from prior activities. We wanted to collect user feedback on the drivers behind users' reactions to www.asha.org. Most important, we wanted to learn about users' mental models of where information should be located on the site.

ASHA has a group of people responsible for approving topics for focus groups. H&CI worked directly with these experts, as well as with the ASHA Web team, developing a plan that set out goals and topics for the focus groups. For each four-hour focus group, there was a core set of topics and topics to introduce if time allowed.

One manager and two staff members participated in the Action Center focus group. Topics were based on what we had learned observing staff at work in the Action Center. Sample discussion points included the following.

- Let's come up with a list of the ten questions that callers and people who e-mail ask most often.

- Sometimes you refer questions to other people at the ASHA National Headquarters. Let's talk about those questions.

- Sometimes you add pages in the ASHA site to your favorites list because you frequently find answers to users' questions on those pages. Let's put together a list of the pages that you bookmark.

- I'm going to give each of you some sticky notes. On each one, please write one thing that you think is important content for the site.

Because we could not schedule enough school-based SLPs, the second focus group had a wide representation of ASHA members—three school-based SLPs, two school-based audiologists, an audiologist in a management position for the Maryland State Department of Education, and a recent graduate who was serving a clinical fellowship in audiology.

Topics for member SLPs and audiologists focused on learning what information they needed from the site and how it should be organized. Discussion points included the following.

- (Opening the site to show the focus group participants the entry page for the first time during the session) When you first come to the ASHA site, what is your first impression?
- What kind of content do you look for on the ASHA site?
- Let's talk about your experiences locating content on the ASHA site.
- What is your impression of graphics on the site?
- What is your impression of language on the site?
- I'm going to give each of you some sticky notes. On each one, please write one thing that you think is important content for the site.

At the end of each focus group, the participants pooled and grouped their sticky notes (similar to a card sorting activity). These groupings became the building blocks of a new information architecture.

It's difficult to take enough notes and impossible to remember everything that goes on during a focus group. So, we videotaped the sessions for later analysis.

Focus Groups Findings

The focus group report updated 28 expert review recommendations, either revising them or changing their priority. It added 48 recommendations, bringing the total to 629. It was organized into 18 categories that corresponded to the participants' principal concerns. It backed up recommendations by references to the same usability principles, standards, and guidelines used in the expert review.

The most emphatic findings were common to both focus groups. The site was not meeting its potential to support members, its most important users, in their practices. Information and functionality weren't where participants expected to find them. All participants wanted fast and easy navigation to the right destination. They complained of "too many clicks" between pages and too much empty screen space. They said they'd prefer longer pages with lots of information.

Members all felt the site had great potential. They wanted to be a part of its success story. They had strong convictions about the kind of information they wanted to find on the site. They wanted ASHA to continue to provide information on continuing education in members' fields. They also needed information to support them in their work, for example, by helping them keep up with advances in their fields.

Much of the functionality and information members said they needed actually existed on the site. In some cases, they didn't know it was there. In other cases, they knew it must be there, but they couldn't find it. For example, members didn't notice navigation links in the side bars. They wouldn't recommend the existing site to others.

Both groups had developed lists of the information and functionality they wanted. Then they had arranged this content into groups. Members were surprised about what happened next. They agreed on what content they wanted, but disagreed on where to locate some of that content. When the site had content aimed at more than one set of users, the usability engineering solution was to make that content accessible from more than one place. Everyone agreed on one site organization strategy—let members navigate directly to speech-language pathology or audiology content from the site's entry page.

Both focus groups expressed a need for short information sheets, what the members called "Quick Sheets" to give a quick overview of facts and issues. They needed these to easily and quickly keep up-to-date in their fields and to give to clients. This idea sounded a lot like the printouts that ASHA staff had prepared to respond to members' questions.

A surprise from the members was a strong call for a new look—one with "pizzazz." They especially disliked the way the site used color. The day of the members focus group, the site's entry page featured clip art. The members called for swapping the site's clip art, as shown in Figure B.6, with photographs that showed the "friendly face of ASHA." They praised a photo montage already on the site (see Figure B.4). This was the kind of graphic they wanted.

The ASHA Web team was interested in language on the site, especially language that impacted navigation. Both focus groups reported that some labels were mis-

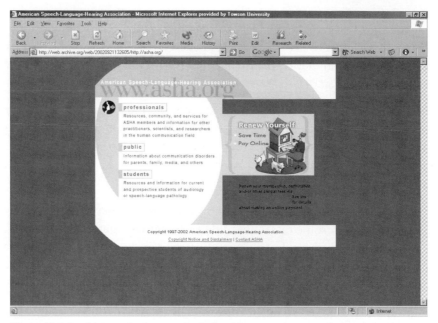

Figure B.6 Looking at the legacy site helped focus groups zero in on important topics. For example, we learned members wanted to swap the site's clip art for photos of people.

leading. Members agreed that the name of one of the site's three sections, "Professionals," needed to be more specific. They wanted to see "SLPs and Audiologists."

Functionality labeled "ProServ" provided information about members who practiced outside of the schools. At the time of the focus groups, out of 53,000 eligible members, only about 5,000 had registered to include their information in this online professional referral service. The Action Center team reported that members didn't know they had to register and sometimes called to ask why their name wasn't included. Members reported that they didn't know about the service and that the name didn't tell them what it was. They came up with a variety of solutions. Their favorite was "Locate Services/Providers in Your Area."

This led to another discovery. Participants reported that other functionality was difficult or too time-consuming to use. The members considered each other valued resources. They wanted easier ways to connect to each other. Members repeated what the academics had told us—having to remember a user number for login was too much trouble. They wanted an easier-to-use search functionality.

Outcomes

The focus group report stressed UCD. It didn't embrace user-driven design. It reported participants concerns, but users' remedies that violated good usability practices did not become recommendations.

A more inviting and information-intensive site entry page became part of the plan for the prototype. The ASHA Web team decided to experiment with some new labels and a new color scheme. There would also be more photo montages. But, the focus group's recommendation of pizzazz did not coincide with stakeholders' vision for the site's professional look and feel.

The ASHA and H&CI team decided that to improve users' success and satisfaction in finding what they sought at the ASHA site, the user observations should focus on a new information architecture and users' experiences navigating that architecture. The team concentrated on speedy navigation to the information and functionality users needed. The focus groups' ideas for content and information architecture became input to this effort.

We had gathered a lot of information to inform UCD. Everything we had learned up to this point had to come together during the user observations.

Prototype Design and Building

H&CI had to administer user observations without bias toward any design approach. While H&CI could answer questions about usability during prototyping, it wouldn't participate directly in design. So, at the beginning of the usability study, we planned that ASHA would develop the prototype independently.

The ASHA Web team concentrated on a new look and feel that would be more interesting, yet still promote the professional look and feel that had been the site's hallmark. They developed a prototype that introduced a new look for major pages on the first two layers of the site. Not all navigation routes were activated.

The prototype, as shown in Figure B.7, presented a new information architecture and navigation scheme. The site entry page was longer and held more information. Its original three sections increased to four and introduced new section labels—For ASHA Members Only, For All Professionals, For Students, and For the Public. Menus and submenus outlined the contents of each of the four sections.

Fly-out menus in the left bar offered the same options as drop-down menus under each of the section titles. By giving users more than one way to navigate,

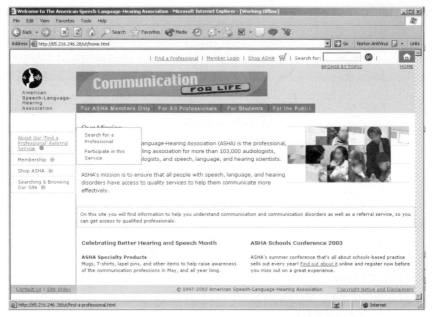

Figure B.7 The prototype ASHA produced during the usability study featured four navigation paths and fly-out menus.

this approach followed an important usability principle—accommodate users' work styles. These menus directly accessed the site's third level. The Members Only submenu gave SLPs or audiologists a direct route to content specific to their professions.

And for those users in a hurry, there was a placeholder for a search box on every page of the prototype. It wasn't functional—that would come in a later version—but it showed users that ASHA was going to address their need for speed.

There was a new color scheme. Photos replaced clip art. Brackets disappeared from titles. The ASHA Web team experimented with new labels—ProServ became "Find a Professional." The site's opening page was full of content that emphasized what the members' focus group had called "the friendly face of ASHA." The value that the site offered was obvious to users from their very first glance.

Usability Testing: User Observations

At the start of the study, H&CI made a commitment to ASHA never to use the term "testing." This was part of an effort to build a strong collaborative environment. Because the word "testing" has the judgmental connotations of passing and failing, we agreed to use the word "evaluation."

The goal of the usability evaluation (see Figure B.8) was to assess user success and satisfaction with a prototype by observing users performing typical tasks. The users added another goal—even though we didn't request it, they often compared the prototype with the legacy site.

The budget allowed for one user group. The ASHA Web team chose the site's largest, school-based SLPs. Any changes we made to improve their experiences would most likely make the site more usable for other user groups too.

Users' tasks documented during requirements gathering became scenarios for user observations. We started with a quick and easy "comfort scenario" to let users settle in and relax. So, users would navigate to a Web site of their own choosing.

ASHA User Observations: Scenarios

User No. _____   Date: _____

Finding Information on Stuttering for a Parent

Background: You have just returned from a parent conference with the mother of Lucy Hansen, a 13-year-old you are treating for stuttering. Lucy's mother has requested some easy-to-understand information about stuttering. You have promised to send the information home with Lucy tomorrow. You have five minutes before your next parent conference. You decide to see what's available on the ASHA prototype Web site.

Tasks

1. Find information on stuttering to send to Lucy's mother.

2. Look through the information to see if it's easy to understand.

3. Print this information for Lucy's mother.

Figure B.8 The users' background/task sheet for a scenario gave the background and tasks but never told the users how to accomplish the tasks.

Eleven scenarios for data collection each incorporated an information-seeking task that the team had chosen. Each scenario started with a short background that set out the user's role. Then there were tasks, but never any clues about how to accomplish them.

We gave the users a separate background/task sheet for each scenario. We didn't expect everyone to finish all the scenarios, so we started with the most important and finished with the least important. We asked users to read the scenarios out loud as they worked.

We quickly learned that we had chosen relevant scenarios. During the observations, the SLPs nodded and commented that this was "real life."

Observing Users' Working with the Prototype

Five users all performed the same tasks in the same sequence so we could collect the same types of data during all the user sessions. We call this parallel data.

We worked with each user individually, each on a different day. We stressed the fact that it was the prototype, not the user that was being evaluated. As a matter of fact, it was the user who was doing the evaluation. The rest of us were only observers.

Each user consented to being filmed and sound recorded. Keystroke-recording software captured data on users' success—types and numbers of errors, and whether users completed tasks. We noted critical incidents—times when users had to stop because they didn't know what to do next. We watched for latency periods—times when users paused, trying to figure out what to do next.

While they worked with the prototype, we encouraged users to "think aloud," sharing their expectations and reactions. At specified points in the scenarios, we asked the users questions about their satisfaction with the prototype.

Users who finished the planned tasks with time to spare had the opportunity to test drive the prototype on their own. We collected the same types of data as we had with the scenarios, but, this data was not parallel because the users chose their own tasks.

User Survey

With ASHA's survey experts, we wrote a survey to collect data on screen elements that the SLPs used during the scenarios. In the survey, users described their experiences and gave opinions using a rating scale that went from five (best) to one (worst). They always had the option of not answering by choosing N/A (see Figure B.9.) The survey offered plenty of opportunities for users to elaborate on their answers or to share comments on topics that the survey didn't address.

5	4	3	2	1	N/A
I always find the information I want			I never find the information I want		

Figure B.9 Users rated their experiences on a scale from five (best) to one (worst).

The survey started by asking users about themselves. This not only gave us valuable information, it put users at ease because they were starting with a topic they knew well. One section focused on language in the prototype and another on its features and functions. We asked about users' satisfaction with the prototype—finding information, the look and feel, moving around the site, and the new menus. We asked the users to prioritize the information needs that we had learned about during requirements gathering. They also had an opportunity to add to the list.

After a break, users viewed the site on two different screens—an LCD (liquid crystal display, such as the screens of portable computers) and a CRT (cathode-ray tube such as glass screens in older monitors and TVs). At this point, the survey addressed colors and graphics. It asked them how they thought the site would work for them in their jobs.

Interviews

After the observations, we interviewed the users, starting with a few prepared questions. We came prepared with written directions to make sure that we asked the same questions in the same sequence (see Figure B.10).

We invited users to talk about any aspect of the site or their experience that they wanted to discuss. We also captured users' reactions to issues the Web team was considering, but couldn't explore with the prototype. For example, we collected metric data on their satisfaction with alternative versions of some of the labels.

The H&CI deliverables were a report and a presentation to the ASHA Web team on findings. The user observations brought the number of recommendations

15. Draw user's attention to the **Member Login** link at the top of the page. Pointing out the link, ask: What does "**Member Login**" mean to you?

Expected answer: to get to members-only information, information that is not available to people who are not members AND who are not registered on the site. If any other answer is given, explore it.

Administrator will tell the user that this functionality isn't available in the prototype.

● How would you expect to use this?
● Do you have any other comments to share about this?

Figure B.10 The usability engineers had instructions to make sure that they asked post-usability evaluation questions in the same way.

to 647—more strengths to build on and issues to address. It revised three recommendations.

User Success

One of the greatest strengths of the new architecture was that it quickly and simply led users directly from the homepage into four major categories of information. It appeared that this structure would scale up to a site of 4,000 pages.

The users tended to navigate the site within the context of their own professional roles. There was a strong tendency to navigate through the Speech-Language Pathology and SLPs link on the Members Only drop-down and by using an SLPs in Schools page. Just like the focus group, they wanted to be able to navigate directly to information about their professions from the homepage.

Users' positive experiences with the drop-down and fly-out menus pointed out another strength. The menus sped users to major information categories. The report recommended adding another level to the menus to lead users deeper into the information architecture and to increase the likelihood that they would find the content they sought. This recommendation came with a caveat. The prototype only contained a small part of the site's content. We couldn't be certain that the prototype's menu and submenu option categories would accommodate users' mental models for the wide range of content a fully populated site would offer.

All of the users preferred a search box over a menu as their primary means of finding information. In a future version with a functional search box, and the functionality to search by topic, the ASHA Web team would be giving users exactly what they wanted where they expected to find it.

Users found that most of the new labels were easy to understand. They were able to get to members-only information easily. ProServ had become the Find a Professional Referral Service. The new name made more sense to users than ProServ. The site informed members that they had to register to be included in this service.

The prototype contained some sparsely populated pages. While these pages filled in slots in the navigation scheme, they generated more steps for users. UCD called for eliminating these pages.

In the survey, users had prioritized their information needs. Their needs were very similar to those of other users we had worked with. They wanted information to help them in their work and information on the continuing education that their profession required.

User Satisfaction

During interviews and focus groups, members' responses to satisfaction questions about the legacy site had been negative. Survey answers to those same questions told us that user satisfaction with the prototype was higher than satisfaction with the legacy site.

Users gave ratings between three and four, out of a possible five, for ease of using various features, moving around the site, text organization, overall look, and finding information. Their satisfaction was in the positive range for titles, labels of links, menus, and menu sub-topics.

Most importantly, users gave a 4.5 out of a possible 5.0 rating on their impressions of being able to get to their information destinations at the site. The prototype had addressed users' strongest concern and fulfilled a most important usability principle—users felt they were in control of their experience.

There was a disparity between users' comments during "think aloud" and interviews and their color ratings in the survey. During the scenarios and interviews, users did not like the site's color scheme. In the survey, users gave a better-than-neutral 3.5 rating to color viewed on an LCD screen. Satisfaction went below the neutral range, to approximately 2.5 for color viewed on a CRT screen. In the prototype, photos had been re-colored to use the site's new color scheme. The ASHA Web team was on the right track using photos, but users wanted true-to-life, full-color photos. This was the reason why satisfaction went below the neutral range and into the dissatisfaction range for photographs viewed on both the LCD and CRT screens.

Outcomes

Had we achieved our big goal? Was the team on the way to making the Web site the most valuable and valued benefit that ASHA offered its members? In the best tradition of UCD, we asked the users. There was one make-it-or-break-it question in the user observation survey. We asked if participants would recommend the ASHA prototype site to a colleague looking for information on speech-language pathology. They said "yes" with an average rating of 4.25 out of a possible 5.0. As one member put it after working with the prototype, "I think the new site would benefit my colleagues." "Benefit!" Our goal, exactly!

Then, we posed another show-stopper. Would the prototype help the users in their work? Would they recommend the prototype site to parents? The users' approval came through loud and clear with an average rating of 4.5 out of 5.0, much better than earlier findings for the legacy system.

Users transfer their impressions of a Web site to their impressions of the site's providers. Did the prototype shed a good light on ASHA? In the words of a member during the user observations, "This Web site has made me view ASHA in a more positive way."

The user observations had validated that the ASHA Web team was on the right track. They considered this a milestone, but not a grand finale. They remained committed to iterative improvement. We had arrived at the most important point in a usability study. After the user observations, the time came for the ASHA Web team to apply everything we had learned to make important decisions about the new look and feel of www.asha.org. The task list was challenging, but doable.

ASHA decided to publish the site with the new navigation scheme and labels. They continued to use photos, but wanted to investigate the color issue more before deciding whether to keep it or change it. They would continue to work on accessibility. In the next round of design changes, they would build on their success in meeting users' expectations about navigation. For starters, they would have the ASHA logo on each page link back to the site's entry page. The to-do list included helping senior citizens change font size; remembering users' login information; explaining .pdf files; and helping users download a .pdf reader.

Step by step, many of the topics the focus groups had stressed found their way into drop-down menus on the site's entry page, categorized to meet users' expectations (see Figure B.11). SLPs and audiologists had direct paths to their own content. Search boxes appeared at the top of all pages—complete with options for Boolean searches. "Quick Facts," "Quick Sheets," and "Fact Sheets" answered the call for short, easy-to-understand information presentations.

The site maintained its professional demeanor, but presented the "friendly face of ASHA" in photographs of smiling people. The entry page more than tripled in length to put the site's best foot forward with previews of interesting content. From the first glance, the site announced its great value and delivered users directly to it.

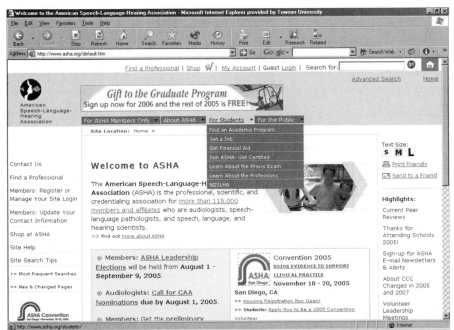

 Also in the
Color Insert

Figure B.11 Step by step, the site became more responsive to users' needs.

Conclusions

Although ASHA published its redesigned site, this is a story without an ending—which is a very good thing. ASHA commits to monitor its Web site continually and make improvements as needed.

The ASHA Web team reviewed all of H&CI's usability engineering recommendations, considering the wide range of factors beyond usability that come into play. Throughout the study, they accepted some recommendations, making them requirements, decided against others, changed some priorities, and added new requirements. The requirements list would continue to evolve with the needs of ASHA and its site's users. And, as we saw throughout the usability study, there are always surprises along the way.

ASHA's membership has grown and its mission statement has expanded: "To promote the interests of and provide the highest quality services for professionals in audiology, speech-language pathology, and speech and hearing science, and to advocate for people with communication disabilities." Their new Web site will be a valuable and valued asset in helping them achieve that mission.

Even without an ending to our story, some conclusions are obvious. The ASHA Web site users have a more usable site, a site with a higher potential for user success and satisfaction. And, the Web team is firmly on the path to making www.asha.org the most valuable and valued asset for ASHA members.

CancerNet—

How the Usability-Led Redesign of CancerNet.gov Helped to Change the Thinking about Web Design at the National Cancer Institute

Sanjay Koyani
Senior Usability Specialist

Craig Lafond
Senior Information Technology Specialist

Web Management Team
U.S. Department of Health and Human Services

Janice Nall
Manager, User Experience Group
Office of E-Gov Solutions
General Services Administration

Overview

The federal government began building Web sites in the early- to mid-1990s with a modest communication goal to just "get it up on the Web." Many of the federal government's early Webmasters and communications planners who worked with Webmasters saw cyberspace much as others who were using it for the first time—they simply viewed it as another place to put their collection of information. If the uploaded information was accurate, spell-checked, and grammatically correct, it was fine. The Web was not much more than an alternative location for information that was traditionally transmitted by phone, fax, mail, or from citizens making a visit to a federal agency. Little thought was given to *how* the information was presented on the Web.

How times have changed. A couple years in the technology world is like several decades in another industry, given the rapid pace of change. But today, as technology has evolved, professionals who are responsible for government Web sites are considering the way that information is presented on the Web. Web surfers have become Web users and are no longer willing to tolerate poor design or disorganized sites. Visitors to government Web sites are beginning to ask themselves: How many screens do I have to scroll/click through to get to the information I want? Is this information so valuable that I am willing to click through seemingly endless screens to obtain it? On the other side of the coin, Web developers and other government communicators who work with the Web are beginning to ask, will people return to my Web site if they have trouble accessing information the first time around? Do our category labels make sense? Does our navigation help users find what they are looking for or does it confuse them even more?

The fact that these questions are even coming to mind is a testament to changing attitudes about Web sites, and it validates the work that was done by the National Cancer Institute's (NCI) Communication Technologies Branch (CTB) in NCI's Office of Communications. The branch, created in 2000, led innovative usability initiatives in the federal sector and broadly shared what it learned about producing usable information-based Web sites to its colleagues throughout the federal government and even outside government.

The Communication Technologies Branch—Why Is a Cancer Organization Involved in Usability Engineering?

The Communication Technologies Branch (CTB), which led usability-related efforts at NCI from 2000 to 2003, was responsible for ensuring the usability of

NCI Web sites and various other communication technologies that distribute important cancer information to the public and the cancer community. However, CTB did more than usability testing. It was involved in the whole range of usability engineering—information architecture, user data collection, prototype design, and graphic design, among other things. The branch also collected information and mined extensive research to determine—based on supporting evidence—the best approach to designing Web sites and disseminating cancer information in other digital formats as well, including newer and emerging technologies like personal digital assistants and handheld devices. CTB's job was to make cancer research information easier to find and more understandable when the public received it. CTB was formed as a branch of NCI, part of the National Institutes of Health, U.S. Department of Health and Human Services, because of what was learned during the redesign of NCI's CancerNet Web site.

This Case Study focuses on that redesign project. It provides an in-depth look at how the practice of usability engineering can lead to better sites that are easier to use and easier to learn.

CTB devoted significant energy to sharing the knowledge it acquired. The key enabler of this sharing is a signature site containing a wealth of new user-centered design research and resources, usability.gov. The site includes CTB's well-regarded and first-of-a-kind *Research-Based Web Design & Usability Guidelines*. Another popular section of the innovative usability.gov Web site, which was cited in 2002 for an E-Gov Trailblazer award, is an area called *Lessons Learned*, where Web developers and others can access details about the CancerNet Case Study and other lessons learned.

CTB used three tools to share information and lessons learned.

1. Research-Based Web Design & Usability Guidelines. Published online at http://usability.gov/pdfs/guidelines.html, these new guidelines provide specific, evidence-based strategies and tips for creating usable Web sites. The tips result from extensive testing and analysis of Web site usability. These guidelines address such topics as font size, use of icons and buttons, unused space on a page, page layout, content organization, and the development of effective prototypes for usability testing.

2. Usability.gov. This site is a compendium of information about how to develop usable, useful, and accessible information-based Web sites. The site provides evidence-based recommendations for developing Web sites that are designed according to user-centered principles. A host of resources for developing usable Web sites is also offered on the site. The site generates about 30,000 visitors a month.

3. Communication Technologies Research Center. This state-of-the-art facility provides space and equipment for usability testing, training, communication technologies evaluation, demonstrations, and other related services for CTB and its partners. The 3,300-square foot center features

- formal usability labs where test participants are observed performing specific tasks on prototype Web pages

- seminars and training programs designed to improve the usability, access, and usefulness of communications technology products and services

- testing and demonstrating a variety of emerging technologies— hardware and software—so information developers can see these new tools in action

Note: Usability.gov and the *Research-Based Web Design & Usability Guidelines* have been relocated to the Department of Health and Human Services as a broader department wide initiative that will allow a more cross-agency approach with broader participation and learning.

CancerNet has now been renamed Cancer.gov. CancerNet was re-launched early in 2002 under the new name, with many of NCI's existing Web sites folded into it. In its previous iteration as CancerNet, the site won numerous awards and was considered the most authoritative government resource on cancer on the Web. CancerNet had established a reputation as the "go-to" place for official information about cancer, from cancer types, to cancer treatment, to cancer genetics, to cancer causes, risk factors, and prevention. The awards were earned for CancerNet's site design and usability.

Because CancerNet reaches a very diverse audience of cancer patients, researchers, medical professionals, and health policy decision makers, the redesign created some interesting challenges in user-centered design. For example, what a researcher needs to know about cancer may be entirely different from what someone who has just been diagnosed with breast cancer needs to know. In redesigning CancerNet, the reality of a broad, diverse audience made user experience and user preferences even more important in creating a functional design. This Case Study describes what took place and how, during the core redesign.

Defining the Mission and the Target User Population

Many Web developers can identify with the early days of the CancerNet redesign, when the team was trying to figure out where to start. There was a huge diversity of opinions about what the new site should look and feel like, and what it should do. A workable timeline also had to be developed for the project. A tough aspect of the CancerNet redesign was deciding how to implement the decision to take a new approach to site design, turning the focus away from the organization and/or the developer toward the user.

Traditionally, new Web projects begin with intense discussions among creative-minded developers and designers about graphics and design schemes. What color scheme should the site display? Should the site be built with frames or not? Where should the navigation buttons be located? What role should multimedia play? In what amounted to a paradigm shift, these kinds of discussions gave way to talk about the users—Who is using the site? What specific information are they looking for? What terminology do they use? Do people's eyes scan left or right when they first hit the page? What is the most effective way to present links to users? What fonts are easiest for Web users to handle when scanning the page?

In retrospect, the creation of CTB and the emphasis on usability was a well-timed move, affirmed by the following data.

- More than 60 percent of Web site users cannot find the information they are searching for, though they are at the right Web site, according to User Interface Engineering, Inc.

- Approximately 40 percent of Web users do not come back to a site after their first visit if they have a negative experience, as noted in a Forrester Research study.

Requirements Gathering with Users: Learning What Users Want

The data collection effort was a two-and-a-half month project to obtain feedback from CancerNet users. It was the first key step toward the redesign. Through an online survey, the team learned what information users wanted to see on the site and what terminology they used. The survey also covered current users' opinions about the existing site. A total of 615 users responded to the online survey.

One of the greatest revelations of the survey was that one-third of CancerNet's users were first-time visitors. That was surprising new information to the team. With so many new users coming to the site, usability became an even greater issue in CancerNet's redesign. The challenge was to create a user-centric site that was easy enough for first-time users to learn, for repeat visitors to re-learn quickly, and for frequent users to find the information they need quickly.

One of the lessons learned was how a combination of specific and open-ended questions works best to elicit useful responses on a feedback form (see Figure C.1).

Specific	**Open-Ended**
In what state do you live?	Describe any difficulties you encountered using the Web site.

Figure C.1 Comparison of specific and open-ended question styles.

NCI turned to health-care facilities to find real users to interview to validate the information gleaned from the online survey. Patients, family members, nurses, physicians, and social workers were interviewed individually, and they confirmed the data collected online. By interviewing participants in person, the team was able to get a wealth of in-depth information from people's facial expressions as well as other nonverbal cues and voice inflections, to detailed experiences in searching for cancer information.

A major finding of the data collection process was that open-ended questions worked better on questions where the response could give you feedback on terminology issues. In addition, this format does not limit the way that users could provide their answers, creating the opportunity for Web developers to glean much more information from users about usability issues than if users were asked to respond to narrowly defined questions. Some sample interview questions follow.

Questions for a Physician in a Data Collection Interview

- Do your patients bring you information from the Web?
- How do you respond?

Questions for a Cancer Patient in a Data Collection Interview

- How do you ask your physician for information?
- How does your physician respond to your information requests?

This data gathering experience also taught us that the online survey should be kept short, with best results coming from asking 10 or fewer questions. As a result, we included just four or five questions about site use in the questions, while several more related to demographics. Research shows that people are more likely to fill out forms if the forms are simple and short. CTB purposely did not include any questions about the design in order to keep users focused on core concerns such as what information they were looking for, what information the site lacked, and other feedback. Tables C.1 and C.2 provide data from the responses to the questionnaire.

Interestingly, a large percentage of the survey respondents said they wanted information about a specific type of cancer—"I want everything you have on lung cancer." Another surprise from the data collection was the makeup of the CancerNet

Table C.1 "What information are you looking for?"—Data from survey responders.

Major Categories	%
Information on specific type of cancer	23
Treatment information	19
Symptoms, causes, risk factors …	8
Statistics (e.g., incidence rates, survival)	3
Clinical trials	11
Access to other resources (e.g., treatment facilities, physicians)	3
Drug information	3
NIH organization (e.g., mission, employment)	—
New treatments	5
Ordering NCI publications	2
Recent findings	—
Type of tumor (not by cancer name)	7
Cancer literature	5
Patient support	4
Side effects	3

Note: Respondents could select more than one category.

Table C.2 "Which of the following best describes you?"—Data from survey responders.

	N	%
Family/Friends	169	28
Cancer Patients	85	14
Educators/Students	—	—
Researchers/Scientist	41	7
Nurse (non-Oncology)	15	2
Oncology Nurse	14	2
Oncologist	60	10
Physician (non-Oncology)	22	4
Journalist/Media Professional	—	—
Librarian	29	5
Patient Advocate	8	1
Other	91	15
Not specified	81	13
	615	

audience. As it turned out, CancerNet's biggest users were caregivers—not patients, physicians, or other medical and health-care professionals as was speculated. This information certainly had a significant impact on the redesign.

Information Architecture and Site Navigation

Once user feedback was collected and CTB had a good profile of users and what they wanted, it was time to start developing a prototype site and do usability testing to determine its effectiveness in meeting users' needs. Data collection clearly affected prototyping, and the survey results actually drove the site layout. Through iterative prototyping and testing, CTB was able to develop a better product because it allowed developers to resolve problems during the redesign rather than at the end of the process, when it is much more costly. Usability testing of early prototypes was used to help determine the information architecture and site navigation. Examples of the site navigation appear later in this case study.

Usability Testing

Usability engineering was key to the CancerNet redesign. The benefits of months of data collection and developing user-centered prototypes became evident when it came time for usability testing. More than 140 people (in groups of 8 to 16) participated in various stages of the usability testing process for CancerNet. The testers were recruited by professional recruiting firms and by CTB staff attending various medical conventions. In fact, some of the testing was conducted on-site at medical conventions in Atlanta, San Francisco, and New Orleans.

Two types of usability tests were conducted. In some settings, we tested at medical conferences (in hotel rooms with a portable usability lab). We also conducted usability testing in formal lab settings with complete usability setups. We found little difference in the test results in these different testing environments.

The usability testing focused on testing the site's new features and functionality, testing the search engine functionality as well as the site's information architecture, including second- and third-tier pages. In addition, CTB tested the site's graphics, but graphics were applied and tested at the end after the information architecture and navigation were firmly established and refined through testing. In a departure from the usual practice, CTB used the usability testing results to refine the new site by building the interface first and the programming second. Often, programming decisions precede the selection of the interface. The usability engineering approach allowed users to drive the layout and design rather than having the technology drive the users.

Testing included giving users a set of scenarios—or tasks—to complete. Those tasks included having users complete an exercise in which they located basic cancer research information and tracked down descriptions of different types of cancers on the site. As users completed these tasks, their progress—or lack of it, along with their frustration—was recorded according to time and end result. The scenarios were realistic tasks identified in the online user survey. Following are some of the tasks from user testing.

- "You are being treated for cancer and are having problems with depression, nausea, and vomiting. What can you do to alleviate these problems?" In this scenario, users must browse through the Web site to find the information that addresses this task. The information is definitely located on the site, but the real test is in how much time and how many wrong paths users took to reach the information.

- In another scenario, users were told, "You have been diagnosed with stage IV colon cancer. Your doctor has recommended chemotherapy, and you want to know if there are other treatments." Again, users had to go through the site and locate this specific information with observers paying careful attention to how the test participant went about seeking the information and in what time frame. Observers were also interested in why users selected certain links, why they ignored certain links, and how they scanned a page.

Based on our experience, CTB recommends the following usability testing techniques.

Have Users/Test Participants Perform Actual Tasks. Having test participants perform specific and realistic tasks on the site helps measure efficiency and clarity of the site's navigation structure as well as its content. Ideally, during testing, you want users to search for specific information located on the site. Did the users go through the desired number of clicks? Did users miss any signals on the page? Are items clearly labeled? Did users give up the search in frustration?

Ask Probing Questions to Elicit Additional Information. Another lesson we learned is to be forthright when asking users about a Web site's structure and terminology. During the testing phase, some users may be reluctant to bring up certain issues, or they may be unclear about what it is they are experiencing. By asking the right questions, you can get useful responses that provide clues about how to fix Web site problems *before* you launch. For example, ask, "Did that link take you to where you thought you should go to get the information about colon cancer symptoms, or did you just end up at the right place by trial and error?" That may elicit a more useful answer than "Did you find the information on colon cancer?"

Take Detailed Notes on What Users Say and Do during the Tasks. It is imperative to record as many user actions and comments as possible during testing. From our experience, notes from the testing should be as detailed as possible to allow the preparation of a thorough report and the collection of user information that will clearly identify site problems.

Record the Session on Videotape for Future Reference. Videotaping carries important benefits, allowing facilitators to review a usability session to determine whether certain kinds of questions can elicit useful answers. Much like athletes and coaches, usability engineers can learn from reviewing the "game tapes," which can help point out specific problem areas to management, content developers, or programmers.

Focus on Performance, Not Opinion. Test a user's *performance* on a site. Don't ask them for their preferences. If getting the user to the proper information is the goal of the Web site, then you must test performance. Testing showed that users' preference often contradicted their performance on a site. For example, users may say they are comfortable with hyperlinked text that appears in red, green, or yellow, but when their performance is observed, they navigate sites faster and smoother when they see familiar blue hyperlinks.

Lessons Learned from Early Usability Testing of CancerNet

- It is impossible to predict the range of responses from users. It is difficult to predict accurately how users would go about searching for information on the Web. Only a test can truly demonstrate that experience. Certain features of a site may seem important or usable to designers, but real users may find those same features to be a hindrance to using the site efficiently.

- Usability testing clarifies terminology. The usability testing of CancerNet made it clear to our team that some people were not using the site the way we had anticipated, apparently, because they misunderstood the terms and descriptions we had used (see Figure C.2).

- Complex user interactions need to be tested extensively. Web designs that call for users to operate complex tools on the site must be tested extensively. Instruction-heavy tasks requiring users to enter a variety of information in specified fields, make calculations, or read and analyze data as part of using the site, make such experiences labor intensive. It adds to users' frustrations when the process is not well thought out. For example, the CancerNet PDQ Clinical Trials database requires users to complete a complex search form that involves data entry in several fields and makes selections based on the information that is submitted and processed. Usability testing the form to learn what fields made sense, weren't necessary, or needed to be reordered, ensured that it was usable by all users.

Web Designer Term	User Preferred Term
Glossary	Dictionary
Supportive care	Coping with cancer

Figure C.2 Web designer terminology versus user-preferred terminology.

Launching the Site

The final piece to the puzzle was the most delicate. The risk of making major changes to a site, even if the changes improve the site—especially a high traffic site—is the loss of some of that traffic in the transition. When people notice a redesign of a familiar site, and when that redesign takes them by surprise, they can be intimidated by the changes and go elsewhere. The team was very careful to plan for announcing site changes to regular users.

Clearly, people are more willing to accept change when they are told about the changes in advance. The team recommends the following strategies for informing the public about major site changes. These approaches were successful in alerting the audience to the upcoming changes on CancerNet.

- Tell users what is happening and when the site change will occur.
- Use high visibility screen space on the current site to announce coming changes and show a picture or screenshot of the new homepage.
- If you can, put an announcement on another site that is visited by the same audience.
- Announce the changes in e-mail newsletters, print newsletters, or other print or electronic sources users may read.
- If URLs change, be sure users are quickly redirected to the new pages.

Lessons Learned Overall

The Web is maturing. Clearly, people surf less. Now, they log on more often to go directly to information and services that affect their daily living—health, finance, career, and travel sites are among the most popular. As this transition continues, it is very likely that the Web user will continue to grow in prominence as the focal point of Web design and usability. This is becoming even more important to government and other public sector Web developers, as recent research shows a growing popularity of communication with government via the Web. One study, by the Washington, D.C. nonprofit Pew Internet & American Life Project, found that

- The number of Americans seeking information from the government via the Web rose 70 percent in two years.
- Users primarily access tourism information, research topics for school projects, or government forms for downloading.

- Seventy-six percent of people rated government Web sites good or excellent.

Finally, the CancerNet Case Study shows clearly that for all that the Web has become in such a short amount of time, it still remains a frontier. Projects like the redesign of CancerNet will continue to advance the technology and the body of knowledge in Web design as the Web's role in people's everyday lives expands.

The iterative prototype testing process for CancerNet produced a series of lessons learned that are worth passing on, including:

1. Use a common signature/brand or logo to brand the site. Users need a frame of reference throughout the site so they know they are on your site. Each page needs a common signature or masthead across the top of the site that is constant throughout. (Figure C.3)

2. Put critical global navigation elements together in the same place on each page. Critical global navigation elements such as Home, Help, Dictionary, and Search, need to be present on every page as aids to navigation. (Figure C.3)

3. Prioritize the information. Information should be presented in the order that users identified (in online feedback forms and interviews) as being most important. For example, the majority of users were most interested in information about different types of cancer—which is why this category is positioned in the top left of the page. (Figure C.3)

4. Separate critical core information from secondary information. Page layout must help users find the important information. Primary information should be placed in the center of the page. Secondary information should be placed less prominently on the page. (Figure C.3)

5. Package related information. All information related to one topic should be grouped in one place. This minimizes the need to search the site for related information. It also makes updating much easier. (Figure C.4)

6. Put a table of contents to be used as drop-down links at the top of each page of information. In our site, a table of contents with hyperlinks is located at the top of each cancer topic page so that users can see all their options in the first screen. For example, links to all information on breast cancer, from treatment to publications, is on one page. (Figure C.4)

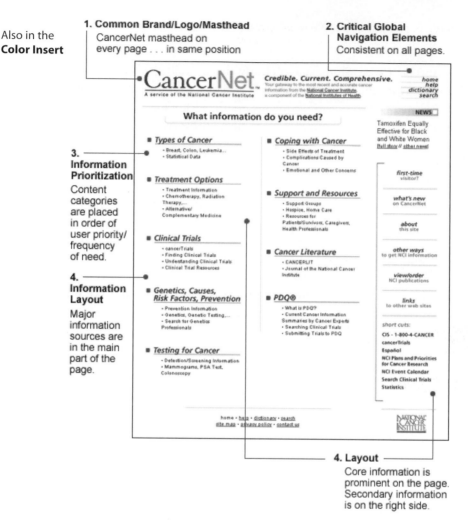

Figure C.3 Separate critical core information from secondary information.

7. Provide multiple paths to the same information. Not all users search for information using the same paths. Different users try different ways to find information depending on their own interpretations of a page. Establishing several access points helps users find what they need no matter where they start. (Figure C.5)

8. Use headings, subheadings, and lists. Users locate information faster when it is presented through headings, subheadings, and short bulleted phrases

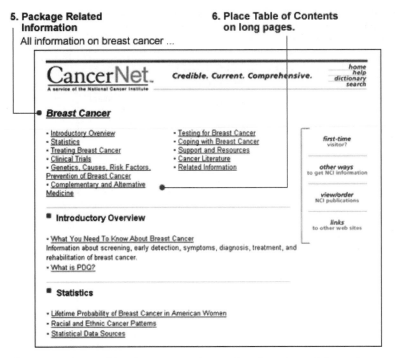

5. Package Related Information

All information on breast cancer ...

6. Place Table of Contents on long pages.

Figure C.4 Put a table of contents to be used as drop-down links at the top of each page of information.

rather than in undifferentiated paragraphs. Using subheadings ensures that some subcategories are not overlooked and also informs users of what they can expect to find. (Figure C.6)

9. Raise information to the highest level. Critical information should be provided as close to the homepage as possible. This minimizes the need to dig deep into the site, which may be difficult for some users. (Figure C.7)

10. Provide assistance to first-time visitors. In our case, more than a third of respondents (36 percent) were first-time visitors. We created a page to give these users extra help in navigating the site. (Figure C.8)

11. Provide easy access to all levels of information. On our site, users want to see information for both the health professional and the patient versions of the documents without first having to declare themselves a health professional or

7. Multiple Paths.
Treatment Options, Type of Cancer, and other pages go to the
Breast Cancer page.

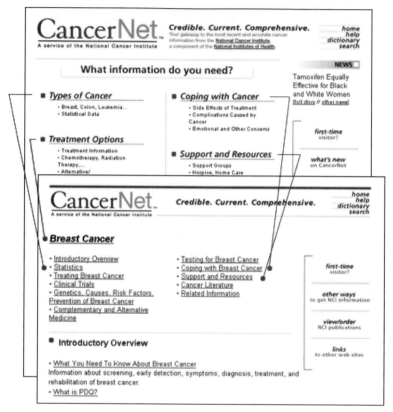

Figure C.5 Provide multiple paths to the same information.

a patient. Therefore, all users navigate the same homepage and second-tier pages. It is not until the document level that users select type: "professional" version or "patient" version. (Figure C.8)

12. Write simply and directly. Users want to get to the point as quickly as possible. They do not read paragraphs of information. They skim for hyperlinks so they can quickly accomplish their goals. We simplified the publications ordering page to bring publications categories up to the top level (see Figures C.9 and C.10).

8. Headings

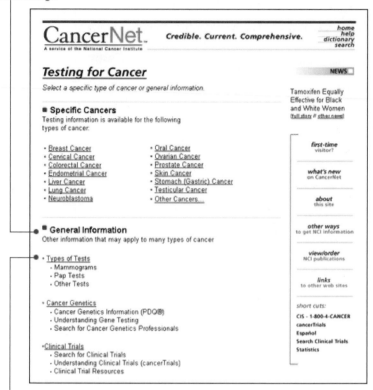

Subheadings

Figure C.6 Using headings, subheadings, and lists.

9. Every major topic of information is listed on the home page.

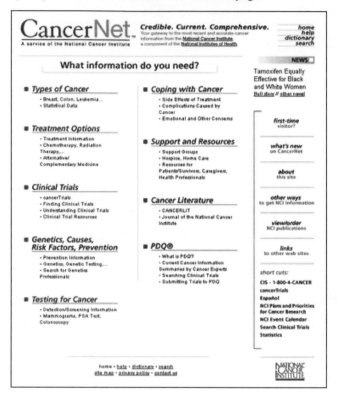

Figure C.7 Raise information to the highest level.

10. First Time Visitor

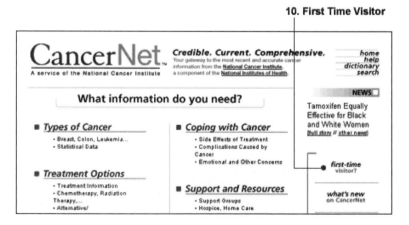

Figure C.8 Provide easy access to all levels of information.

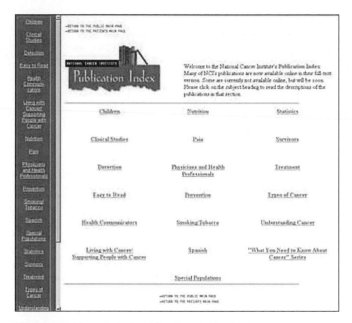

Figure C.9 The original publications index had numerous overlapping categories. It was not clear that users could order free publications through the site.

Figure C.10 Topics are consolidated and don't overlap on the redesigned publications page. The layout and order of topics follow the same format as the rest of the site. It is clear that you can browse or order the publications.

D

PlayFootball.com—
Key Factors in Developing a Positive User Experience for Children on the Web

Jorian Clarke
President
Circle 1 Network/SpectraCom Inc.

Introduction

The National Football League (NFL) faced a significant challenge of how to attract and maintain the next generation of football fans. Because of school athletic program cutbacks, fewer children were taking up football. There was also increased competition from other sports such as soccer and basketball, and athletes such as Michael Jordan, who play without protective face gear, were more recognizable than face-covered football athletes.

To meet these challenges, the league had its share of popular activities for children. The annual Punt, Pass & Kick competition drew more than three million boys and girls from all over the country, with the finals and winners televised nationally during a playoff game. Gaining ground as a marketing vehicle for children was NFL Flag, a series of leagues that played flag football under the auspices of the NFL. The league was adding teams on a regular basis and had a national championship. Still, other sports were gaining ground with America's youth.

Meanwhile, the NFL was enjoying unparalleled success with its Web site, NFL.com. Regularly ranked as one of the most visited sites on the Internet, NFL.com was proving to be one of the flagship marketing tools for the league.

Defining the Mission and Target User Population

While exploring options to bolster the game's image with young people around the world, the league decided to build on its success with NFL.com. Thus, a key strategy employed by the NFL to boost interest among children was to launch a Web site aimed specifically at the 8- to 14-year-old audience. Baseball and hockey already had such endeavors, with reportedly good success. The challenge for the NFL was to develop a site that would appeal to the young audience, build fan support, and encourage a steady flow of young talent into the sport.

The NFL did a search for a development team with expertise in the development of online content specifically targeted to youth. Circle 1 Network, an online publisher with three sites targeted at youth, was the vendor chosen. Their experience with kids age 3–7 with www.kidscomjr.com, tweens ages 8–12 with www.kidscom.com, and teens with www.yazone.com, indicated an understanding of developing content through all youth age cycles. In addition, having been online since 1995, they had experience with maintaining content, doing online customer research, and understanding privacy issues as mandated by the COPPA law. As of April 21, 2000, COPPA mandates that verifiable parental consent must be obtained from a child's parent before collecting, using, or disclosing personal information from a child under the age of 13. This experience was essential due to the start date of the project, falling already within the season and with the Super Bowl looming on the horizon. Circle 1 Network also had a relationship with SpectraCom, an online marketing company with extensive research experience. These two organizations together, which are privately owned, conducted research with children at each step of the development process of the site.

Requirements Gathering

To aid in the development of the site, SpectraCom conducted observational playgroups, focus groups, online surveys, and usability studies with children. The goals were to determine children's preferences for the site's creative design and content and to learn more about how children interact with the Internet. The research that was conducted also helped the site development team gain an understanding of children's interest in playing and watching football, and their level of knowledge about the game. After the initial site was completed, further usability testing was conducted with children and enhancements were made to PlayFootball.com based on what was learned from the children's experiences with the site.

Observational playgroups helped the PlayFootball.com team learn more about how to engage children on the Web. The methodological approach of these groups was to observe children at play in a somewhat natural environment. Although the groups were held in a focus group room, the recruited children were paired with a friend, and the environment was structured to resemble a lab-type setting in computer rooms at school. An adult was present in the room to act as a resource if the children had trouble with the computers. Note takers and members of the development team observed the groups from the focus group observation room, behind a one-way mirror. To facilitate later analysis, each session was recorded using a VGA-to-NTSC converted video recording of the screen contents and a synchronized audio recording of any comments made by the children, in a setup similar to a usability lab.

Two play sessions of four children each were held. Each of the two sessions included two girls who were friends and two boys who were friends—providing eight participants. In the first session, the children were third graders (8–9 years old) and in the second session, they were sixth graders (11–12 years old). All children were pre-screened for interest in football and Internet use. The children all reported liking football and either playing or watching a game within the last six months. Each child also used the Internet at least three days a week at home or at school. Each participant was given an honorarium of $40. The children were given a list of 15 popular child-focused Web sites to play on and were allowed uninterrupted play on any or all of the 15 sites. The children were not directed to play in any special way and were free to interact with each other as they chose.

After observing the children's behavior, the researchers tried to draw some conclusions about how children play on the Web. Although these findings can be used only as guidance due to the small sample size, they were supported by previous quantitative work with significant sample sizes on similar topics.

Findings from the Observational Play Groups

Children are drawn to games and they judge a children's site based on the games. When making their selections on a site's homepage, the children almost exclusively chose games. If children had difficulty with the first game they attempted, they often left the site without further exploration. There were a few exceptions. Girls seemed to be more comfortable with their reading and writing skills, so they frequently gravitated to content areas that used those skills. For example, some girls left the games to interact with content areas, such as the *Be an NFL Reporter* contest, which involved a writing activity.

Children will continue playing a game or activity as long as they are having some success and fun. They don't need to experience total mastery; they just need to have some initial success to engage them. Within the first minute of game sampling, children need to be able to accomplish one or more parts of a game or activity. This initial success encourages them to continue further in the activity or game in which more skill is needed to obtain success. For example, the younger boys played the *MicroManiacs*, a racing game on FoxKids.com, for almost 30 minutes, while the younger girls were composing a story for the *Be an NFL Reporter* contest for 30 minutes. Both of these activities had components that utilized the skills of the target audience. Boys liked the movement of the race game; girls liked the writing creativity and collaboration of the story activity. For boys, the play patterns involved being able to race in simulations of racing, even if they didn't win the race, and for girls the creativity of collaborative writing engaged them even if they didn't win the contest. These times of play were engagement successes that encouraged the children to continue playing those activities.

Children like being able to master a game and will play several times to increase their skill level. Many children and especially boys will opt to learn by experiential knowledge building rather than to read instructions prior to game play. The children were good at discerning strategy by observation and they learned by trial and error as they played. While playing the *MicroManiacs* racing game, the younger boys gradually learned strategies and discovered how the results were scored. For example, they discovered that the race was scored frame by frame when one of the boys won by advancing to the next frame. The older girls played a game called *The Monster Match Game* and in the second trial experience, they were excited to discover that the same questions were asked so they "knew all the answers."

The "too difficult" grid shown in Figure D.1 was defined by the observers as games or activities that were abandoned quickly by the children. In playing these games or activities, children had difficulty mastering the basic skills required to progress

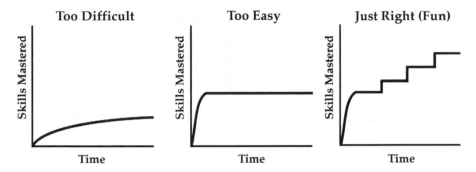

Figure D.1 Game skill learning curves.

in the play of the game. In repetitive play, they did not increase their success or mastery of the required game skills so they found these games frustrating.

The "too easy" grid was defined by the observers as games or activities that were easily mastered (a steep initial learning curve) but then required no new skill mastery to continue in play so there was no excitement generated by a "new" challenge. These games were also abandoned quite quickly. The children thought these games were boring because there was no mix of mastery and ongoing challenge.

The "just right" grid was defined by the observers as games or activities in which children could experience some mastery but also had gaming components that still offered challenges leading to repetitive play and longer play per play session. In playing these games or activities, children could master the basic game skills quickly and then continue to progress in play, adding new skills at a slower rate.

Children are often competitive, but they can also be collaborative. When playing a two-person game, the younger boys would let each other win phases of the game in order to keep the entire game from ending. The younger girls tried to enter both of their names on the *Be an NFL Reporter* contest form because their story had ideas from both of them. When playing single-player games the children would sometimes take turns. The girls did this more often than the boys. In some games, the children divided the game tasks assigning the differential activities to the child in the group who was judged the most skilled for that game or activity challenge area.

Children do not read blocks of text. Children spent little time reading on any of the sites. They would lightly scan or skip the instructions before playing a game.

Sometimes they went back to read instructions if the game was sufficiently engaging. When playing *Zip* on BurgerTown.com, the girls quickly closed the window containing health information that pops up between games without reading any of it. The children sometimes started to read text that was scrolling on the screen. None of the children was observed reading an entire block of scrolling text.

From this research, the development team created a checklist of criteria to use when designing games. Some of the criteria were

- make some component of the game easy to understand and play initially
- incorporate different levels of play to keep a child's interest
- limit the amount of reading required to play

Toward a Homepage: Site Navigation

Focus groups were conducted in two geographical locations to aid in the selection of a creative design for the homepage and to evaluate proposed content for the site. Forty-eight children participated in six focus groups during the development process. All children were pre-screened for interest in football and Internet use. The children all reported liking football and either playing or watching a game within the last six months. Each child also used the Internet at least three days a week at home or at school. An honorarium of $40 was given to each participant. A balanced mix of boys and girls was recruited for each group. Three groups consisted of second and third graders and three groups consisted of fourth, fifth, and sixth graders. The focus groups were videotaped to aid in analysis.

In each focus group the Web site developers asked the children about their offline football experiences and any online football experience they had. To show the image large enough for all to see clearly, the developers used a computer connected to a projector to show a variety of children's and adults' sports Web sites. We asked the children where they would want to go on the sites and what they would expect to find. The developers also showed two different PlayFootball site prototype designs and asked for the children's expectations for each area of the site. The children also took turns playing a selection of online games in each group. The games were chosen to display different types of game play such as trivia games, racing games, and word games. These game play observations formed the creative direction for the game development.

The Web site developers found that in these groups, children had trouble identifying what they would like to have on a site, besides games. They also had difficulty visualizing a verbally described activity. The children were more successful in developing ideas for site content when they had examples to react to and expand upon. The quality and quantity of information Circle 1 was able to gather increased when we searched on existing Web sites for activities that were similar to what we were proposing and showed them to the children.

The children were asked to evaluate two creative designs for the site. (see Figures D.2 and D.3) The goal of the site design was to communicate to children that this was a fun site about football for boys and girls who are 8 to 14 years old.

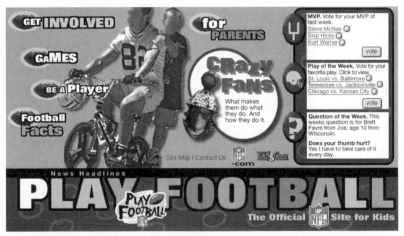

Figure D.2 Initial homepage design #1.

Figure D.3 Initial homepage design #2.

Focus Group Findings

The focus groups revealed that children have strong feelings about which Web sites are for them and which sites are for adults. They consistently mentioned a number of features that earmark a Web site as a site for children. They look for bright colors, interesting and varied fonts, movement and sound, and photos and/or illustrations. They take the cue that the site is for them by the presence of photos or illustrations of children on the site. For example, they suggested that the photo of a professional football player be replaced by pictures of children playing football on the site, which was done for the final design (see Figure D.4).

From previous research Circle 1 had conducted with children, it was known that children show distinct preferences for designs that appear unstructured by adult standards. They feel that linear navigation and content layout combined with large amounts of text indicate that the site would not be fun and interactive. When they see these site components, they assume the site is designed for adults. Looking at an adult sports site, one of the children commented, "There is a lot of information and no fun here."

Children are visually literate. The football field and animated play diagram at the top of design 2 readily communicated "football" to the children. The children

Figure D.4 Final homepage creative design.

identified this image with football more than they did with images of uniformed players or the word "football." This finding was incorporated into the final design.

Children look for interactivity on a Web site. They especially gravitate toward games or activities in which their choices control the outcome. Site content areas that are interactive, such as polls, surveys, or trivia, often are considered by children to be games, even though adults may describe them as activities. The final design included some of these types of interactive elements that were present in both initial designs.

The findings from the focus groups were quantified with an online survey with children ages 4 to 18. For this online survey Circle 1 Network's tween site KidsCom.com was used. The site has a special online survey area that is open to registered kids who have parental approval for KidsCom.com access. This research area is set up to award KidsKash points for participation in surveys. These points can be redeemed for products on the site. A total of 1,238 children participated in the first online survey.

The children evaluated each design on a variety of attributes; they were asked who the site was for (boys/girls, younger/older kids), how interesting the site looked, if it was easy to read, if the navigation was confusing, and if it looked like it was designed for them. After evaluating each design, they were asked to choose their favorite design and explain why they preferred it and how it could be improved.

The children's comments relating to the two site designs (see Figures D.2 and D.3) were perceptive and provided enormous insight to the team for creative and content development. Some of the direct comments from the children follow.

Comments on the Homepage Design

What would you change about the homepage design?

Design #1

- I would not change any thing except I think they should put at least 1 girl on it. Because I am a girl and I love football.
- To make it super cool everybody would love it. hundred thousand games oh I would love it a lot.
- Make it more colorful and not have pictures of a dad and son, it would be better if it had pictures of both parents and a girl and a boy

- Just make it more interesting, put neon colors in it.
- A qb throwing a football not riding a bike
- Change the color of the back round to green. It will probably make it stand out a little bit.
- I would have more pictures and more color so it attracts the eye!
- Don't make the kid and the player on a bike for 3 year olds.
- I would take the kid and the adult off the bike, and show them playing football.

Design #2

- I would have the football player doing a touch down dance.
- You should put more stuff like cheerleaders of the teams because most girls dont like sports but I do and I am a girl
- I might change of how small the polls are. I can read them but some people might not be able to read them.
- Not much because it was almost perfect the only thing is that it needs a little more action like things moving around all over the place
- Have more pictures of people playing football.
- Well it is just so boyish I along with some of my friends think you should make a cheerleading page with different cheers and flips kids can do at home
- I would change the pictures with something more realistic. You should take the writing off the bottom and put something more interesting.
- This site is a lot better set out then the other one so I say leave it the way it is except put in some trivia games etc
- There isn't much wrong with this site but maybe some highlights from some of the previous superbowls would be a good idea. Or maybe only the results of the superbowls.
- Make it more of a girl and boy thing.
- The homepage design is ok as it is. You might want to add something that might interest girls.
- I like the logo, and I like the fact that it is nice and big. However, there isn't much pictures or colors or any wild fonts, and it doesn't catch my eye as much as the first. However, I do like the football field in the

background and I think the moving positions is clever. But I would make everything else more "crazy"—the fonts, layout, etc.

Why do you like that homepage design the best?

Design #1

- I like the football icons when you click on them they move, I like how the polls are lined up on the side of the page and that crazy fans icon it's totally cool.
- It looks more interesting! and it is bright so it will catch your attention.
- It makes me want to look around and get involved. The idea of putting games on it is good. I like playing those sorts of games.
- I like it because it shows interaction with the kids and other people that visit the Web site.

Design #2

- It shows more about football
- I think the designs and topics are better.And the one I picked can be for kids just not for adults.
- Because the 2 one looks as its more for kids
- I like #2 better becauuse it let's you be more a part of the site.
- Because it is bright and it catches my eye. And I also like how the x's and the o's move.
- I like it the best ,because it looks like a football site and bike riding has nothing to do with football.

Finalizing the Homepage

The final homepage created by Circle 1 Network incorporated the input from children to make the page more dynamic. The creative team added a three-dimensional look to the pages, gave additional prominence to selected games, made the promotional areas for content more irregularly shaped, and made the fonts more colorful. They replaced the photo of an adult football player with rotating images of children playing football. In addition, selected text headings and the image of the football play at the top of the page were animated to satisfy the children's desire for "lots of things happening at once."

Children's acceptance of the final design (see Figure D.4) was verified using a quantitative online study with a sample size of 1,025 boys and girls age 4 to 18. Again, this online survey was a joint effort with SpectraCom developing the survey and analyzing the data and Circle 1 Network fielding the survey and handling customer service issues. Boys and girls of all ages liked the site design and agreed that the site looked as if it were made for boys and girls age 8 to 14.

Page Design

As shown in earlier research, games were the most popular content areas proposed by children for PlayFootball.com. During six focus groups, children were asked to play and comment on a number of games targeted toward children. Each child was able to play one game in each focus group. The rest of the group was allowed to provide verbal help and give comments and reaction to the games as they were being played. Games on PlayFootball.com and other Web sites were used in the focus groups.

The content pages, similar to the homepages, relied on kid-friendly design, color, movement, fun graphics, and sound as attractive game elements for children. The focus groups confirmed that children don't read the game instructions. Children want to be able to start game play without reading the instructions. If they were challenged sometimes, they then went back and checked on the instruction game play details. To allow children to access instructions at anytime during a game, a button or link to the instructions was included on all game pages.

The games also needed to download quickly to keep the attention of the children. Children may decide the game is "broken" and go off in search of something more entertaining if they have to wait a long time. Content was added to occupy the time while the game downloaded, to help keep the children's interest.

Children like to feel they have some control over the game they are playing. They want to be able to change and control the game by selecting a difficulty level or by customizing the players, the team, or the rules. They also like to be able to control the speed of play as long as it doesn't appear to "punish" them for lack of performance. For example, games that required questions to be answered within a timed interval proved to be unpopular, especially with the younger children. They said it was "too much like a test in school," and therefore not fun. However, games that required motor skills to be employed in a timed format were acceptable. The game designers removed timing from all quiz games and provided support to achieving success by incorporating a button that the children could click for helpful hints, if they choose.

Surprises and "magic" elements that appear in a game are also very popular. Although children liked the sports figures in the games to appear somewhat realistic, they welcomed the unexpected appearance of space aliens, animals, and other fanciful creatures in their games. Magic potions and other "helps" were also very popular with children. The development team added unexpected sounds and other funny elements, such as a dancing umpire and a clothes-stealing tornado to the games.

Children don't always rate their satisfaction with a game by their ability to play it correctly and successfully. For example, randomly guessing the answers to football trivia was fun for the younger children, as long as the game play didn't end with wrong answers. In the trivia game being tested, multiple-choice answers disappeared one by one until the correct answer was left. Children were excited about trying because they could jump in to answer at any time without "punishment" for guessing wrong. Guessing right early led to more points, giving positive, rather than negative reinforcement.

Children also showed interest in learning about their favorite NFL team, individual football players, and the game of football itself. The content developers had to determine the children's level of knowledge in each of these areas to design interesting content that would not be considered too difficult or too easy. Although many young fans watch professional football games on a regular basis, they often do not completely understand the rules and the referee calls. By knowing their knowledge gaps, the developers were able to define content that was of an appropriate level and of interest to children.

The development team developed the content of games but they also included content as an interactive feature of the site since children perceive interactivities as games. For example, in learning the basics of the game, children could move their mouse over a picture of a football player to get details about the equipment the players wear. This was not a game from a content developer's standpoint, but the children looked on it as fun and game-like causing it to be an activity that resulted in repetitive visits.

Usability Testing

After the first phase of site development was completed, usability testing was conducted on the site. Five children in the target market were invited to participate in one-on-one usability interviews. The children were asked to explore the site to find the answers to two questions ("How tall are the goal posts at each end of a football field?" and "How many countries broadcast the Super Bowl?") and then asked to find the answers to these questions on the site. The children were not instructed to talk aloud about their activities, although they were not discouraged from making comments as they played. The developers found that, especially when playing games, children became distracted when the research moderator prompted them to talk about what they are doing. After searching for the answers to the questions and playing each game, the children completed a questionnaire. The children were also interviewed after each activity about their experience.

The usability research helped the development team understand which content areas were not well understood or accessed successfully by the children. For example, some children had difficulty situating the mouse cursor on relatively small promotional buttons highlighting content areas. In response, the development team increased the size of the buttons or enlarged the clickable areas.

Another area, *Game Highlights*, contained video highlights of recent NFL games. The children lost interest in the area while waiting for the video to load, and some even thought the area was "broken." To address this obstacle, the development team added an explanation to hold the children's interest while the content downloaded.

As in earlier research findings, the development team observed that children enjoyed playing the games. Again, children often skipped the directions to the games, but if they were able to begin play, that encouraged them to return to read the directions later as they needed help. Based on observing the play, the team made the directions easily accessible at any time during the game and tried different techniques to make the instructions more like play than like text reading.

Summary and Conclusions

Developing a sports Web site for children holds many design challenges. The site needs to have a clear structure, but appear unstructured. It needs to deliver information, but be interactive and visually interesting at the same time. Children of this generation like to have lots of things happening at once, but they also want to feel they have control over their online experience.

Games, including interactive activities, are the best vehicle for delivering information to children. Games engage the children by allowing them to gain knowledge or build skills while enjoying a visually stimulating interactive experience. Design components such as simple and easily available instructions, some initial game mastery within initial play, and literal visuals engage children.

By integrating user involvement throughout the development process, PlayFootball.com achieved its initial goals of building strong communication with young fans. User-oriented research combined with a development team experienced in developing online content for youth led to the development of a site with both educational and fun elements to build football sports awareness, and unique NFL experiences to encourage football fan development. Site statistics show a high degree of loyalty to the site with more than half of the visitors coming back. The site has continued with only minor changes (see Figure D.5).

Also in the
Color Insert

Figure D.5 Current PlayFootball.com site.

Index